Praise for *Digital Strategies for Powerful Corporate Communications*

"The global conversation sometimes referred to as Web 2.0 is alternately seen as a curse and a blessing. But one thing is clear: It represents a fundamental new reality for all businesses, one that is challenging long-held beliefs about marketing and communications. In *Digital Strategies for Powerful Corporate Communications*, Paul Argenti and Courtney Barnes provide an insightful and practical compass for communicators and brand stewards, navigating this new ocean of globally distributed information, expertise and relationships."

—Jon Iwata, senior vice president,
Marketing and Communications, IBM

"It's time to get out of your conference room. Social media enables our customers to virtually walk right next to us in our hallways. They are ready to share ideas, coshape our brands, help their peers and guide us in the marketplace everyday. Argenti and Barnes have made a clear case for why companies should embed this expertise into the DNA of their organization. Every function in a company will be transformed through social media. It's time to welcome your new partners—your customers—to your team."

—Bob Pearson, president of the Blog Council

"Argenti and Barnes have written the right book at the right time. Embracing digital communications is no longer a strategic business option for brands and their managers; it is a necessity. Their book is thoroughly researched, incorporating case studies and interviews with business leaders. Most importantly, it offers practical and effective digital approaches to help brands win with their customers, employees, and other stakeholders."

—Brian J. Sheehan, associate professor of
Advertising, S.I. Newhouse School of
Public Communications, Syracuse University

"New digital media have completely changed the dynamic between companies and their stakeholders, greatly amplifying the "vox" in "vox populi." *Digital Strategies for Powerful Corporation Communications* should be required reading for both corporate communicators and C-level executives who seek to master their strategic grasp of this new world. This is where they'll learn the landscape and be prepared to interact continuously in an authentic, transparent and empathetic way with stakeholders and help maintain their most valuable asset—their reputation."

—Bill Margaritis, VP of Corporate Communication
and Investor Relations, FedEx

"Argenti and Barnes recognize the dialectic between control and credibility. Communicators need to inform the on-going conversation instead of relying on messaging."

—Richard Edelman, president and CEO, Edelman

"This is *the* definitive handbook for digital communications executives. Every aspect of the new corporate communications function is investigated and analyzed with respect to its impact on the rest of the organization; real-life examples of how it can and should be done are generously shared. Digital communicators will have a much more significant seat at the table with this guidebook. My only regret is that the book wasn't available before I started my job."

—Scott Monty, Global Digital Communications,
Ford Motor Company

"*Digital Strategies for Powerful Corporate Communications* is a sweeping overview of the rapidly changing landscape for corporate communications. It presents a compendium of case studies to make its case for the best and smartest approaches for tackling social media. Argenti and Barnes not only justify the new and broader role of corporate communications professionals—they insist on their embracing expanded powers."

—Laurel Touby, founder and senior vice president,
mediabistro.com

DIGITAL
STRATEGIES

FOR

POWERFUL

Corporate
Communications

PAUL A. ARGENTI

AND

COURTNEY M. BARNES

New York   Chicago   San Francisco   Lisbon   London   Madrid   Mexico City
Milan   New Delhi   San Juan   Seoul   Singapore   Sydney   Toronto

The **McGraw·Hill** Companies

Copyright © 2009 by Paul A. Argenti and Courtney M. Barnes. All rights reserved.
Printed in the United States of America. Except as permitted under the United States
Copyright Act of 1976, no part of this publication may be reproduced or distributed in
any form or by any means, or stored in a database or retrieval system, without the prior
written permission of the publisher.

1 2 3 4 5 6 7 8 9 0   DOC/DOC   0 1 5 4 3 2 1 0 9

ISBN 978-0-07-160602-8
MHID 0-07-160602-5

McGraw-Hill books are available at special quantity discounts to use as premiums and
sales promotions, or for use in corporate training programs. To contact a representative,
please e-mail at bulksales@mcgraw-hill.com.

This book is printed on acid-free paper.

Library of Congress Cataloging-in-Publication Data
Argenti, Paul A.
    Digital strategies for powerful corporate communications / by Paul A. Argenti and
Courtney M. Barnes.
        p. cm.
    ISBN 0-07-160602-5 (alk. paper)
    1. Business networks–Computer network resources. 2. Communication in
management–Computer network resources. 3. Digital communications–Economic
aspects. 4. Communication in organizations–Computer network resources.
5. Barnes, Courtney M. I. Title.

HD69.S8.A74 2010
658.4'5–dc22   2009011081

I dedicate this book to my wife, Jennifer Kaye Argenti, with love and gratitude for all of her support throughout this project and in my life.

—Paul

I'd like to dedicate this book to my mother, Sue Rowell, who taught me the difference between sacrifice and defeat, and to my father, Bill Barnes, who taught me the difference between a good thing and too much of it.

—Courtney

CONTENTS

ACKNOWLEDGMENTS

As is always the case with a project of this scope, we couldn't have done it without the help of so many individuals and groups. We collectively want to thank our editor, Donya Dickerson, first and foremost for seeing the potential in our proposal and bringing the idea to fruition so gracefully. Her expertise and professionalism—as well as that of the entire team at McGraw-Hill—made what could have been a painful process anything but.

Second, we couldn't have written this book without the help of Anthony DeRico, whose commitment to the project was unwavering and invaluable from the very beginning. His contributions—namely with Chapter 8, which his background in law and politics made possible—enriched the content in ways we couldn't have accomplished without him.

We also want to thank all the executives who lent their insights into this profoundly enormous topic. Their perspectives, achievements, and in some cases, failures shaped the book and brought each example to life. Each individual mentioned in these pages made himself available wholly and without hesitation, highlighting the strategies that have turned these organizations into success stories that others aspire to emulate.

We are immensely grateful to the individuals who contributed their time, research, ideas, and advice to us during every stage of this project—namely, Annette Lyman, Jennifer Farrelly, Adam Carson, Abbey Nova, Peter Verrengia, and Kimberley Tait. Each of you provided unique support that enriched the final product. We are also appreciative of the professionals at the Corporate Executive Board Company, who were generous enough to make their vast network of research available to us, and whose work for corporate executives around the world continues to advance the communications discipline in unprecedented ways.

More specifically, Paul would like to thank his wife, Jennifer Kaye Argenti, to whom this book is dedicated for her support every day in every way; his daughters, Julia and Lauren, for allowing him to see the world through eyes young enough to understand what we have written about; to the Tuck School for research time and financial support; and finally, to Courtney, who convinced him that digital was more than just another channel and did an amazing job on this book.

Courtney would like to thank her family and friends for putting up with her for the weeks and months leading up to the deadline. Thanks to her mother and father, Sue Rowell and Bill Barnes, to whom she dedicates this book, for always being so supportive of her dream to be a writer and for forgiving her absence at so many family functions while she worked to complete this manuscript; to her step-father, Bob Rowell, and her siblings, Lindsay, Taylor, and Ashton, for being encouraging every single day; to her Nana and Popooh, Shirley and Art Hendrickson, for providing a retreat and many home-cooked meals when the sprint to the finish line began; to her boyfriend, Fabian Menges, who endured innumerable moments of hysteria, panic, and frustration and who always kept her grounded; to her Mimi, Josephine Barnes, who has always been and will always be an inspiration; again to Anthony DeRico, who spent many long days and nights across the table from her, editing and writing and reminding her that the blood, sweat, and tears would be worth it; to Cheryl Clements, her best friend and roommate, for always knowing when to pour a glass of wine; and last but not least, to Paul, for giving her a chance to prove herself.

PREFACE

This book grew out a challenge from one generation to another. Courtney Barnes started working with me as a researcher and then joined me in a consulting capacity before returning to her passion, which is writing. After working on two other book projects with me, Courtney became interested in working on yet another book—this time as a coauthor rather than a researcher/writer. The topic she was interested in was digital communications and social media.

What I knew about this topic two years ago was limited to what I had overheard in conversations with my daughters, read about in the business media, or learned from my colleague and now coauthor, Courtney. After speaking at a conference at which I made what today seems like a barbaric claim that digital was just another channel in my tried and true corporate communications strategy model, Courtney took me aside and said, "Argenti, you need to learn about what amounts to a revolution in terms of how people are communicating today."

We decided that if both of us worked on a book together, I would learn everything I possibly could about this revolution, and she would try to think about it in a more disciplined way. We pitched it to my editor at McGraw-Hill—Donya Dickerson—and the rest, as they say, is history.

What I have discovered in the last two years is that applying digital strategies to corporate communications changes the rules of the game in every part of the field. From the most obvious changes in how the media operates, to who is a part of the media, to ways in which digital strategies are affecting investor relations, crisis communications, and corporate social responsibility, everything we knew about communications has been turned upside down in the last decade. Stakeholders control the means of production in communications today as never before. Giant companies can be brought to their knees by lonely bloggers operating in every part of the world. And the opportunity for corporations to seize this as an opportunity rather than to see it as a threat offers us one of the most exhilarating challenges of our time.

As we complete our work on this book, the world is in the midst of one of the worst financial crises in history. As one of my clients said to me recently, "I wish we could have a moratorium on the news for a few days!" But the story that is not being written about the revolution in communications is likely to have a greater effect on all of us in the years ahead than the financial crisis, which will pass eventually. I hope that those of you who are middle aged and wondering about what this revolution is all about will find it as exciting as I do and take the time to think about what effect it has on your business, on your relationships with stakeholders, and on how you will communicate with everyone in the years ahead. And for those of you, like Courtney, who already live and thrive in the digital age, I hope that you will be excited to learn about how all this can be applied to the field of corporate communication.

At this point, Courtney will tell you her side of the story.

I met Paul when I was brand new to the communications industry and, really, to professional life in general. I was 20 years old, fresh out of college, and working as a reporter for *PR News* (a publication I would leave for an opportunity to work directly with Paul and later return to as editor). We crossed paths at industry events, in which he was always a keynote speaker and I was the token journalist sent to cover the day's proceedings. At that time, his schtick was measurement and/or strategic communication, two topics he had single-handedly pushed to the forefront of the business world.

Our relationship began as interviewer-interviewee and evolved into a friendship when he caught wind of both my understanding of the subjects he was passionate about and my determination to be successful (to this day, I'm not sure which characteristic had more of an effect on his decision to mentor me, but either way, I'm eternally grateful). I was green—very green—and, like many members of my generation, hungry for challenges, quick to react (postively and negatively), impatient, impulsive, and I'll admit, more than a little sassy. But Paul saw potential and created tests that I unknowingly passed to ultimately gain his respect. Once that was established, he dangled carrots of opportunity in front of me, first to be his research assistant, then to be his associate at Communications Consulting Worldwide, and finally to be his coauthor.

When the idea for this book was born (over dinner at a Chinese restaurant on Manhattan's Upper East Side, by the way), Paul was hesitant. I was adamant that his presentations on measurement and strategic communication were still brilliant (flattery gets you everywhere), but they were becoming tired. What's more, I was becoming tired of researching and writing about them. Lucky for me, Paul knew it was time for him to write a new book. Lucky for both of us, I had an idea as to what it should be. I pitched it over kung pow chicken, and he ... well, didn't sound too excited.

"I don't know Barnsie. I don't know much about that digital stuff. And who knows if it'll even be around by the time the book would be published?" But I was so relentless that he acquiesced in his usual manner; in other words, he told me to do a ton of work to prepare a proposal, and maybe if he thought it was good enough, he would send it to his publishing contacts—*maybe* being the keyword.

And here we are. I'd be lying if I said it came easily, because anyone who is trying to integrate digital communications strategies into their business models knows that getting buy-in from more vintage executives is easier said than done. But, as someone who's done it in her own way, I can tell you that it's a war worth fighting, even if you are poised to lose battles along the way. Paul's resistance and my persistence proved to be exactly what was required to complete this project successfully. He personified senior management's skepticism to all things digital, and I embodied the modernity that is toppling traditional business approaches. And little did he know that his own advice is what inspired this book—or, at least, that inspired my determination and his ultimate agreement to make it happen, come hell or high water: "Rules are for other people, Barnsie. Just figure it out."

Okay...maybe that's not exactly what he said, but it's all I heard, and *that* is what made all the difference.

Paul Argenti
Courtney Barnes
New York
March 28, 2009

WELCOME TO THE JUNGLE
AN INTRODUCTION TO THE NEW BUSINESS ENVIRONMENT

The business of managing relationships—and therefore, business itself—has changed dramatically in the last decade. Stakeholder empowerment, as it's come to be known, has shifted the corporate hierarchy of influence from the hands of elite business executives to those of their once-passive audiences, including employees, consumers, media, and investors. The complex modern business environment, driven by these individual stakeholders' needs, wants, opinions, and whims, underscores a harsh reality for corporate leaders: They have all but relinquished control over their organizations' reputations and messaging to a dissonant public. Whether you are a corporate leader or a self-described member of said public, this reality affects almost every interaction you will have with the institution of business.

While this evolution—some would say revolution—in business didn't happen overnight, it was prompted by a juggernaut of catalysts that emerged and metastasized so rapidly that many executives were left without any strategies for thriving—let alone surviving—in this new environment.

A number of instigators sparked this swift transformation, but one stands out as having the most impact, endurance, and longevity: the emergence of digital communications platforms, including blogs and social communities. These platforms sparked a complete overhaul of the business environment, especially in the context of communication.

Before the digital explosion at the turn of the twenty-first century, corporations' reputations were shaped by one-dimensional messaging that the senior-most managers pushed down the corporate ladder and disseminated to stakeholders separately and without discussion. As summarized by the 2007 Authentic Enterprise CEO Report, commissioned by the Arthur W. Page Society, "Companies used to control their identities, value propositions and the content of the messages about themselves. Companies used to segment and target audiences. Companies used to have distinct expertise in and control over the channels of communication."[1]

The report's use of past tense is indicative of the seismic shift that occurred to empower "target audiences," otherwise known as stakeholders. A *stakeholder* is any individual or group that can affect and be affected by the actions of a corporation. Universally, the most common and influential stakeholders include employees, customers, media, investors, community members, analysts, nongovernmental organizations, lobbyists, and activist groups. In the past, these stakeholders had limited interactions with corporate entities. Messages were created by executives to meet the needs of a specific group, and that group received these messages with limited means for commentary or reaction.

Now, an ever-growing list of interactive digital platforms, all of which reside beneath the umbrella of "Web 2.0," gives stakeholders the ability to communicate with one another, to build communities around shared interests, to disseminate their own messaging about an organization, and ultimately, to threaten companies' increasingly vulnerable reputations (for more information about Web 2.0 versus its earlier iteration—Web 1.0—see the section "Y2K" below). Corporate executives still create and disseminate messaging to stakeholders, but these individuals and groups are now empowered to "talk back" through digital channels. Perhaps more intimidating, they can converse with one another, comparing notes, so to speak, and interpreting corporate information in their own way, which may or may not be accurate.

This uneasy reality requires business leaders worldwide to redefine their strategies and brands in the context of digital communications platforms and the power these platforms grant to stakeholders. Control of messaging and reputation may seem all but lost, but executives are in a position to emerge from this cyber jungle with renewed authority and influence. First, however, they must learn to harness the power of digital communications by integrating these platforms into all business strategies and applying them across every business function.

This book sets out to define the current business environment as it is shaped by these new technologies and to offer executives strategies for understanding them and (finally) using them to the advantage of their organizations. While revising long-held business beliefs and practices, this approach will empower an often-overlooked organizational function—corporate communication—to lead the movement to digital supremacy.

To begin, this chapter will outline the catalysts that instigated stakeholder empowerment and its role in business and then define the specific digital communications platforms discussed throughout this book. It then will describe what all these changes mean for corporate leaders and specify how corporate communication fits into the big picture.

The Business Environment Version 3.0: The Evolving Corporate Landscape

The more things change, the more they stay the same. This adage might be true in some contexts, but business certainly isn't one of them. Over the course of the last decade, a number of factors came together to catalyze a massive change in the way business is conducted around the world. Most senior executives entered the corporate world in a very different era, and they now face a business landscape that is very different from what they once knew.

For starters, corporate reputations have become extremely vulnerable in the wake of scandals that rattled the public's trust in business. While corporate malfeasance was by no means unheard of in the twentieth century, scandals became ubiquitous in recent years, beginning most notably in 2001 with the infamous dissolution of energy company Enron after a series of fraudulent accounting procedures became public.

From that point on, one could argue that the situation went from bad to worse. Trust in business institutions plummeted, with only 44 percent of the population saying they trusted business to do the right thing.[2] Likewise, by February 2002, approximately 81 percent of surveyed investors "did not have much confidence in those running Big Business."[3] These grim statistics set the tone for what would become a common theme for corporate leaders: Their credibility—along with their organizations' reputations—was declining in the face of increased scrutiny by every stakeholder group, be it consumers, investors, or even employees. What's more, this sentiment of skepticism has endured to the present day. The 2008 Edelman Trust Barometer revealed that, globally, only 51 percent of respondents (made up primarily of elites) trust business to do what's right.[4] (For a complete breakdown in confidence in leaders of various institutions from 2001–2008, see Table 1.1.)

Here's an even sadder story just waiting to be told: As far as confidence in the leaders of various institutions is concerned, the public ranked major companies only above Wall Street, organized labor, law firms, the press, Congress, and the Executive Branch of the government.[5] Again, the confidence that corporate leaders seem incapable of engendering places additional pressures and responsibilities on the corporate communication function because it must position senior executives as trustworthy thought leaders while still enhancing the perception of the organization as a whole—a charge, we will argue, that is made possible by the power of digital communications platforms.

If You Build It, They Will Come: The Rise of Online Media

While the widespread distrust and doubt in companies and their leaders may not be so detrimental on its own, imagine it taking place in tandem with another trend: the fragmentation of media. This phenomenon developed as Internet usage became more ubiquitous in the 1990s, during which time it was estimated that Internet users grew by 100 percent each year, with periods of even more explosive growth within this time frame.[6] Prior to that time, the Internet had existed in its most basic form, operating as a series of internal communication networks for the likes of governmental agencies, military outfits, and university research teams. It wasn't until 1989 that the Web as we know it was invented by an English scientist named Tim Berners-Lee. Then, on August 6, 1991, the European Organization for Nuclear Research (most commonly referred to as CERN, the acronym for the organization's French moniker, Conseil Européen pour la Recherche Nucléaire) publicized its

Table 1.1: Confidence in Leaders of Institutions (2001–2008)

"As far as people in charge of running (READ EACH ITEM) are concerned, would you say you have a great deal of confidence, only some confidence, or hardly any confidence at all in them?"

Those saying "a great deal of confidence"
Base: All Adults

	2001 %	2002 %	2003 %	2004 %	2005 %	2006 %	2007 %	2008 %	Change 2007–2008 %
The military	44	71	62	62	47	47	46	51	+5
Small business	X	X	X	X	47	45	54	47	−7
Major educational institutions such as colleges and universities	35	33	31	37	39	38	37	32	−5
Medicine	32	29	31	32	29	31	37	28	−9
Organized religion	25	23	19	27	27	30	27	25	−2
The U.S. Supreme Court	35	41	34	29	29	33	27	25	−2
Public Schools	X	X	X	X	26	22	22	20	−2
The courts and the justice	X	X	21	17	22	21	21	16	−5
Television news	24	24	21	31	16	19	20	16	−4
The White House	21	50	40	31	31	25	22	15	−7
Major companies	**20**	**16**	**13**	**12**	**17**	**13**	**16**	**14**	**−2**
Wall Street	23	19	12	17	15	15	17	11	−6
Organized labor	15	11	14	15	17	12	15	11	−4
Law firms	10	13	12	10	11	10	13	10	−3
The press	13	16	15	15	12	14	12	10	−2
Congress	18	22	20	13	16	10	10	8	−2
The executive branch of the federal government	20	33	26	23	X	X	X	X	X
Harris Interactive Confidence Index	**55**	**65**	**57**	**55**	**53**	**52**	**53**	**44**	**−9**

X = Not asked
Source: "Big Drop in Confidence in Leaders of Major Institutions," The Harris Poll #22, February 28, 2008.

World Wide Web project, and the basic applications and principles that had defined the Internet until then finally were given a public interface.

Web technology's subsequent exponential growth, aided largely by the lack of central administration and protocol, happened organically. This would be the public's first taste of the unrestricted power of connection that would soon govern their professional and personal communications, as well as their media consumption habits.

This brings us to the fragmentation of media and its effect on modern business. As the Internet's presence infiltrated homes and businesses throughout the 1990s, major news outlets began to explore the role the Web would play in their own operations. On January 19, 1996, the *New York Times* on the Web—www.nytimes.com—went live, giving readers around the world access to the newspaper's content on the night of publication.[7] The *Wall Street Journal Online* was launched that same year, and most national and international media companies quickly followed suit.

The expansion of media online happened synonymously with the public's rapidly changing consumption habits. Multiple distribution channels, including search engines and site aggregators, made it easier than ever for consumers to find information. The 2007 Media Usage Survey conducted by the USC Annenberg Strategic Public Relations Center sums this trend up nicely:

> *The continuous creation of new technologies is speeding up the pace of news gathering and dissemination and providing numerous media outlets for consumers to turn to for their daily dose of information. That means that the time consumers devote to media consumption is more fragmented than ever—presenting multiple challenges for communicators attempting to reach their target audiences.*[8]

These challenges become even more salient when you look at the statistics that support the fragmentation of media:

- The percentage of Internet users that went online for news consumption "yesterday" (indicating that they do so daily) went from approximately 20 percent in the fall of 2000 to nearly 40 percent in December 2007.
- The Web is becoming a more integral part of people's lives. Eight in 10 Americans 17 years of age and older now say that the Internet

is a critical source of information—up from 66 percent in 2006. According to the same survey, more Americans identified the Internet as a more important source of information than television (68 percent), radio (63 percent), and newspapers (63 percent).

- In 2007, as the number of people going online grew, so did the frequency with which they went there, as well as how much time they spent. Overall, 75 percent of adult Americans use the Internet, according to data from the Pew Internet and American Life Project gathered from October 24 to December 2, 2007. That number is up from the 70 percent during the same time in 2006.[9]

These statistics are only a brief glimpse into the complex mechanisms that drive the shift in the public's media consumption habits. While these mechanisms will be discussed further in Chapter 4, suffice it to say here that they have contributed to a monumental shift in the way organizations reach their key stakeholders. As the propensity for online consumption increases, companies must ramp up their digital presence by creating dynamic, interactive, and original content around the clock.

Of course, many organizations noticed this and acted accordingly. On June 25, 2000, the *New York Times* and the *New York Times Digital* inaugurated a continuous news operation, providing updated news and analysis around the clock.[10] This decision was four years in the making because the first incarnation online was simply repurposed content from the printed publication. However, greater demands for more content more often from consumers forced *Times* executives to approach the Web site not just as an extension of the printed product but as a viable brand in and of itself.

Y2K: The New Millennium Marks More than a Calendar Change as Web 1.0 Matures into Web 2.0

Before exploring the forays of companies into online brand extensions, it's important first to understand the technical and semantic differences that separate the earliest version of publicly accessible information online—Web 1.0—from the interactive, dynamic Internet that we know today—Web 2.0.

Web 1.0 is the Internet version of primitive corporate communication strategies, in which executives pushed out messages to stakeholders, who digested them without many means for responding. This isn't to say that one-way messaging from corporate executives to stakeholders was strictly due to the absence of the Internet. On the contrary, by 1996, the Web 1.0 Internet was composed of approximately 250,000 sites and 45 million global users (see Figures 1.1 and 1.2). However, these sites were static, populated primarily with read-only information programmed in basic HTML code and accessed by users via dial-up Internet connections—in other words, "surfing the Net" was more akin to wading through a poorly catalogued library of seemingly random information. In its earliest stages—circa 1996, when major news outlets began publishing their printed products online—the Web was a

Figure 1.1: Web 1.0 versus Web 2.0

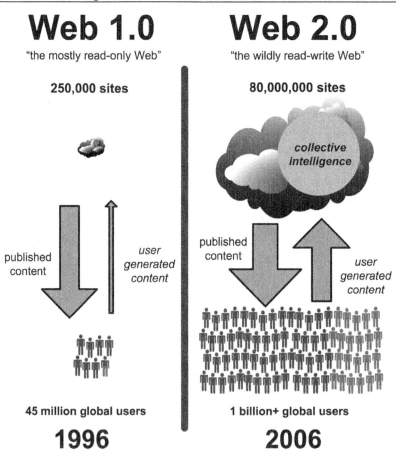

Figure 1.2: Elements of the Web's next generation

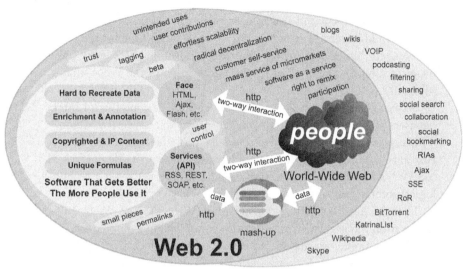

Source: Dion Hinchcliffe, Hinchcliffe & Company, http://content.zdnet.com/2347-9595_22-10672-10673.html?seq=1.

resource for few and a curiosity for many. Major network service providers such as AOL and Delphi had already connected their proprietary e-mail systems to the Internet, so the adoption of e-mail as a personal communications tool began to crescendo. Likewise, corporate use of Web technologies began to increase steadily as tools for taking corporate messages online began to emerge, from internal communications networks to corporate Web pages.

With the entrance of these technologies came a slew of Internet-based companies, also known as *dot-coms*, whose rapid escalation to market dominance shined a blinding spotlight on the Internet. The stock market reacted kindly to these companies, many of which defied standard business models by focusing more on market share and less on the bottom line. Venture capitalists swooped in to fund these speculative business propositions, and stock values soared. The success of these organizations was predicated primarily on growing consumer bases as rapidly as possible, so public awareness campaigns were of critical importance. By 2000, the dot-com bubble reached its pinnacle, with the Nasdaq peaking at 5132.52 on March 10.

But, as the old adage goes, what goes up must come down, and even the dot-com bubble couldn't overcome the law of gravity. Its meteoric rise halted abruptly and unceremoniously in March 2000, and the fallout would linger for years to come. It was a rocky time for the economy and for business in general, but the dot-com bubble's burst was a major catalyst for the birth of the next generation of the Web—that is, Web 2.0.

Between December 1996 and December 2006, the number of Internet users skyrocketed from approximately 36 million to nearly 2 billion.[11] This explosive growth straddled the dot-com bubble's wave of success turned to failure, and the flurry of online business activity democratized the Web to a large degree, transforming the Internet from a technological interface into a dynamic platform.

Therein lies the difference between Web 1.0 and Web 2.0— observation versus participation, static versus dynamic, monologue versus conversation. Some organizations were quick to identify this critical shift; for example, as previously stated, the *New York Times* had updated its Web presence to include continuous news updates around the clock by 2000. Constant content updates aren't the defining characteristic of Web 2.0, however; it is the collaborative environment that facilitates the creation and exchange of user-generated content via dynamic channels, including blogs, wikis, and social networks.

The Perfect Storm: Technology, Trust, and Media Fragmentation Beget Stakeholder Empowerment

Up to this point, the stage on which modern business is conducted has been partially built: Widespread corporate scandals crippled the public's trust in corporations, all while the fragmentation of media online cultivated a place for consumers to get information and communicate freely with one another. But these two factors are just the building blocks of the current business construct because they enabled the creation of the Web 2.0 platforms that enhance collaboration, communication, and community building among users.

The proliferation of these platforms occurred almost anarchically over the course of the last five years. There are a number of platforms and iterations therein, but for the purposes of this book, the following will be the focus because they are most relevant to corporate communications and strategic management (a thorough dictionary of terms can be found in Appendix A):

- Blogs
- Social networks
- Video-sharing platforms
- Search engine marketing and optimization
- Corporate Web sites/online newsrooms
- Wikis
- Mash-ups
- Viral/word-of-mouth (WOM) marketing

These platforms have been embraced and implemented by the most successful, innovative organizations; alternatively, others have ignored them at their own risk and to great detriment. Examples from both categories will be explored in the following chapters. For now, though, it is most important to have a thorough understanding of what these digital communications platforms have collectively enabled—stakeholder empowerment. The "Authentic Enterprise" report mentioned earlier explores the stakeholder empowerment phenomenon, stating

> In addition to the familiar intermediaries and constituencies with whom corporations have interacted in the past, there is now a diverse array of communities, interests, nongovernmental organizations and individuals. Many of these new players represent important interests, while others are not legitimate stakeholders, but rather simply adversarial or malicious. Regardless of motive, all are far more able to collaborate among themselves around shared interests and to reach large audiences. At the same time, companies and institutions themselves are seeking similar kinds of engagement with multiple constituencies.[12]

In addition to these effects of stakeholder empowerment, the power to interpret messaging and communicate with other individuals has another profound effect. Now, anyone with an Internet connection and an opinion is a journalist for all intents and purposes. A particularly salient example can be seen in the announcement of Tim Russert's death in 2008. When the moderator of NBC's *Meet the Press* died suddenly of a heart attack on June 13, 2008, the official news of his passing didn't come from an NBC correspondent; it came via an update made on Wikipedia approximately 40 minutes before the official announcement was made.

This realization instigated a debate among media representatives and the general public. After all, the story was deliberately kept quiet until Russert's wife and son, who were traveling in Italy, could be notified. Other news outlets agreed to hold the story out of respect for Russert's family, but it didn't matter. The Wikipedia update, made by an employee of a Minnesota-based company that provides Web services to local NBC-TV stations, sparked conversations prematurely and proved the Internet's power once and for all.

This is just one example of the "citizen journalists" who find and influence audiences online in a 24/7 news cycle. Traditional journalists, too, have found their way online, and many host blogs and communities that influence audiences worldwide. Now, almost all major news outlets have a roster of blogs that cover everything from business to media to the economy. The statistics that frame both traditional and citizen journalists' activities in the blogosphere tell the story of a proactive and prolific population (for more on citizen journalists and digital media relations, see Chapter 4):

- Technorati, the Internet search engine that tracks and indexes new media activity, tracks 112.8 million blogs and more than 250 million pieces of tagged social media.
- According to Technorati, more than 175,000 new blogs are created every day. Bloggers update their blogs regularly to the tune of 1.6+ million posts per day, which is equivalent to more than 18 updates per second.

These numbers aren't limited to the activity of media stakeholders because the Internet also empowers consumers; they are becoming the ultimate brand evangelists (or brand destroyers) based on the power of communications granted by digital platforms. Beyond creating their own content, these stakeholders also turn to their peers for brand references and testimonials before requesting information from companies themselves. The 2008 Edelman Trust Barometer supports this tendency, revealing that the highest percentage of respondents—58 percent—trust "a person like me" as a source of information about a company.[13]

In a similar vein, employees at every level of the organization now have more collective influence than C-suite executives, who until recently were the top-down decision makers. Now, employees have more channels through which to communicate their dissatisfaction with management, policies, workplace, etc. And whereas senior leaders could at once dismiss this discontent—or even punish it—they are now compelled, if not required, to listen up. With that, the human resources (HR) function becomes increasingly integral to the C-suite's communication with employees. The integration of HR and communication as employees take on greater roles in their organizations' reputations and bottom-line success will be discussed at length in Chapter 5; for now, suffice it to say that employees as a stakeholder group have been empowered by digital platforms, and their influence is driving change within organizations.

Externally, another stakeholder group that has always wielded a great deal of power—investors—also finds itself even more influential with the dawn of digital communications. Publicly traded companies now face increased pressure from investors owing to a boom in shareholder activism that has been enabled by the ease with which investors can communicate with other stakeholders to influence management.

The combined power of these stakeholders, which will be discussed individually in subsequent chapters, punctuates the current business context. Corporate leaders find themselves at the mercy of the people they once controlled, and their organizations' reputations hang in the balance.

Business Models Version 3.0: Evolving Corporate Strategies

This anarchic business backdrop has severe implications for global corporate executives, the majority of whom have been forced to change their business strategies accordingly (see Figure 1.3). While recent economic upheavals reshuffled the cards for many global organizations, much of this transition took place at the turn of the century, when the Internet bubble burst, the economy faltered, the American political system revealed critical flaws, and the United States experienced the largest-scale terrorist attack in history—not an inconsequential list of events to have taken place between 1999 and 2001. With these landscape-altering revisions to the direction of business, coupled with the explosive growth of new digital communications platforms, institutions themselves moved from a proverbial Web 1.0 mind-set to a Web 2.0 reality (see Figure 1.4).

Figure 1.3: Implementation of new business strategies

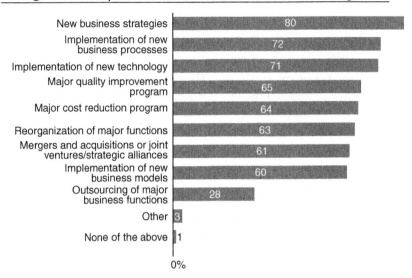

Q: Which of the following changes, if any, has your organization implemented in the past 3 years? (Base: All respondents 1,150)

Source: PricewaterhouseCoopers 11th Annual Global CEO Survey, 2008.

Figure 1.4: How to survive and thrive in business today with 2.0.

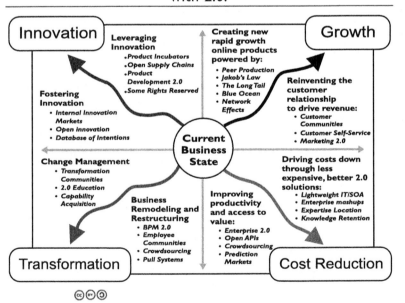

Source: Dion Hinchcliffe, Hinchcliffe & Company, 2008, http://hinchcliffeandco.com.

Figure 1.5: Top causes of business model transformation

"Which three of these issues will require the biggest changes to your business model in the next three years?"

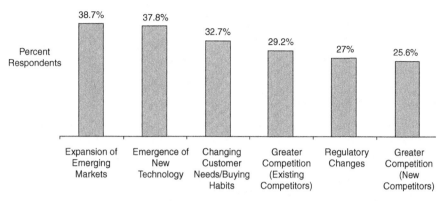

Source: "Business Model Transformation," Marketing Leadership Council, Corporate Executive Board, 2007.

This general transformation process offers a visual overview of a more specific transformation process—that of business models. In fact, the 2008 IBM Global CEO Study revealed that virtually all CEOs would be adapting their business models over the next three years, and two-thirds planned to implement extensive innovation (for types of innovative business models, see the sidebar "Types of Innovative Business Models").[14] Complementing these findings is a study conducted by the Corporate Executive Board's Marketing Leadership Council that found that in 2007, 93 percent of surveyed executives planned to make changes to their business models in the next three years. These executives cited all the trends discussed earlier in this chapter as drivers for remodeling their strategies, placing the greatest weight on the expansion of emerging markets (38.7 percent) and the emergence of new technology (37.8 percent; see Figure 1.5).[15]

TYPES OF INNOVATIVE BUSINESS MODELS

- *Enterprise model:* Specializing and reconfiguring the business to deliver greater value by rethinking what is done in-house and through collaboration (as Cisco has done by focusing on brand and design while relying on partners for manufacturing, distribution, and more).

- *Revenue model*: Changing how revenue is generated through new value propositions and new pricing models (as Gillette did by switching the primary revenue stream from razors to blades).
- *Industry model*: Redefining an existing industry, moving into a new industry, or creating an entirely new industry (think music industry and the Apple iPod and iTunes).

Source: "The Enterprise of the Future," IBM Global CEO Survey, 2008, p. 49.

The influence of these issues over the transformation of business models can be seen directly in corporate leaders' increasing interest—and, more important, investment—in intangible business drivers, including research and development (R&D), investment in building organizations, and internal and external organizational communication (see Figure 1.6). The latter drivers will be discussed at greater length in later chapters, but for now, consider it a noteworthy shift in the collective corporate mind-set from tangible to intangible investments.

Case in point: Research shows that the economic boom experienced in the 1990s can be correlated directly with an increase in intangible investment dollars. The National Bureau of Economic Research's report of R&D investments shows that R&D relative to gross domestic product (GDP) grew by 30 percent between 1994 and 2000.[16] More indicative is the fact that net intangible investment in the business sector was an estimated 3 percent of GDP prior to 1990 and rose to more than 8 percent in the late 1990s; this level dropped back down to the first approximation in 2001, which coincides with the proverbial dot-com bubble's burst. Finally, research shows that one indicator of increased intangible investment is the increased funding of R&D (aided and abetted by rapid technological advances), as well as the dramatic increase in mergers and acquisitions.[17]

Development innovations have been the crux of pharmaceutical maker Eli Lilly and Company's healthy sales growth, even in the face of its peers' general malaise. From 2002 to 2007, its sales increased at a compound annual growth rate of 11 percent[18]—an accomplishment widely attributed to its constantly evolving collaborative business models. For example, in 2001, Lilly launched InnoCentive, a Web site on which organizations can anonymously submit scientific challenges to a diverse network of more than 140,000 "solvers" from

Figure 1.6: Web 2.0 for the enterprise

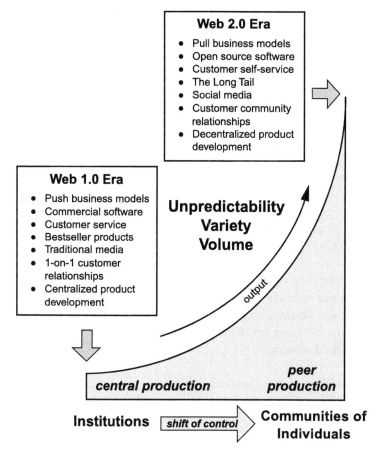

Web 2.0 for the Enterprise
New Network-Powered Business Models Offer Major Opportunities But Disrupt the Competitive Landscape

Web 2.0 Era
- Pull business models
- Open source software
- Customer self-service
- The Long Tail
- Social media
- Customer community relationships
- Decentralized product development

Web 1.0 Era
- Push business models
- Commercial software
- Customer service
- Bestseller products
- Traditional media
- 1-on-1 customer relationships
- Centralized product development

Unpredictability Variety Volume

output

central production   ***peer production***

Institutions | shift of control | **Communities of Individuals**

Source: Dion Hinchcliffe, Hinchcliffe & Company. http://blogs.zdnet.com/Hinchcliffe/?p=135.

175 countries. Then, in 2007, the company established an agreement with Nicholas Piramal India Limited (NPIL) under its newly minted status as a Fully Integrated Pharmaceutical Network (FIPNet)—that is, a model based on pioneering risk-sharing relationships aimed at

facilitating research and development.[19] The combined effect of these collaborative business models helped to reduce the company's costs, increase development capacity, accelerate the drug development process, and leverage the assets of both Eli Lilly and its external partners.[20]

Hindsight is 20/20: Times Changed, and We Should Have Too

Alongside the increase in intangible investments, which perhaps many executives committed to unknowingly—or at least impulsively—the increase in Web 2.0 platforms precipitated involvement by those who were at the forefront of the participatory age. However, for those who weren't, hindsight has proven to be 20/20 in the most clichéd sense. According to a 2007 article in *McKinsey Quarterly* entitled, "How Businesses Are Using Web 2.0," when asked what they might have done differently to make previous investments in Internet technologies more effective, 42 percent of surveyed executives said that they "invested at the right time, but should have invested more in our company's internal capabilities." Twenty-four percent said that they "should have invested sooner in technology that in the meantime had a significant impact on our industry"[21] (see Figure 1.7).

In terms of business leaders' investments specifically in social media in 2008, the following breakdown illustrates the commitment of significant financial resources:

- $149 million on social networking
- $78 million on Really Simple Syndication (RSS)
- $64 million on blogs
- $63 million on wikis
- $39 million on mash-ups
- $33 on podcasting
- $29 million on widgets

Plus, social media spending is expected to surge between 2008 and 2010 from an estimated $800 million to nearly $2 billion.[22]

But what does all of this research have to do with corporate communication's shifting role in business strategy and development? As Chapter 2 will reveal, it represents the catalysts that sparked a complete

Figure 1.7: Given hindsight

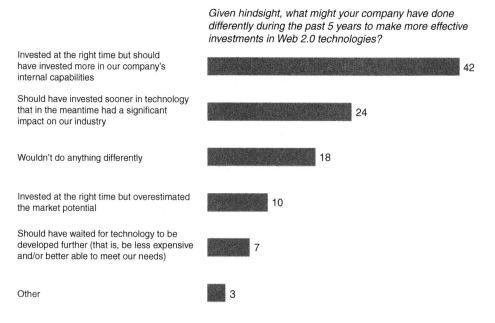

Given hindsight, what might your company have done differently during the past 5 years to make more effective investments in Web 2.0 technologies?

Invested at the right time but should have invested more in our company's internal capabilities — 42

Should have invested sooner in technology that in the meantime had a significant impact on our industry — 24

Wouldn't do anything differently — 18

Invested at the right time but overestimated the market potential — 10

Should have waited for technology to be developed further (that is, be less expensive and/or better able to meet our needs) — 7

Other — 3

transformation in the way the corporate communication function is viewed by corporate leaders, as well as the reorganization of strategic business units within the overall company (in terms of reporting relationships, etc.). Of course, technology and emerging digital communications platforms also play a role in the need to transform business strategies via increased intangible investments; their influence over stakeholders' ability to affect business' success or failure forces senior managers to at least consider substantial revisions to their strategies to respond to changes.

Besides acknowledging the rapidly changing business environment, companies must adapt without changing what they stand for or compromising their principles. In effect, companies must invest resources to establish an intimate understanding of their stakeholders' identities and preferences, a clear picture of the innovations that will enhance their brand identities in a digital context, and a thorough awareness of the risks and challenges that could derail even the sturdiest of business strategies.

Conclusion

This chapter introduced the modern business environment in the context of the profound changes that continuously redefine the way companies interact with their stakeholders, especially in terms of the two-way conversations facilitated by digital communications platforms. In the following chapters we will provide the strategies and tactics needed to exploit these digital platforms to regain the control over messaging that has been ceded to stakeholders, leaving corporate reputations—and, in turn, bottom-line business results—vulnerable to irreversible damage. But first we will consider the changing environment's impact on organizations in terms of structures and reporting relationships, with a specific focus on the corporate communication function's emergence as a key player in leading companies into this new era of business.

CHAPTER 2

CORPORATE DARWINISM
ORGANIZATIONAL STRUCTURES EVOLVE TO MEET CHANGING STAKEHOLDER DEMANDS

When Charles Darwin developed his evolutionary theory around natural selection and the concept of survival of the fittest, he couldn't have known how well it would translate to twenty-first-century business. Based on the trends identified in Chapter 1, including heightened public scrutiny, emerging digital communications platforms, and the subsequent stakeholder empowerment these platforms enable, corporations have been forced to adapt to a new environment. Those that haven't, suffer the consequences and, in many cases, become vulnerable to extinction.

This chapter will consider the theory of corporate evolution in a number of contexts—the need for corporate leaders to evolve their business strategies to remain competitive and to protect their organizations' reputations, as well as corporate communication's evolution from a backroom function to one that is integral to senior management's decision-making processes. The chapter then will introduce the concept of integration and its relationship to the alignment of many organizational subfunctions, including media relations, investor relations, and human resources. Finally, the chapter will offer an in-depth look at each subfunction that now resides under the umbrella of "corporate

communication" and explain the significance of emerging digital platforms to each platform's interactions with the others and with the organization as a whole to strengthen corporate reputation and, ultimately,
the bottom line.

The Global Village: Globalization's Impact on Organizational Communications

The drastic shift in the business landscape, complicated by the ongoing
changes that continue to transform it, has a number of significant implications for corporate leaders. With control over corporate reputation,
brand, and messaging shifting from senior executives to their stakeholders, corporations must evolve their overall business strategies to
place an increased focus on the communication function.

Of course, this impetus to redefine strategies with a more respected
view of the contributions of communications wasn't based solely on the
loss of power to stakeholders discussed in Chapter 1. Consider the rep-
utation-damaging crises that happen with a higher frequency and are
more difficult to anticipate, especially with the influence of digital communication channels over a global 24/7 news cycle. These crises, fueled
by the harsh, often-impulsive criticisms of stakeholders that gather and
converse online, can only be weathered if a reputation is strong enough
to endure the storm.

An ever-growing number of examples illustrate this point, which
we will focus on in later chapters. However, one example that demonstrates the Web's ability to take an issue and elevate it to crisis status in
no time flat involves Dell. The computer manufacturer's reputation was
thrown for a loop when in June 2005 an irate blogger by the name of
Jeff Jarvis lambasted the company for poor customer service. Within
hours, hoards of consumers who were in agreement with his claims
posted comments on Jarvis' blog as well as their own, thus creating a
maelstrom of negativity throughout the blogosphere. The company
remained in the doghouse for months after failing to address the discontent properly in cyberspace; however, beginning with the launch of
its own blog (Direct2Dell) in July 2006, executives finally joined the

online conversation and began to slowly rebuild the company's tarnished image.

The blog was put to good use when another potential crisis—a widespread battery recall—hit. Dell's chief blogger, Lionel Menchaca, addressed the issue in a human voice and enabled customers to comment freely. Michael Dell even launched IdeaStorm.com in February 2007 and implored customers to give the company advice. New metrics show that the company's customer-service rating has risen significantly.

This is just one example of the modern business climate's impact on corporate reputations and the crises that threaten them. Business leaders also must consider the dramatic increase in global mergers and acquisitions (M&A) volume, which surpassed the $3.4-trillion record set in 2000 by reaching $3.8 trillion in 2006.[1] M&A activity places pressure on executives to merge often-disparate corporate cultures and to rebrand the organization with a new identity (see Chapter 3 for more on branding/rebranding).

An additional element that has profound effects on organizations, whether or not they are involved in M&A activity, is corporate culture. After all, today's tumultuous business environment is ripe with reputational risks such as Apple's dependence on Steve Jobs, who is a cancer survivor facing further illness, or the connection between the evil financier Bernard Madoff and several fund managers. As a result, companies need to change and evolve. In doing so, though, they can't build strategies without first aligning the organization's identity, mission, and goals. And when two companies—and, therefore, two cultures—combine, this alignment is critical.

It comes as no surprise that digital communications channels ease this alignment because they provide platforms for interacting with employees regardless of location. Hewlett-Packard (HP) executives realized this early on in their 2002 merger with Compaq Computer Corporation, a move that brought together more than 88,000 employees across 178 countries. To improve information management and cultural alignment during this time, HP executives, with the help of public relations (PR) agency Porter Novelli, created @hp, a business-to-employee intranet portal that acted as a gateway to the merging HP and Compaq legacy intranets. This platform would serve as the infrastructure to communicate messages to all 88,000+ employees in multiple languages and at multiple locations.

According to Porter Novelli Senior Vice President Peter Eschbach and Account Manager Jeremy Morgan, both of whom worked with HP to develop the intranet:

> *A shared sense of community would be critical to the integration of the two organizations. . . . [Our intranet's homepage] needed to embody and propagate elements of the new corporate culture, while also promoting the numerous professional and personal communities of interest to be found within the new company. The two companies [HP and Compaq] worked together to establish an internal communications infrastructure that harmonized intranet-related messaging and coordinated employee outreach to ensure that communications were delivered at the right time to the right internal audiences.*[2]

This merger experience highlights both the challenges associated with combining two disparate cultures and the opportunities offered by digital platforms. But it isn't the only example: In late 2006, Dow Jones began the process of acquiring Factiva from Dow's venture partner Reuters. The acquisition took a great deal of communications prowess. In addition to the usual challenges presented by M&A activity, one unusual circumstance was thrown into the mix: Factiva was owned as a joint venture between Dow Jones and Reuters but always had operated independently. As a result, many Factiva employees weren't familiar with the Dow Jones culture, to which they would be required to assimilate.

This question of corporate culture—so relevant during a merger or acquisition, but increasingly more important to any public company thanks to stakeholder empowerment—will come into play in later chapters. In the case of Dow Jones's acquisition of Factiva, though, it was certainly top of mind for executives, as was their use of technology to communicate. According to Diane Thieke, director of global public relations for Dow Jones:

> *Making good use of technology enables you to build a corporate culture worldwide. Our head of internal communications and I [worked closely during the acquisition process]..., and our philosophy was to be completely transparent with all stakeholders, and particularly with*

employees. You must keep employees up-to-date and informed before [acquisition-related] external messages go out.[3]

Crafting messaging during a merger or acquisition isn't solely a function of communications, though, as evidenced by Dow Jones Executive Vice President and Chief Marketing Officer Alan Scott's participation. During the Factiva acquisition, he said:

Corporate communications, PR and marketing executives all got together to decide where we had the most brand equity overall, and then what the best way to move forward would be in terms of leveraging that equity and creating a go-to-market strategy. Then, [it was about] ... putting together a polity that allows the organization to be seen and act as a thought leader.[4]

From the Backroom to the Boardroom

Up to this point, we have considered the modern business environment, the catalysts that brought it to its current condition, its impact on corporate leaders, and the reasons that these leaders are now inspired (or should be) to give greater attention to the communication function. Our focus is on digital communications platforms and the role they play in empowering stakeholders but also communicators. Before we go any further, though, it is important to understand the function itself.

Corporate communication, formerly described more basically as PR, grew up within organizations to meet the need of responding to external stakeholders. The earliest iteration of the function was communication at its most basic level; it was largely tactical, with employees responsible for PR-related activities that focused mostly on generating publicity through press releases and, when trouble arose, keeping the press at bay. A common complaint these professionals had was their inability to "get a seat at the table," which refers to their lack of representation at C-level meetings, when high-level strategies are shaped and executed.

Management's argument, if it could be defined as such, hinged on the misunderstanding that PR was a cost to the organization and offered very little return. After all, PR executives dealt largely with intangible assets such as reputation, whereas the marketing executives down the hall could justify their budgets by demonstrating the return on investment (ROI) of advertising campaigns. When faced with the choice of giving money to PR or to marketing, then, management historically favored the latter, encouraged by the hard numbers this function could bring back to show the effect of its work.

In conjunction with the competition historically brought on by the marketing discipline, it's also worth considering the corporate communication function's counterpart: external PR agencies. Their rise in prominence over the course of the last decade helps to set the stage for the current role corporate communications plays in companies.

In the economic boom of the late 1990s, PR agencies went on a proverbial shopping spree, hiring new and expensive talent to meet their clients' voracious appetites for services. Then the terrorist attacks of 9/11 and the dot-com bust crippled the businesses that had, mere weeks earlier, been fat, happy, and more than willing to write checks for service firms, including PR agencies. Executives within these agencies responded to the financial hit accordingly, firing their most expensive assets—the senior-level strategists—and relying on cheaper junior staffers to do most of the client work. Traditional consultancies, à la McKinsey and Bain, recognized the crater left by the void of senior PR talent and began to offer their clients strategic counseling services that once fell within communications' parameters. This commoditization of PR left an industry that was on the upswing after years of battling a negative image back in the doghouse; once again, these professionals were defined by their ability to write press releases and little else. Redefining their roles from tacticians to strategic counselors became another top priority. Whether this is a necessary shift in focus or merely a manifestation of preferences in diction remains to be seen, but there is certainly an argument to be made that in the current business environment, moving completely away from tactical skills isn't a wise approach.

"Despite the fact that most everyday PR activity focuses on tactics, the tendency within most PR circles is to overemphasize the strategic aspects of public relations and to subordinate the tactical. To be taken seriously, it seems, everyone with a PR responsibility feels the need to self-identify as a strategist," said Mark Weiner, CEO of PRIME Research North America, a global PR and corporate reputation research-based consulting firm. "The implications for PR's heavy emphasis on strategy are clear: Strategy is the superior mental and managerial activity, and tactics can be relegated harmlessly to the lower echelons. In reality, this argument is simply wrong."[5]

Rather, to accommodate increasingly complex organizational needs, PR professionals must hone strategic *and* tactical skill sets to both set objectives and achieve them. According to Weiner:

> *Those who choose to marry tactics with strategy will almost certainly succeed. In the first place, tactics must be fully considered as a part of the strategic process if anything is to come as a result of conducting a campaign. As the Chinese general and philosopher Sun Tzu wrote in 500 B.C., "Strategy without tactics is the slowest route to victory. Tactics without strategy is the noise before defeat."*[6]

Thanks to digital communications developments and the 24/7 news cycle, slow routes to victory are not an option for corporations, nor are noisy defeats (made all the noisier by stakeholders' online grumblings). That said, these challenges, coupled with the increase in M&A activity to the commoditization of PR, have come full circle to position communication professionals to take a leading role, strategically *and* tactically, in their organizations. While getting "a seat at the table" and scraping by on shoestring budgets are still legitimate struggles among some PR/communication executives, the situation quickly began to change in recent years because senior leaders are increasingly confronted with heightened public scrutiny, stakeholder empowerment, a more stringent regulatory environment, and of course, emerging digital communication platforms.

According to Jon Iwata, senior vice president of marketing and communications at IBM Corporation:

> *There are pretty clear implications of message control and segmentation of audiences. [Digital media] . . . has created a great deal of complexity, but it has put a potentially powerful array of new tools into the hands of communicators. We are in the business of building and selecting channels of communication, but now we can build networks of relationships with the . . . [stakeholders] we care about.*[7]

Thus, as more management teams recognized the need for developing relationships via communications, PR began its transition from a backroom mechanism to a central function within corporations. No longer dismissed as a cost with diminished returns to the organization, today's most successful companies, such as IBM, view the corporate communication function as a profit center, even going so far as to transfer funds that historically went to marketing into communication's budget or to merge the two functions.

The backroom-to-boardroom evolution happened concurrently with the increased importance of brand and corporate reputation, two intangible assets that communicators are best equipped to handle based on their inherent skills in building and maintaining relationships with stakeholders. While marketers, for example, create campaigns to move customers to take action (usually in the form of purchasing a product or service), they don't have the inherent propensity for nurturing the relationships with stakeholders that ultimately define the strength of the organization's reputation and the viability of its brand—a difference that will be explored in greater depth in Chapter 3.

"New media models give [communication professionals] additional ways of reaching audiences with messages. But this is not about expanding channels of communication. It's about building networks of relationships," said IBM's Iwata. "But it starts with a recognition that we are no longer in control of our company's messages and channels—which we don't have anyway. Once we liberate ourselves from that illusion, we can begin to adopt and embrace new ways, tools and approaches."[8]

Ultimately, suffice it to say that emerging digital platforms have put communications executives in the position to reassert and reinvent themselves as valuable leaders within their organizations, which is a natural segue way to the next step of communications' repositioning in companies—a completely refined job description that bestows these executives with newfound responsibilities across every business function.

Form Fits Function: Integration Redefines the Role of Corporate Communications

With recognition of the corporate communication function as more strategic than tactical, senior executives are now inclined to integrate it into the overall organization. However, inclined is the operative word because this inclination, in many cases, stalls in the earliest stages of development. But the situation isn't as hopeless as it may sound. The communication function has received more kudos—and, in turn, more responsibility—as the changing business environment becomes apparent to corporate leaders. According to "The Authentic Enterprise CEO Report" by the Arthur W. Page Society:

> *In earlier eras, a company's principles, credos or beliefs—like its strate-gies and processes—were typically dictated from the top. However, we now live in a world of distributed, dynamic enterprises and shifting workforce attitudes and expectations. This demands increased delega-tion and empowerment, while maintaining consistency of brand, customer relationships, public reputation and day-to-day operations.*[9]

Speaking of increased delegation and empowerment, research shows that communications professionals do enjoy a marked improvement regarding their prominence as strategic counselors (see Table 2.1). The "Fifth Annual Generally Accepted Practices Study," released by the Strategic Public Relations Center at the University of Southern California on May 18, 2008, revealed that a growing number of companies recognize the value of corporate communications and are adapting their budgets and internal structures accordingly. For exam-ple, the study showed that PR/communications budgets increased by 10 percent between 2002 and 2007 for all responding organizations. And when asked to describe the extent to which communications

Table 2.1: Relying on PR Counsel: Aside from internal/ external communications in which of these areas do you involve your PR counsel?

Function	Total (Percent of CEOs)
Managing corporate reputation	70.8%
Recruiting top talent	64.6
Launching new products	62.5
Developing company strategy	59.7
Engagement with community leaders	59.0
CSR (Corporate Social Responsibility)	57.6
Boosting investor/analyst perception; perception of your company's well-being	57.6
Retaining top talent	55.6
Green/sustainability/environmental issues	55.6
Weathering a crisis (product recall, etc.)	53.5
Shaping your corporate brand	50.7

Source: Burson-Marsteller/PR Week 2007 CEO Survey, November 12, 2007.

functions were integrated in their organizations (1 = not at all integrated; 7 = extremely integrated), respondents specified a solid level of integration (4.92) compared with 2002 (4.64).[10]

To understand the concept of integration fully, though, an in-depth examination of companies' organizational structuring is required. *Organizational structure* refers to the way that people are arranged within their companies in terms of both reporting relationships and divisions of responsibility.

In the context of organizations and their subfunctions, historically, structuring could be categorized loosely as centralized or decentralized. *Centralized* communications functions describe those in which all communications activities report to one senior officer at headquarters. Conversely, *decentralized* activities allow individual business units to handle communications independently. There are pros and cons to both approaches. In the past, more centralized models provided an easier way for companies to achieve consistency in and control over all communications activities. With increased globalization and fragmentation of media, however, this model is becoming obsolete because companies now need to have communications capabilities that extend into every area of their business and that address specific needs as they arise.

The decentralized model lies at the opposite end of the spectrum; it gives individual business units more flexibility in adapting the function to their own needs. This model was ideal for an organization as large and diversified as Johnson & Johnson (J&J), for example: With more than 110,000 employees in more than 200 operating companies in 57 different countries, complete centralization of communications would be difficult, if not impossible. Instead, Bill Nielsen, the legendary former corporate vice president of corporate communication at J&J, described the function as "a partnership of professionals in communication."[11]

These black-and-white approaches were more effective in an era when stakeholders received messages passively; today, it is more difficult to manage communications in "silos," thus requiring managers to reshape their organizational structures to reach highly targeted audiences with customized messages. Finding a middle ground between a completely centralized and a wholly decentralized structure is the best way to maintain an effective communications strategy in today's environment. For example, a centralized functional area can be supplemented by a network of decentralized communications executives who adapt the function to meet the special needs of individual business units.

While every company is structured slightly differently to meet its own needs—be it centralized or decentralized—there are, almost without exception, always certain positions that report directly to the CEO and subsequently define the rest of the organization's reporting relationships. Traditionally, a common C-suite would include (but not necessarily be limited to) the chief executive officer (CEO), chief marketing officer (CMO), chief financial officer (CFO), chief information officer (CIO), and chief operational officer (COO). However, the modern business environment has precipitated something of a boom in the creation of chief communications officer (CCO) positions—a role that, in the past, often fell under the chief administrative officer (CAO) umbrella.

In fact, a 2008 study released by Weber Shandwick and Spencer Stuart revealed a strong correlation between a company's corporate communications organization and its ranking on *Fortune*'s "World's Most Admired Companies" list. The study, dubbed "The Rising CCO," compared responses from 141 top communications executives in the "World's Most Admired Companies" with those from "contender companies" to find that the former class of executives has more prominent organizational statuses and longer tenures than their counterparts.[12]

Perhaps more significant, though, is the connection drawn between communication and an organization's reputation: Approximately 34 percent of CCOs from the most admired companies cited corporate reputation as their number one priority for 2008, compared with fewer than 21 percent of CCOs at contender companies. According to Dr. Leslie Gaines-Ross, chief reputation strategist at Weber Shandwick, "Our research identifies how the corporate communications function can be a critical force in driving a company's reputation in good times and bad. With the right organizational structure and partnership at the top, the best CCOs can significantly contribute to building shareholder value and corporate reputation."[13]

This nod to the importance of CCOs within companies brings us back to the factor that is so imbedded in the collective evolution of organizational structures—integration. As the PR profession began to transform into an empowered carbon copy of its former self, communications executives took more aggressive steps to integrate their activities with those of other functions; not coincidentally, this transformation happened as "international" companies became truly multinational corporations. It was not until the 1980s, when trade barriers were dropped and the privatization of state-owned companies occurred regularly, that a company's organizational form could become increasingly efficient. The rise of the Internet in the 1990s only served to highlight that the economic and industrial rules of the game had changed.

Thus traditional means of structuring reporting relationships became inefficient. According to Sam Palmisano, CEO of IBM:

> *It's about culture and how decisions are made. The old model of the corporation was vertically integrated, whereas today, the most important kind of integration—the most important way to be "one"—is horizontal. For IBM today, being one means figuring out ways for 370,000 IBMers, expert in virtually every industry and working in 170 countries across the globe, as well as literally millions of business partners and other members of IBM's global ecosystem, to exercise their own judgment and imagination ... but at the same time produce work that is consistently and recognizably "IBM."*[14]

Note that this antisilo organizational approach emphasizes the importance of both fostering a consistent brand and allowing employees to exercise their imaginations and foster innovation; in other words, communication—among employees, managers, and external stakeholders—is of paramount value.

According to IBM's Iwata:

> *[In 2006], IBM's business consulting unit surveyed more than 750 CEOs from all over the world on the subject of innovation. The CEOs had a lot to say. They emphatically agreed that innovation is a top priority for them and their companies, and they see themselves as personally driving the innovation agenda. They said that innovation today meant more than novel products and services, and that it extended to innovative business processes and models and to how they manage their workforces and evolve their corporate cultures.*

Significantly for communications executives, the CEOs identified as top sources of innovative ideas their own customers, business partners and the general employee population. This is excellent news for communications executives. It means that CEOs are asking for help to drive systemic change across the enterprise. It means that CEOs are looking for ways to engage employees in meaningful, two-way dialogue, and to find ways to open up their companies to collaborate with customers and business partners. The fact that they need all of this but are scratching their heads as to how to get it done spells opportunity for progressive communications leaders who rise to the challenge.[15]

INTEGRATION'S CATALYSTS, APPROACHES, AND BENEFITS

Catalysts:

- The legal and regulatory environment
- Sophisticated overlapping constituencies
- Organizational growth and complexity
- Technology

Approaches:

- Reporting relationships
- Creation of informal communications councils
- Creation of a unique communications integration manager position
- Leveraging technology

Benefits:

- Preservation of the corporate brand, enhanced reputation
- Ability to weather crises more effectively
- Optimization of business outcomes

Source: Paul Argenti, "The Power of Integration: Building a Corporate Communication Function That Is Greater Than the Sum of Its Parts," Tuck School of Business at Dartmouth for NIRI's Center for Strategic Communication, Hanover, NH, September 2005.

Ultimately, this shift in mind-set has precipitated the increasingly prevalent role of communications in an organization's reporting structures. Case in point: Many companies have gone so far as to completely restructure their reporting relationships in recent years to place more focus on corporate communication, especially its role in protecting and enhancing reputations. As mentioned briefly early in this chapter, the usual structures—centralized and decentralized—met the needs of most organizations until relatively recently, mostly owing to the one-way communications that took place between a company and its stakeholders.

Now, with the number of multinationals growing exponentially and the continued emergence of digital communications platforms, organizations that rely on these approaches find themselves less and less successful in communicating with their target audiences (for specific catalysts of integration, see the sidebar "Integration's Catalysts, Approaches, and Benefits"). In light of the challenges presented by the modern business environment, then, how *should* senior managers consider restructuring in the context of the corporate communication function—and how can digital platforms facilitate the process?

Matrix Reloaded: An Integrated Organizational Structure Gives Communications the Lead

A third category of organization structures is the most ambiguous, with its malleability helping to meet the ever-changing needs of corporations. Matrix structures, which first gained popularity in the late 1970s but were implemented originally with relatively little success, came back into style with improved results in the late 1990s and 2000s because this era's economic and corporate environments were better suited to this type of management. According to the Corporate Leadership Council, these structures most often define flat, horizontal corporations that are organized around teams and that have a greater drive to increase customer satisfaction.[16]

Reasons for the relative success of the matrix structure include its ability to leverage core competencies across horizontal companies, to stay plugged in with local stakeholders (in the case of global organizations), to react responsively to the needs of different markets, and to keep up with shorter production cycles. In short, products and individual brands within a corporation often drive organizational structures. According to Georg Baur, CEO of BMW Financial Services, "Products have to be local with a global brand. I see us as a globally integrated organization with a local presence and localized products."[17]

However, while products and brands are key to organizational approaches, the ability to develop relationships "on the ground" with local employees and consumers often determines the use of one organizational approach over another. A more modern, "digital minded" iteration of the matrix structure that focuses on relationships within the organization, as well as between the organization and external partners, is the networking model, which focuses on the interests of individual communities and stakeholders and develops value propositions around them accordingly. As corporate leaders move to embrace integration, the majority—60 percent of them, according to IBM's 2008 Global CEO Survey—are taking largely global approaches by leveraging networks and local partners (see Figure 2.1).

According to Rupert Stadler, chairman of the board of management of Audi AG:

> *Networking plays a substantial role at Audi. We're a company with branches in 130 countries around the world. You can't make this business model work unless you have partners that you can trust. The biggest opportunity of this networking model is that you make use of available skills and conserve your own resources. We assume that our local partners know their market much better than we do and can do a lot better than we could from Germany. As for risk, the big risk is mistrust.*

Figure 2.1: The two most common approaches to organizational structure

The two most common approaches are more global. One focuses locally. And the fourth falls in the middle between both extremes.

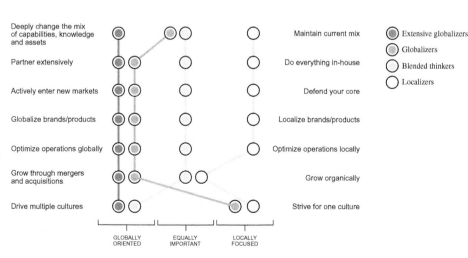

Obviously, in a collaborative relationship, you are completely dependent and at your partner's mercy. This means one has to think about how to manage everything. But I think good networks and good partnerships are characterized by both parties continually moving forward to address these issues. One has to cultivate a culture of discussion.[18]

Indeed, research suggests that corporate culture is the most important factor in determining the success of a matrix structure, as well as being one of the intangibles cultivated and maintained by the corporate communication function. While this will be discussed in greater detail in Chapter 5, Mike Davies, global director of communications for PricewaterhouseCoopers, notes that his organization adopted a matrix structure after its 1998 merger (between Price Waterhouse and Coopers & Lybrand):

Communications is paramount when you are trying to bring together two organizations, or when you are trying to communicate worldwide. Communications has to be very high up on the agenda. I have a central team of 10 that deals with communications issue, but then we work in close cooperation with the communications leaders around the world.[19]

Davies offers these best practices when considering a modern matrix structure:

- "You must be able to explain to people who are driving the business that it isn't just a case of money and resources. It's about spending time to manage and communicate both internally and externally."
- "Execution can differ widely from country to country, so you have to understand and accommodate local need. You can have a core message, but you have to tailor that to the marketplaces you disseminate to."
- "News travels very fast these days, so you need to be close with your network in order to get the right intelligence and then react to situations. You can always make things better when bringing on new technology. Though it's not the answer, it is part of the solution. You have to make the message worth reading."[20]

These strategies are overarching themes in any modern communications effort, and they help to address restructuring challenges. The point becomes even more salient when illustrated by another company's journey to true integration, which optimized the internal economic, cultural, and political forces that already existed and then delivered a value proposition for individual stakeholders and, ultimately, for the company as a whole.

And the Walls Come Tumbling Down: Diagnosing and Implementing Effective Organizational Structures

The value of centralized, decentralized, and matrixed organizational structures is certainly company-specific, but changes in the global business landscape discussed thus far have forced almost every corporate leader to reevaluate his or her company's internal processes. One of the greatest challenges is diagnosing which structure will optimize business performance, facilitate development, control costs, and enhance employee development—all at the same time. Choosing the wrong structure and moving forward to implement it can have devastating effects on brands and bottom lines. HP executives, for example, spent 16 years alternating between centralized and decentralized organizational structures, losing critical business assets with each transition.[21] More recently, HP executives began leveraging digital assets, including the intranet, as we mentioned earlier in this chapter, to streamline internal communications and integrate business units after its 2002 merger with Compaq.

DaimlerChrysler, on the other hand, couldn't pull off the reorganization instigated by the 1998 merger, thus failing to realize the hyped synergy that would never be brought to life. While it was true that there may have been very little overlap between the product lines of the businesses (Mercedes built high-end, exclusive automobiles, whereas Chrysler operated in mass-market mode), achieving synergy is never a given. More is needed, such as the willingness to integrate supplier relationships. Looking to become a global behemoth, the company abandoned the core supply management principles at the unit level that had differentiated the Chrysler brand under Lee Iacocca, reverting back to pressure tactics to squeeze the best possible prices from its suppliers.

As late as 2002, analysts noted that DaimlerChrysler appeared to be running two independent product lines. Worried about diluting its luxury brand, Daimler never followed through on its promise to share patents and vehicle architectures between Chrysler and Mercedes-Benz models—a key selling point of the original deal. And questions have always persisted about whether the traditional hierarchical management model prevalent in Germany, with its silos of reporting levels, was able to be flattened as easily as Daimler anticipated. Less than a decade into the merger, in August 2007, DaimlerChrysler completed the sale of Chrysler to Cerberus Capital Management, a private equity firm that specializes in restructuring troubled companies.

What HP's and DaimlerChrysler's struggles with structures do highlight is key for all business leaders: No single organizational structure is a panacea for business challenges. Even a matrixed approach, which on paper appears to solve many of the problems associated with pure centralization or decentralization, has proven to be ineffective. Giving equal power to different leaders throughout a corporation presents conflicts of interest that can be resolved only if one party agrees to cede power. This structure is also prone to disconnects in management's communications with employees company-wide, thus prompting their trust in leadership to suffer.

Does this mean that there is no real solution? Yes and no. Before the emergence of digital technologies, corporate leaders were forced to be married largely to one structure and one structure only because any mixing and matching usually led to gaps in communications. But digital communication channels facilitate cheap and immediate connections between offices around the world; they also provide mechanisms for executives specifically to communicate goals and strategies for reorganizations to employees themselves, as General Electric (GE) did via its GE Reports blog on November 18, 2008. Executives posted the company's new organizational chart for its GE Capital Division and also used the forum to explain the reasons for the reorganization and to post a video interview with Bill Cary, COO of GE Capital, and Communications Director Marissa Moretti that discussed the change.[22] Thanks to the ability to streamline communications around restructuring, many companies have begun to embrace a buffet approach to reorganizations, taking a little of this and a little of that to meet their specific needs and seeing no real reason to label it one way or the other. Most organizations today are too complicated for labels anyway.

As IBM CEO Sam Palmisano summarized:

The challenge for IBM—given our complexity, geographic dispersion and the breadth of our businesses—is to define what is common, shared and enduring. That's what being "one company" is about for us—and it's not synonymous with centralization or top-down control. It is not at all the same thing as rigidity, conformity or even alignment, which are actually fairly easy to impose as management systems.[23]

Adidas is a prime example of an organization whose recent restructuring had very little to do with alignment, let alone a "one company" vision. Beginning in 2000, its leadership began planning a reorganization that would position the Germany-based company for massive growth in all its markets. That strategy has largely been realized, especially since its 2006 acquisition of Reebok. Once organized under a matrix structure that divided the company into brands and regions, Adidas now takes a combined centralized and decentralized approach, leaning toward one or the other based on specific units' needs. For example, the company no longer organizes according to region; all divisions are brand-specific, falling under either Adidas, Reebok, or Taylor Made (in 2006, all products that didn't fall under these brands' core subsets of golf, sports shoes, or sportswear were sold[24]). These brands and their related activities—all of which are consumer-facing—are decentralized, each having its own leaders (who report directly to the CEO) and brand identities (i.e., logos, design, marketing, etc.). This approach has a number of benefits: The individual brands' employees can focus on one mission and corporate culture, and consumers aren't confused by convoluted messaging or branding that detract from the products.

Global Operations, then, hovers above these three brand divisions on the organizational chart. This is a centralized cluster of functions that handle all non-consumer-facing activities, including the coordination and optimization of production planning, inbound and outbound logistics, and supplier relations (Adidas' production is completely outsourced). Thus the brand identities—from the perspectives of both employees and consumers—are Adidas' competitive advantage, and they guide organizational strategies accordingly. Said Herbert Hainer, CEO of Adidas, "The management of brands is our core competence, and we are sure that we can reach a bigger target audience with separate world-class brands."[25]

Meanwhile, Dutch firm Philips Electronics, led by CEO Gerard Kleisterlee, underwent a restructuring of its own, seeking to identify the tie that binds its employees to the company and, in turn, increase synergies and enable cooperative efforts among all organizational functions.

The crux of the strategy to achieve this goal was to ensure that the values and beliefs of Philips' core businesses resided within its employees rather than on a piece of paper in a strategic plan. After all, even in a technologically advanced world, there is only so much that enterprise resource planning systems can do to facilitate true integration. Bringing a company to its potential today is not about nature versus nurture but rather about how, in bringing together global units, a company can take advantage of the competitive environment through culture changes and aligned communications—a philosophy that can be described in short as "one company."

Unlike other companies, which have undergone transformation mainly in response to competitive pressures or the sometimes culturally harsh realities of postmerger euphoria, Philips' Kleisterlee instinctively understood the inherent value of the one-company tenets and the bottom-line effect those could have on his company. At the beginning of his tenure as CEO, Philips consisted of an armada of independent ships each with its own identity, about which he said, "I was determined to change them to one effective fleet joining forces aimed at serving customers' needs in an integrated way."[26] Until the late 1990s, Philips' strategy was the accumulation of individual divisional strategies focused primarily on its high-volume electronics value chain. Unfortunately, that wasn't where the company was making money. Medical devices and lighting were where the action was.

Philips' first step was to establish consistency in its communications, making sure that the messages and media the company was projecting were aligned in its external and internal platforms—in other words, that they were truly integrated. Accomplishing such a goal involved taking a tough look at the consistency in the look and feel of media, as well as the themes and messages conveyed. Part of the process was checking to see that redundancies were avoided and that there was no "local" messaging within departments that was out of step with the effort.

In addition, tracking progress in the degrees of employee alignment (as measured by desired behavior) will allow management to be in control of the change process—enabling managers to press the right buttons at the right time.

Philips has been using a tool assessing the degree of employee alignment at a global level for years. The tool enables it to see figures corresponding to the awareness, attitude, understanding, and actual behavior of Philips' people at divisional and country levels. Kleisterlee uses these figures not only to be aware of the failures and successes of the change process but also to create awareness about the fact that the "Towards One Philips" strategy really was serious and that he could see who was a follower and who was an opponent.

Measuring alignment among employees with corporate strategy is fundamentally different from traditional employee satisfaction surveys. While the former is a proxy for risk assessment regarding the implementation of the intended strategy, the latter is a proxy for the degree of retention within a company. To put it simply, alignment research provides an answer to the question, "Do my people do what I want them to do?" whereas employee satisfaction studies focus on the question, "Will my people still work for me next month?"

Realizing a one-company philosophy is not a simple goal to achieve, and without clear ambition from top management to become a unified business, many companies will fail in the effort to make the transformation.

For Philips, as for most companies, the most convincing argument to reaching consensus on aiming for one company boils down to anticipated improvements in the marketplace thanks to a balanced approach that serves customer demands in a more efficient way. For Philips, its key account management system—which showcased clear bottom-line gains—was the turning point in gaining company-wide acceptance of Kleisterlee's internal "One Philips" campaign. As just one example, Philips' communications and HR teams were able to offer proof of lowered costs for attracting capital, which, in turn, increased the corporate brand's prestige and lowered recruitment costs.

This example of Philips' process to achieve integrated communications is ideal for setting the stage for the organizational subfunctions that, thanks to integration and organizational restructurings, now reside beneath the corporate communications umbrella:

Marketing

Historically, the marketing function has been PR/corporate communications' greatest competitor in terms of both budgets and respect from senior leadership. The Corporate Executive Board defines marketing as the "organizational function and set of processes for creating, communicating and delivering value to customers and for managing customer relationships in ways that benefit the organization and its stakeholders." As will be discussed in Chapter 3, integration and digital technologies abetted the process of transferring the responsibilities of customer messaging from the marketing to the communication function.

Media Relations

While the old-fashioned PR function focused almost exclusively on dealing with media relations may be a thing of the past, the subfunction now referred to as *media relations* is still central to the corporate communication function; so too is it evolving almost as quickly as the function itself, given the fragmentation of media and the concurrent proliferation of digital media channels. Regardless of the monumental changes occurring in this subfunction, it still refers to the processes of communicating an organization's news to media, be they traditional journalists or, as they are more and more frequently, bloggers.

Internal Communications

Once owned primarily by human resources (HR), internal communications—which encompasses talent management and employee relations—has an increasingly prominent role in the corporate communication function as companies focus on retaining a contented workforce in the face of changing values and demographics. While strong internal communications always have generated a more engaged, productive, and loyal workforce, the business themes discussed thus far have further necessitated strong communications channels between management and employees to win back employee trust and loyalty. More and more, companies are making sure that their employees understand the new marketing initiatives they are communicating externally and are uniting the workforce behind common goals and corporate strategies. This type of communication requires the expertise of strong corporate communicators who are also well connected to senior management and the corporate strategy process.

Additionally, difficult economic times, layoffs, and uncertainty require open, honest communication from senior management to all employees. The sensitive nature of some of these messages further speaks for the involvement of seasoned communications professionals alongside their HR counterparts and, most important, of the CEO or of senior executives who are the individuals communicating messages to internal and external audiences most frequently.

Finally, owing to the merging of stakeholder groups, companies must recognize that employees now also may represent investors and members of community advocacy groups—making thoughtful communications even more critical.

Investor Relations

Traditionally, investor relations (IR) was handled by the finance function, often reporting to the company's CFO, but the focus in recent years has moved away from "just the numbers" to the way the numbers are actually communicated to various stakeholders. IR professionals deal primarily with shareholders and securities analysts, who are often a direct source for the financial press, which this subfunction cultivates in conjunction with experts from the media relations area. IR professionals interact heavily with both individual and institutional investors. They also are highly involved with the financial statements and annual reports that every public firm must produce.

Given the quantitative messages, as well as the need for IR professionals to choose their words carefully to avoid any semblance of transferring inside information, the IR subfunction must be a coordinated effort between communications professionals and the IR team. The need for this coordination has only increased in recent years with more stringent regulatory demands in the age of Sarbanes-Oxley and Regulation Fair Disclosure (Reg FD), both of which will be discussed in greater detail in Chapter 6.

Corporate Social Responsibility

Today, reputational risks and rewards transcend simply staying out of trouble; rather, stakeholders are far more proactive in seeking out information about corporations, and corporate social responsibility (CSR) now plays a much larger role in forming these groups' perceptions. Study after study shows that how good a "corporate citizen" a company is directly correlates with the strength of its reputation, brand, and bottom line.

As the CSR discipline—also referred to as *corporate citizenship, philanthropy, sustainability*, or *green*—evolved, the corporate communication function quickly adopted it. Pressures to have a positive impact on communities, employees, consumers, and investors (in other words, stakeholders) mounted, and simply *doing* good had far less impact than *communicating* the good that was being done. And with increased globalization and international corporate expansion, stakeholders' expectations for corporate citizenship also have grown more global in scope. In turn, many companies are publishing environmental and social performance information in the same manner as they traditionally would report financials. This, along with other CSR and green-marketing-related endeavors, will be discussed in depth in Chapter 7.

Public Affairs

Public affairs, also referred to as *government relations*, traditionally was more important in some industries than in others; however, the democratization of information online, coupled with heightened public scrutiny, increased government regulation, and an increasingly litigious business environment, makes this subfunction at least tangentially relevant to most organizations.

Staying connected to what is happening in local, federal, and international governments through a well-staffed and savvy government relations team is important to virtually all businesses given the far reach of government regulations within industries from pharmaceuticals to computer software. As companies expand internationally, building or outsourcing government relations efforts in key major foreign hubs—for example, in Brussels to concentrate on European Union legislation—will become equally important. Public affairs as it relates to companies' digital communications efforts among stakeholders will be discussed at length in Chapter 8.

Crisis Communications

One of the most profound effects of the changing business environment on companies and their corporation communication functions is the exponential increase in risk factors that could lead to a devastating crisis, be it financial, legal, reputational, or otherwise. The proliferation of digital communications channels only exacerbates the risk because news travels at warp speed across the autobahns of cyberspace, reaching audiences all over the globe with the click of a button.

Chapter 9 will highlight crisis management strategies in the context of both anticipating challenges and leveraging opportunities provided by digital communications platforms.

Conclusion

The changing business environment described in Chapter 1 has had a monumental impact on the way businesses operate, both internally and externally. As this business landscape evolved to encompass emerging digital platforms, increased globalization, and a more stringent regulatory environment, the importance of communications—and, specifically, the corporate communication function—has morphed from a backroom tactical department to a strategic liaison between the organization and its many stakeholder groups, all of whom have significantly more control over companies' reputations and bottom lines.

Because of organizations' new vulnerability to stakeholder demands, the corporate communication function, naturally skilled in relationship building and reputation management, became a central organism whose tentacles extend to every internal department, be it marketing, public affairs, or investor relations. Corporate leaders have been required to reshuffle their organizational structures accordingly, integrating functions that were previously siloed to incorporate communicators' intrinsic skill sets, especially in the context of the challenges and opportunities presented by digital communications platforms.

Whether a company is in the midst of a merger, shifting from a centralized to a decentralized organizational structure, or just trying to remain competitive in an increasingly complicated environment, modern reputational risks and rewards require senior executives to rethink the way they position themselves internally to have a positive impact on the actions of external stakeholders. The biggest lesson: The devil's in the digital, and corporate communicators are stepping up to lead their brands out of the inferno and into the future.

CHAPTER 3

THE DIGITAL MEDIATOR
ONLINE PLATFORMS CREATE COMMON GROUND FOR MARKETING AND CORPORATE COMMUNICATIONS

By introducing the concept of integration, Chapter 2 teased the notion that prior to public relations' (PR's) transformation into the modern-day corporate communication function, marketing executives enjoyed greater prominence within corporations, thanks in part to their inherent ability to quantify the impact marketing campaigns had on the bottom line of the business. Today, though, PR's kissing cousin—and once its greatest competitor for budgets and access to the C-suite—has been humbled by stakeholders' decreasing responsiveness to the one-way message dissemination on which the marketing discipline is founded. To marketers' dismay (and perhaps PR executives as well), the discrepancies between the two disciplines have faded to gray, and many organizations such as the powerhouse IBM and the embattled Citigroup have acknowledged this by restructuring reporting relationships to include marketing within the umbrella of corporate communications.

This chapter reveals how the rapid growth of digital communications channels has been the key driver in this integration because marketers traditionally are trained to handle one-way outreach (in the forms of advertising and publicity), whereas PR professionals are more inclined toward two-way conversations with stakeholders, not to mention reputation building and message development. Because of this, corporations are increasingly relying on the corporate communication function—and, often, outside PR agencies—to engage stakeholders with viral, word-of-mouth (WOM), and buzz marketing initiatives to drive action through engagement.

This discussion will be framed in the context of an organization's brand and reputation—two intangible factors that marketers are less equipped to manage in the age of digital communications. The chapter then will identify the digital tools best suited for online marketing communications, the best practices for making them successful, and examples of organizations that have already caught the "viral bug" and benefited accordingly.

First, A Word from Our Sponsors: A Brief History of Marketing's Move from Monologue to Dialogue

According to the American Marketing Association, "Marketing is an organizational function and a set of processes for creating, communicating and delivering value to customers and for managing customer relationships in ways that benefit the organization and its stakeholders." This definition suits an anachronistic vision of marketing in which messages are created, communicated, and delivered to customers via one-way channels—namely advertising. Speaking of outdated, in the early 1960s, Harvard Business School Professor Jerome McCarthy defined four elements that collectively comprised the "marketing mix": product, price, place, and promotion. These *four P's*, as they are often called, shaped the process of developing marketing messages for customers:

1. *Product.* Select the tangible and intangible benefits of the product.
2. *Price.* Determine an appropriate product pricing structure.
3. *Promotion.* Create awareness of the product among the target audience.
4. *Place.* Make the product available to the customer.[1]

The four *P*'s approach worked well in an environment where executives had a tangible product to promote, had a well-defined audience to promote it to, and didn't need to consider what that audience might say in response to the message. Plus, for marketers, "that audience" usually referred only to customers; other stakeholders, including employees and investors, weren't direct recipients of marketing messages, so campaigns were crafted without specific attention to these groups.

Of course, thanks to a multitude of factors discussed in Chapters 1 and 2, this narrow approach could not remain effective forever. As digital channels emerged and broke down every proverbial wall that separated the company from its stakeholders and stakeholder groups from each other, protecting corporate reputation and building a strong brand identity became paramount. These two factors, now controlled more by stakeholders than by corporate executives, determine an organization's ability to weather crises, manage change, remain competitive, and reap financial rewards. However, while this reality precipitates the altered relationship between marketing and corporate communication within organizations, it is important first to define brand and reputation against an increasingly digital business backdrop.

Brand Aids: Identity and Image Merge to Create Added Value

Simply put, *brand* is the product of a company's identity (the visual manifestation of the organization as it is conveyed through its name, logo, motto, products, services, etc.) and its image (the reflection of an organization's identity as it is seen from the viewpoint of its stakeholders). Both a noun and a verb, *brand* can describe the embodiment of corporate identity and image, as well as the process of defining (or redefining) this embodiment to stakeholders.

The latter process happens with greater regularity as the business environment shifts to meet changing stakeholder demands. Whether a company must brand itself to a new audience or rebrand itself in the face of a merger, acquisition, name change, or other event, senior executives rely more and more on the communication function to shape messaging around target stakeholder groups and to disseminate them in the most efficient way possible. According to 2008 research conducted by the Corporate Executive Board's Communications Executive Council (CEC), corporate brand strength is a significant predictor of company preference, as well as a stakeholder's willingness to recommend the company—another important behavior to achieve company objectives. The research also revealed that in addition to brand favorability among stakeholders, brand differentiation is a critical lever for corporate communicators seeking to improve levels of company preference: Differentiated brands have 61 percent more impact on company preference than do nondifferentiated brands.[2]

Hewlett-Packard (HP) executives learned the value of brand management and differentiation the hard way, albeit in a slightly different context. As mentioned in Chapter 2, the company merged with Compaq in 2002, thus opening up a Pandora's box of challenges surrounding its culture, identity, and employee communications. But the challenges didn't stop there; HP's marketing—or lack thereof—presented a major problem when then-CEO Carly Fiorina and her board tried to rebrand the company and its new identity to a skeptical marketplace.

At the time, the corporate marketing function reported to HP's chief financial officer (CFO) and had become marginalized over the years. Business-unit marketing teams were organized as part of independent silos— whenever a new product was successful in the marketplace, HP would create a separate business around that product. When Fiorina attempted to nail down each of the product brands that HP promoted in the market, she came up with more than 150 of them, but she saw that each embodied very little of the broader HP brand. "It was reflective of the reality that the 'thousand tribes' has no collective identity," Fiorina would recall years later. "The company was 87 different profit and loss statements."[3]

With that many brands scattered across multiple markets and no consistent messages to unite them, the company faced a situation that no management team would envy: It had one newly united company with two separate identities and, according to Fiorina's estimates, more than 150 unique brands. What's more, its stakeholders, from investors to consumers to employees, weren't sure how to interpret the changes, and profits suffered accordingly.

HP's branding struggle tied into what many would define as a reputation crisis for the company; however, many executives' tendency to think of brand and reputation synonymously could prove to be a fatal— though not uncommon—error. According to the CEC research, 65 percent of surveyed corporate communicators believe that reputation- and brand-building activities are the same, whereas in reality, they are means to very different ends. While the corporate brand signals the organization's unique value proposition to stakeholders, corporate reputation signals the fulfillment of stakeholder expectations.[4]

While also struggling with branding challenges, then, the blows to HP's reputation would keep coming three years after the HP-Compaq merger, when Fiorina was unceremoniously fired after HP missed quarterly profits in 2004, causing shares to plummet by 15 percent. Even prior to Fiorina's dismissal, though, the company realized that a major strategic change would be required to weather this storm. In late 2003, HP executives announced a shift in the company's advertising and marketing strategy: For the first time, the company would focus on ensuring that HP's communications bore a consistent corporate message. The company's senior vice president for global brand and communications, Allison Johnson, told a *Forbes* reporter, "We are in a commoditizing industry, in a marketplace where the brand is more important than speeds and feeds [the metrics of a machine's top performance]. The message is now about the value of the relationship with the company."[5]

That word—*relationship*—is integral to the corporate communication function's success in gaining traction against marketing's dominance over messaging. Case in point: In 2007, Michael Mendenhall (who previously oversaw all marketing and communications for Walt Disney Parks and Resorts) joined HP as chief marketing officer (CMO) and senior vice president of corporate marketing. In contrast to the company's earlier organizational structure, in which corporate marketing reported to the CFO, Mendenhall became the direct report of HP's Office of Strategy and Technology. In a "Productivity Network" interview with the Marketing Leadership Council, Mendenhall said:

My group's current charter is focused around brand reputational management and driving higher brand awareness, brand equity and shareholder value for HP around the world. We are focused on strengthening our customers' and employees' relationships to the HP brand worldwide and leveraging the entire portfolio to profitably grow the business.[6]

Mendenhall went on to say:

There has been a fundamental paradigm shift in the overall media landscape, which has had profound implications on how companies manage relationships with their customers, their reputation and their overall brand. Brands are now being built in the digital net space as opposed to traditional channels. It's an evolution in all communication channels that's happening at a pace that we've never seen before in our lifetime. It's forcing marketers to not only repurpose campaigns and content, but to really look at the digital landscape, and the specific channels that are emerging, and think, "How best can we create the right message and the right level of engagement?"[7]

The paradigm shift illustrated by Mendenhall's comments has staggering effects on marketing functions within corporate entities, especially in the context of protecting vulnerable reputations and building strong brand identities—two things that stakeholders have more and more control over. This reality has sparked a newfound cooperation between marketing and corporate communications (forced or not); these executives may not agree on much, but the need to have a strong brand and reputation turned out to be enough to bring them together.

Show Me The Money: Dollars Inspire Common Sense, Marketing, and Collaborative Corporate Communication Functions

Implementing the practices to build a valued brand and to sustain a strong corporate reputation is becoming a joint effort between marketing and corporate communication executives. That said, *joint effort* is still a relative term because true integration is still a work in progress for many companies.

"There is a long way to go before corporate and marketing communications are integrated," said Mark Weiner, CEO of PRIME Research North America. "Despite the general agreement that integrated marketing and communications is better than silos, and that marketing messages and corporate messages have an effect on one another, there is still a great deal of territorialism to be found. Until CEOs stand up for what works for the enterprise rather than what works for an individual or department, we will continue to see inefficiency, waste and less-than-optimal business results."[8]

But times are changing, and a number of instigators—digital platforms, media fragmentation, and stakeholder empowerment—are proving to expedite the integration between marketing and communications in many organizations. According to Weiner, "The emergence of digital communication platforms is as reflective of the situation as it has always been except that there is 'fresh meat' on the table, and there is a battle over who is to be served."[9]

The corporate communication function is well positioned to become executive chef in this proverbial situation based in its natural propensity to fuel engagement. Likewise, the skills in marketers' toolboxes that hinge on traditional advertising are becoming less and less effective; digital video recorders (DVRs) allow people to fast-forward through commercials on television, for example, and newspaper and magazine readerships continue to decline as consumers turn to the Web for a more interactive experience. In short, the Internet is getting a growing share of advertising spending at the expense of traditional media outlets. For those who believe that numbers speak louder than words, consider these statistics:

- Spending on alternative media will climb 21 percent to $81.67 billion in 2008.
- Alternative media spending will account for 17.7 percent of total advertising and marketing spending, up from 6.9 percent in 2002.
- Traditional ad spending is expected to continue to struggle and remain essentially flat from 2007 to 2012—its share of overall advertising and marketing spending will drop 16 points in 10 years (47.1 percent share in 2002 to 31.5 percent in 2012).
- Alternative media will continue to spur growth in advertising and marketing during the forecast period, posting a 17.6 percent compound annual growth rate (CAGR) from 2007 to 2012.
- Alternative media will account for 26.7 percent of total advertising and marketing expenditures in 2012, up from 6.9 percent in 2002.[10]

But enough statistics. Numbers may speak louder than words, but actions speak loudest of all. The fact that a growing number of corporations are restructuring reporting relationships to facilitate cooperation between the marketing and corporate communication functions, including HP's newfound focus on engagement, is proof enough. There is even a term for this cooperation: *integrated marketing communications* (IMC). According to the *Journal of Integrated Marketing Communications*, published by Northwestern University's Department of Integrated Marketing Communications:

> *[IMC] is a customer-centric, data-driven method of communicating with consumers. IMC—the management of all organized communications to build positive relationships with customers and other stakeholders— stresses marketing to the individual by understanding needs, motivations, attitudes and behaviors.*[11]

The journal identifies four elements that combine to create true integrated marketing communications:

1. *Customer-centric.* Every IMC strategy begins with an acute understanding of the customer. This approach goes far beyond demographics to uncover the customer segments and consumer motivation that drive purchasing decisions.
2. *Data-driven.* Today, marketers have more information than ever about their customers' behaviors and preferences. IMC depends on these data to identify and understand a company's best customers and to make informed decisions regarding how to communicate with them.
3. *Integration.* Customers and other stakeholders—including investors, the media, employees, and others—do not distinguish between messages intended for them and those intended for other audiences. IMC not only integrates the marketing communications disciplines of advertising, direct and e-commerce marketing, and public relations, but it also advocates aligning all of a company's business processes, from product development to customer service.
4. *Effective branding.* When companies respect and understand their target audience, customers demonstrate their appreciation with loyalty to products, services, and corporate brands. These loyal customers reward companies with high retention rates, which, in turn, translate into measurable success and improved bottom-line profitability for companies.[12]

The Periodic Table: Elements of Successful IMC Campaigns

The four IMC characteristics identified in the preceding section provide a basic definition of integrated marketing communications, but additional background about specific campaign components gives executives a more robust understanding about the pillars that make an initiative successful. The Corporate Executive Board's Marketing Leadership Council research aggregates the following components that align to form truly integrated campaigns:

• *Simultaneous media consumption.* As discussed earlier in this chapter, media consumption habits have changed drastically in the wake of media fragmentation and the proliferation of nontraditional channels.

Thus, as the council's research states, "With the continued growth of mobile marketing and increased wireless Internet access outside the home, integrated campaigns leverage the connectivity of new technology to target consumers all the time, multiple times, and often simultaneously."[13]

- *Strategic campaign development.* This element describes the process of ensuring that brand messages align with distribution channels and, ultimately, with the target audience. As the brand message extends across all channels, the failure of the message in one channel may negatively influence all other channels, putting vastly more pressure on up-front planning to construct campaigns that match customer needs.[14]

- *Below-the-line activation.* Below-the-line activities are those that directly affect consumer behaviors by exploiting information networks created and maintained by word-of-mouth communication. This component hinges on creativity and is often viral in nature.

The latter component of IMC is a perfect segue way into the next topic: IMC's transition to the Web.

A Marriage of Convenience: Marketing and Corporate Communications Find Common Ground in Cyberspace

In October 2006, when the concept of Web 2.0 and its related communications channels was still in its embryonic stages, a man by the name of George Wright faced a challenge. As the newly hired vice president of sales and marketing for Blendtec, the Utah-based company that manufactures and sells blenders, he needed to find a way to raise the brand's visibility on a shoestring budget. But budget limitations weren't the only hurdle to overcome. Blendtec's target audience was tough to narrow down, there wasn't a specific "hook" on which to focus messaging (after all, there isn't really a blender-buying season per say), and the products didn't have the "sex appeal" that made for creative ad campaigns. However, after stumbling across a room in the Blendtec warehouse that was filled with sawdust and woodchips, Wright realized he was staring at an enormous opportunity. Apparently, Tom Dickson, Blendtec's CEO, would test upgrades made to blenders by seeing if they could blend two-by-two boards. "That was a normal occurrence," Wright said. "That was just what he did to test equipment."[15]

Collaborating with the company's Web master and video producer, Wright put together a marketing strategy that hinged on the potential for Dickson's extreme blending to go viral online. "Tom didn't really understand what social media or viral marketing was, so I just said, 'Don't worry about it; if I can have $50 for a budget, I'll go out and buy a few things and see what we can do,'" Wright said.

Dickson agreed to the $50 budget, which Wright used to purchase a white lab coat, a rotisserie chicken, a six-pack of Coke, a bag of marbles, a rake, and a URL called *willitblend.com*. Then, armed with a video recorder and a Blendtec Total Blender, the team turned on the camera and asked Dickson to start blending. What resulted were five video clips of Dickson engaging in extreme blending, which the team uploaded to *www.willitblend.com*.

The campaign took off almost instantly, with video clips popping up on video-sharing sites such as YouTube and Revver. Influential bloggers and traditional media alike took note, and Dickson became an overnight celebrity, making appearances on NBC's *The Tonight Show with Jay Leno* and the History Channel's *Modern Marvels* series, among others. Traffic to the "Will It Blend" Web site (*www.willitblend.com*) skyrocketed, thanks in part to a feature that allowed visitors to submit suggestions for what to blend next. ("Victims" of the Blendtec Total Blender now include golf balls, marbles, iPods, a camcorder, six Bic lighters, a tape measure, CDs, and video games. Among the only things to withstand the blender's mighty blades are coins and a crowbar.)

Of course, the ultimate measure of any campaign's success is the generation of sales and increased brand awareness—an accomplishment Blendtec achieved. According to Wright, "We watch how it affects sales and brand awareness. If you look at it in terms of what we spent, 'Will It Blend?' is not a cost center for the company; it's a profit center. We now have companies coming to us asking us to film episodes of 'Will It Blend?' for their brands."[16]

Poison that Needs no Antidote: Viral Marketing Brings Corporate Messages to the Masses

The Blendtec anecdote is one of many modern-day campaigns that combine marketing and communications components to identify, target, and engage influential stakeholders via the Web. But what makes Blendtec such a success story? After all, in terms of traditional marketing, at least three of the four *P*'s weren't especially compelling: The product was a blender, the price was relatively steep (listed from $399.95 to $599.95), and the place (point of sale) didn't have any noteworthy characteristics. The promotion, however, became the ultimate selling point; in effect, it alone had all the elements required for a successful viral campaign.

Viral marketing is the love child of Web 2.0 platforms and IMC that uses preexisting online social networks to disseminate messaging and increase brand awareness. As a communications technique, it has all the key ingredients: stakeholder engagement, mechanisms for building relationships, and platforms that enable audiences to "talk back." And, while it and all its variations—buzz, word of mouth, guerrilla, ambush—are tagged with the "marketing" moniker, these disciplines fit the IMC bill.

Viral marketing's success in today's business environment can be pinned to a statistic quoted in Chapter 1—that the most trusted source of information about a company is "a person like me" (see Figure 3.1). ("Shares my interests" and "holds similar political beliefs" are the top two defining factors of "a person like me," according to the 2008 Edelman Trust Barometer.) What's more, 85 percent of surveyed individuals will pass along positive information about a company or discuss negative experiences.[17] This is the crux of a successful viral campaign (and all IMC initiatives, for that matter), not to mention the factor that causes many corporate executives to bristle at the very thought of planning one.

"To fail with viral marketing is to fail publicly," said Jason Alcorn, associate account director at Virillion, Inc., a full-service interactive agency. "[But], as managers become more knowledgeable, they will better understand that public failure is part and parcel of the digital era. You just have to handle this failure smartly."[18]

If they have any drive to success in today's consumer-driven environment, these corporate leaders need to stop digging in the heels of their Oxfords and embrace all that viral marketing has to offer. That said, viral IMC, be they buzz, guerrilla, WOM, or ambush efforts, don't always unfold as gracefully as Blendtec's accidental cyber-blockbuster did. But that doesn't keep many communications executives from operating under the misunderstanding that viral marketing success stories involve nothing more than being in the right place at the right time. On the contrary, the most forward-thinking corporate communications executives go to

Figure 3.1: Communications today requires top-down and peer-to-peer spokespeople.

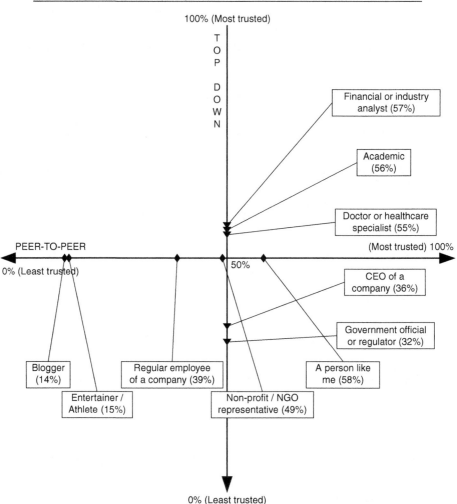

great pains to shape strategies and have them unfold in ways that are organic and true to their audiences.

"There is a lot more control than people give credit to having something go viral," said Blendtec's Wright. "The number one reason is that you want to create content. Marketers and advertisers have been thinking for so long that they need to make an ad. Basically, an advertisement is targeted at interrupting someone's schedule, whether they're watching the television or reading a newspaper. We now need to create content—something that will drive people to want to watch. Maybe it's funny, maybe it's serious, maybe it's a how-to. It can be a lot of things, but it has to be worth watching."[19]

Ready, Aim, Fire: Executing Effective Digital IMC Programs

Having established the background of marketing and corporate communications' ultimate compromise to share custody of brand and reputation (in which, of course, Web 2.0 acted as the mediator), it's time to address the steps executives must take to executive an effective integrated marketing campaign in cyberspace. This section will outline these steps and offer specific examples of the strategies and tactics that work, as well as a few don't-try-this-at-home efforts that . . . well, didn't work.

Hello, My Name is _____: Identifying Your Brand's Target Online Audience

While the very nature of viral marketing makes it difficult to predict what will take off and what will just languish and fizzle out, one thing is for certain: The preliminary step in any communications initiative, viral or otherwise, requires having a thorough understanding of the audience the company wants to target, as well as their consumption habits. This falls within the data-driven component of IMC cited by the *Journal of Integrated Marketing Communications*. Lucky for corporate leaders, as HP's Mendenhall puts it:

> *Greater business intelligence will provide us with the consumer insight that we need to personalize and customize in real time. It puts increased importance on the level of data capture and the back-of-house information that we collect—both contextually and behaviorally on a given customer—and our ability to respond in real time, in a relevant manner, in that specific channel [continues] to be of the utmost importance. Hence, a very robust CI/CRM [customer intelligence/customer relationship management] program [is] critical, and it [allows] us to build this knowledge repository.*[20]

Mendenhall mentions two things that are critical to successful communications initiatives, while being made infinitely easier by the emergence of digital technologies: *customer intelligence* (CI) and *customer relationship management* (CRM). Used interchangeably, these terms refer to the process of gathering, analyzing, and exploiting information about a specific stakeholder group. Before digital channels became a mainstay in everyday interactions, CI and CRM data depended mostly on speech analytics, telephone polling, and on-site customer surveys.

Today, customers' profiles are far more robust, and while digital media didn't force this maturation, they certainly inspired it. "Research has a place in digital communications, just as it has a place in business," said PRIME Research's Weiner. "Typically, research can help the corporate communicator to optimize success and minimize risk by identifying the messages, media, spokespeople, events and vehicles that the target audiences consider to be most credible, most compelling and most differentiating. A digital communications strategy should be researched and conducted as part of an overall integrated approach to understand the interactivity and inter-relationship between digital and traditional media, and other communications channels."[21]

However, it's the "integrated approach" that still can be a sticky situation despite the role digital platforms continue to play in creating synergies among marketing, PR, and communications. That said, the importance of well-researched strategies is only heightened by these platforms because any misstep with regard to diagnosing a target audience's consumption habits—online or offline—could lead to complete failure of a communications effort.

"Research should be the foundation of any communications plan or strategy, irrespective of the channel, [because] PR, which is often a major budget holder, needs to demonstrate its worth at all levels," said Mike Daniels, managing director of U.K.-based media analysis consultancy Report International. "If PR pros want to drive strategic change in their organization and genuinely deliver meaningful results, they will have to (a) work much more closely with (and not be afraid of) market researchers in their organizations and (b) be prepared to invest in undertaking the necessary research to link media analysis outputs to outcomes around sales and consumer awareness/perception. This will show the genuine business benefits of PR in terms the rest of the business understand and accept as common currency."[22]

Thus, adding the intelligence provided by market research to their arsenals enables communications executives to target audiences with greater accuracy. This, of course, is key when attempting to execute an IMC campaign online. Failing to understand the audience makes brands—and, in turn, corporate reputations—vulnerable to ridicule. (See Chapter 9 for more on reputation crises that begin online.)

Executives at HBO can teach communications professionals a thing or two about targeting audiences for viral marketing campaigns based solely on the meticulous research they conducted for the initiative surrounding the September 2008 premiere of the new original series, *True Blood*. The show's premise centers around a group of vampires who manage to control their blood-sucking instincts by consuming "Tru Blood," a synthetic blood substitute. Outlandish as it may sound, HBO's leadership saw potential in the storyline, which is based on the novel series by Charlaine Harris, and they tasked the marketing communications team with building buzz in the months leading up to the premiere. On one hand, homing in on a target audience was easy: Vampire enthusiasts are a narrow, easy-to-identify demographic. On the other hand, the task was as complex as it was unusual: Vampire enthusiasts may be as specific an audience as you'll ever find, but they have as defined and nuanced personalities as a group of, say, stamp collectors or wine connoisseurs.

"In terms of finding [our target audience], it was a matter of researching where the conversations were taking place and then categorizing the types of conversations—on goth sites, for example," said Gregg Hale, partner at Campfire, the interactive creative agency that was tapped by HBO to help develop the branded media campaign surrounding the launch of *True Blood*. Hale also was one of the producers of the box office hit, *The Blair Witch Project*, which was made for $22,000 and grossed $248 million in theaters. "We followed the path to where these people are and then built a map. In *True Blood*'s case, we wanted to start with something that was different enough to cut through the clutter and make people take notice, which is why we decided to go with the dead language mailers."[23]

Hale's reference to the "dead language mailers" is critical to understanding the unique opportunities in the modern marketing communications environment, as well as the need to completely customize messaging to play up the interest of the target audience. One component of HBO and Campfire's approach to targeting a niche audience—sending letters written in Babylonian and Ugaritic, two dead languages, to online influencers—prompted a maelstrom of activity online, where vampire enthusiasts congregated on blogs, social networks, and community forums to help translate the messages.

But the viral marketing efforts didn't stop there. The dead language mailers teased the debut of a Web site that hosted brief prequel episodes to the new series. Additional Web components included two microsites that hosted vampire-related conversations and storylines, a vampire dating Web site, a blog "maintained" by in-story characters, video teasers with behind-the-scenes information, and an online "True Blood" serial comic book. It was the ultimate integrated juggernaut, and its robust content resonated with audiences thanks to the attention to detail.

"To the extent possible, we wanted to emulate the experience of a world in which vampires had come out of the coffin, so to speak," Hale said. "We needed a rabbit hole into this world, digitally; we wanted to have multiple sites where people were getting multiple sides of a complex story. We approached the campaign in three phases: Inside the vampire world, which was exclusive. [Then], once the vampires in the story 'came out,' we launched a media-forward push for the beverage Tru Blood [a product created specifically for the campaign]. We promoted that with the trappings of what people are used to for a product launch. Running parallel to that, we were telling the story of vampires coexisting with humans, where vampires would be facing the civil rights issues that any minority would face when integrating into society."[24]

The multipronged viral approach—the largest ever undertaken by HBO for an original series premiere—appears to have paid off. According to Hale, the first episode captured 4 million viewers; that number increased by 24 percent for the second episode. *True Blood*, then, marks what might become the standard for creative integrated marketing, in which the target audience—not the product—exists at the center of the strategy. True, starting with an intimate understanding of your target audience is key for successful viral campaigns, but the individuals on the cutting-most edge of digital marketing have an even sharper way of looking at it.

"Social media has communities [more so than] audiences," according to Heidi Sullivan, director of electronic media at Cision North America. "People are gathering around blogs, social networking sites, microblogging sites and forums because they actively participate in and share the content on those sites. When identifying key communities, a communications professional should look at the psychographics of their target community, and not just the demographics. Psychographics allow us to ask, 'What is my community truly passionate about?'"[25]

Play-Doh 2.0: Shaping Messages to Meet and Exceed Audience Expectations

Once you have established a specific target audience and, through market research, done due diligence in understanding their consumption habits, it's time to shape the messages that will connect the brand with these targeted stakeholders. In theory, the concept of integration that was discussed so thoroughly in Chapter 2 ensures message consistency, but communications executives cannot take this for granted; all communications must convey a unified brand. Deborah Fell, senior vice president of marketing strategy and integration for Marriott International, says that her organization has a specific strategy for guaranteeing message consistency:

We try to develop our plans around what we call the "central organizing idea." If we have a consumer insight that helps us think about this brand, then we can develop more of a central organizational idea for our plan. That central organizing idea might be a two- or three-word phrase for the positioning, but its purpose is to make sure that the plans and programs tie together. . . . I'm always asking "What's the central organizing idea here? What's the big idea that we're trying to accomplish for the brand that all these different activities can hook onto?" The execution becomes much crisper.[26]

Equally important as being consistent, the messaging must be authentic to the organization's identity and that of the target audience. The HBO example illustrates the point of authentic audience outreach as poignantly as any other campaign could. Reaching out to these vampire enthusiasts with messages that were even a hair off the mark could make the campaign come off as condescending or patronizing of an audience that takes its interests very seriously.

If You Love it, Set it Free: Releasing Integrated Campaigns into the Virtual Abyss

The final tactical piece of online integrated campaign development is choosing the proper mix of distribution channels because IMC inherently implies the use of multiple platforms that work together to deliver unified messaging to a target audience. Without this synergy, organizations will do more harm than good to their brand identities and corporate reputations.

"The barrier to entry is very low. At first, you have nothing to lose," according to Blendtec's Wright. "It's really just a matter of putting together the concept and then placing it. The scary thing is that when you put things out into social media sites, you really can't bring them back, so you have to be careful. There are a lot of corporate executives who struggle to understand, and they see a lot of risk."[27]

One way to minimize this risk is by creating good content in the first place, which leaves much less room for justified attacks. Then, reaching the target audience via the most high-impact mix of distribution channels helps to ensure that the message is being conveyed only to receptive stakeholders. According to Virillion founder Shabbir Imber Safdar, this mix "is entirely based upon the demographics or your audience. Different demographics use different tools. At the base of . . . [distribution], you should be publishing on your own Web site several times a week if you have more than one million people in your audience. You can take this content and adapt it to e-mail, Facebook, YouTube, Twitter—wherever your audience is. But you have to understand that it's not a cut-and-paste job. You need to participate in the conversation and adapt the content for the environment."[28]

This participation is something the HBO *True Blood* campaign executed very effectively, in that it created the participatory platforms— microsites, community forums, etc.—and then fed the fire of conversation by unveiling components of the campaign incrementally. According to Zach Enterlin, vice president of advertising and promotion for HBO, "It's critical to consider the depth of the experience you're providing. Offering consumers the ability to truly immerse themselves in a rich and deep experience across multiple digital platforms can transcend marketing and become true entertainment—storytelling through marketing content. At the same time, it's important to realize that the detailed, immersive experience isn't for all consumers, and the surface-level mass vehicles are just as critical in reaching a broad audience."[29]

Ultimately, giving complete control to the audience with regard to message development and buzz building developed unofficial spokespeople for the series, all of whom participated with the campaign elements and spread information in the most effective way possible—that is, organically.

The Snowball Effect: Managing the Murmur as It Begins to Reverberate Online

This stage of viral/IMC campaigns tends to incite the greatest amount of anxiety in corporate leaders because of the inevitable lack of control they have over what audiences are saying about their brand. What if they respond negatively? What if they begin saying things that aren't true? How should we respond to online conversations? How can we encourage the positive conversations and squelch the negative ones?

So many questions, and so few tangible answers—at least that's what executives' skittishness suggests they believe. But there are specific tools that can be used to monitor online conversations, solving at least one part of the problem about not knowing what online audiences are saying about brands. In fact, many digital technologies have embedded applications that allow for this executive oversight of conversations that follow message dissemination via online channels. Social networks, virtual communities, blogs—all these platforms can be monitored for mentions of a company or brand. The only catch is that no organization has the personnel necessary to manually scour the Internet's infinite acreage.

As tends to be the case these days, this is where technology comes in, having been double-cast as the antagonist and protagonist on the modern business stage. True, digital communication channels can be blamed for the relatively anarchic conversations that agoraphobic executives must join, but these channels have built-in coping mechanisms, the easiest and most accessible of which is Really Simple Syndication (RSS).

Metaphorically speaking, RSS is the gateway drug of experiential online monitoring, if only because everybody is doing it (or at least could be), so to speak. The basic premise of RSS is, as its name suggests, simple: The application syndicates news content by mining for Extensible Markup Language (XML) tags based on keywords chosen by the user. If this doesn't sound simple enough, think of RSS technology as being comparable to digital video recorders (DVRs): Viewers can program their DVRs to record only the television shows they want to watch, and the machine "finds," records, and stores the shows, whether the television is turned on or not. The shows live on the DVR until the viewer wants to watch them; afterwards, he or she has the option to delete or save them.

Similarly, RSS technology allows Web users to choose keywords—say, their company's name or that of their competitors. Their customized RSS reader then will find and aggregate all mentions of those keywords, whether they appear in news stories, press releases, blog posts, or social media commentary, and feed the stories to a central location, either on the user's desktop or in a Web browser. While the process of setting up an RSS platform is simple to execute, however, there are strategies for making the content that you syndicate more digestible and user-friendly.

"It's easy to be overwhelmed with a fire hose of information, so cluster your feeds by priority—not topic," Virillion's Jason Alcorn said. "Have a folder of daily reads (including Google Alerts), a folder of weekly reads, and a folder that you save for the train or airport. There is a whole other level of paid tools and services that are quite valuable, but start here and grow."[30] This starting point alone has a number of advantages for communications executives:

- RSS is cheap (there are a number of providers that are even free) and easy to set up.
- It significantly reduces the amount of time you need to spend trolling Web sites for information about your brand.
- It gives you a media-relations "in" because many reporters use RSS to narrow the scope of their online research.
- It helps you to monitor industry trends, as well as your competitors' activities (just add those company names/brands to your list of keywords).
- You can syndicate your own content to be RSS-enabled, thus increasing your company's visibility online in the context of information you want to be found.

Implementing RSS technology is perhaps the most elementary step in monitoring online conversations about a company or brand, but it is by no means the only step. Many communications executives are going out on a cyber-limb and joining Twitter (*www.twitter.com*), an online messaging application that acts as a platform for users to communicate and stay connected throughout the day (or night). What began as a curious site for only the most maverick members of the tech community has become a common meeting place for millions of industry analysts, communications professionals, journalists, social media influencers, and corporate executives. All you have to do is register (for free), log on, and start "twittering." The only catch? Each post is limited to 140 characters. It's the typical quality-versus-quantity argument, in which the latter doesn't have a fighting chance. However, in an age of attention-deficit stakeholders, this limitation turns out to be an advantage for those who can communicate concisely.

Message platforms like Twitter have proven to be a great place to engage influential stakeholders who frequent the sites, as well as to sit back and monitor what other people are saying about your company.

And, while certainly not a channel for every company or industry, history has already proven Twitter to be worth its weight in gold for some organizations. Comcast is just one example. As a company that is entrenched in an industry that is notorious for customer disservice, the cable/Internet services provider swan-dived into the Web's Wild West, going to the very location where many of its customers were complaining: Twitter. Comcast executives set up a Twitter account under the name "ComcastCares" and kept an eye on conversations (Twitter can be easily searched for musings about specific topics), some of which turned out to be less than complimentary.

One particular "Tweeter," influential tech blogger Michael Arrington, was especially vocal about his negative Comcast experiences. On April 6, 2008, he posted three comments about the 36-hour Internet connection timeout he was experiencing. But, thanks to the company's online monitoring system, a Comcast representative responded to Arrington in very short order. Arrington wrote this on his TechCrunch blog (*www.techcrunch.com*):

> *And then I lost my cool, tearing into Comcast on Twitter. Jeff Jarvis and others picked up the story and blogged about it. . . . And this brings me to the point of this post. Within 20 minutes of my first Twitter message I got a call from a Comcast executive in Philadelphia who wanted to know how he could help. He said he monitors Twitter and blogs to get an understanding of what people are saying about Comcast, and so he saw the discussion break out around my messages.*[31]

Arrington continued by saying that Comcast sent a team out to fix his Internet connection and apologized profusely. While he did note that his situation didn't apply to others who don't complain publicly (read: digitally) about customer-service issues, he did commend Comcast's use of digital channels as "an early warning system to flag possible brand implosions."[32] The technology certainly helped Comcast executives to upend a potential crisis by giving them time to respond before it was too late, and they aren't alone. JetBlue, Dell, and Kodak are among the growing number of companies using Twitter to engage consumers, build brands, and monitor potential crises. Plus, sites such as Tweet Scan make it piece-of-cake easy to use Twitter as a brand-monitoring tool. Just go to *www.tweetscan.com* and type in a keyword. The scanner will conduct a real-time Twitter search and return the results. Executives even can sign up for e-mail alerts or import the application to update in their RSS feed. Ultimately, Arrington's words best sum up the value of monitoring online conversations:

> *And a piece of advice to anyone with a Comcast service problem. Skip the hold time on their customer service line and go on the attack at Twitter instead. You may find your problem fixed in a hurry.*[33]

Testing Your Reflexes: Maintaining Online Conversations

You've built it, and they have come. Now what? Once the messages have reached the target audiences and the conversations have begun to percolate, the corporate communication function's job has only just begun. According to HBO's Enterlin, "It's important to provide opportunities for further engagement beyond initial messaging and allow the community to coalesce. *HBO.com* is a critical component of all of our campaigns, and in the case of *True Blood*, a number of community features, including a consumer-generated wiki for the show, gave fans the opportunity to stay engaged and involved throughout the season.[34]

The ability to sustain positive online conversations and to squash negative ones is critical to the effectiveness of any digital IMC campaign. Doing both requires gumption and, in some cases, an aptitude for taking risks. In terms of sustaining positive conversations, especially in the context of viral initiatives, executives must interact with audiences in the tone of the campaign.

"They need to actively be a part of the conversation and unafraid to adopt it after the start," said Virillion's Safdar. "Perhaps your audience made a joke at your expense. Riff on that joke, and encourage them to continue to talk about your product. I wouldn't suggest demeaning yourself, but by showing you have a sense of humor, people will feel an affinity for your brand."[35]

Now defunct, Circuit City's communication team did just that when, in August 2008, an operations employee realized that an issue of *MAD Magazine*—a publication sold in select Circuit City stores—contained a parody called "Sucker City" that made fun of the electronics chain. She immediately sent an e-mail request that managers remove and destroy all copies of the magazine in stores. Unfortunately for Circuit City, *Consumerist.com*, a consumer-complaint Web site, got hold of the e-mail and posted it. Very quickly, the issue went from a parody that was innocent enough and most likely would have gone unnoticed by loyal Circuit City consumers to a crisis that was largely created by the employee's overreaction.

When Jim Babb and Bill Cimino of Circuit City's corporate communications department heard about the unraveling crisis (on a Sunday night, no less), they acted quickly, sending the following e-mail to *Consumerist.com*'s editor, Ben Popken:

Hi, Ben,

I spotted the article about Circuit City and MAD Magazine on your site.

fyi, I became aware of this "situation" only this morning, and I have sent a note today to the Editors of MAD Magazine.

Speaking as "an embarrassed corporate PR guy," I apologized for the fact that some overly sensitive souls at our corporate headquarters ordered the removal of the August issue of MAD Magazine from our stores. Please keep in mind that only 40 of our 700 stores sell magazines at all.

The parody of our newspaper ad in the August MAD was very clever. Most of us at Circuit City share a rich sense of humor and irony . . . but there are occasional temporary lapses.

We apologize for the knee-jerk reaction, and have issued a retraction order; the affected stores are being directed to put the magazines back on sale.

As a gesture of our apology and deep respect for the folks at MAD Magazine, we are creating a cross-departmental task force to study the importance of humor in the corporate workplace and expect the resulting PowerPoint presentation to top out at least 300 pages, chock full of charts, graphs and company action plans.

In addition, I have offered to send the MAD Magazine Editor a $20.00 Circuit City Gift Card, toward the purchase of a Nintendo Wii . . . if he can find one!

All the best,
Jim Babb
Corporate Communications
Circuit City Stores, Inc.
Richmond, VA

Source: Downloaded from *http://gizmodo.com/5032930/circuit-city-apologizes-for-pulling-mad-magazine-promises-to-get-a-sense-of-humor*, August 30, 2008.

While Babb's response to the situation doesn't fall into the category of integrated or viral marketing messaging, it is a prime example of speaking to the target audience in their "native language"—humor—in a way that is genuine and that ultimately squelched negative conversations and even engendered a positive reaction. Popken posted the letter of apology on his site and summarized why he thought it was such a good move on the part of Circuit City's communications department. Of course, in an ideal world, the situation would have never occurred in the first place, but the outcome reinforces the immeasurable value of transparent and authentic conversations that are completely void of "PR speak." (For more on handling crises online, see Chapter 9.)

The Calm after the Storm: Measuring the Impact of an Online IMC Campaign

Measurement—long considered to be the Holy Grail of communications—has been transformed, thanks to the ease with which campaigns picked up on digital platforms can be tracked. While there is still no one-size-fits-all measurement approach, executives can stay abreast of the traction of their viral/IMC campaigns with audiences online. There are a handful of key metrics to start with: impressions, visits, page views, and click-throughs (for definitions of these terms, see the Appendix). Executives should establish a baseline before launching the campaign—Web traffic/page views, etc.—against which they can then benchmark post-campaign results. Another tactic, according to Virillion's Safdar, "Trick out your social media environment with as many customized URLs as possible so [that] you can see which ones are feeding your traffic."[36]

But that's just one of many facets of measurement in the digital space because engagement has trumped mere media impressions in terms of importance. This relates back to corporate reputation because digital IMC campaigns that fuel stakeholder engagement with the brand in a positive way often lead to actions that boost the organization's reputation. Mark Weiner of PRIME Research drills down into reputation measurement with this piece of advice:

> *To set the stage for corporate communications success and to minimize risk in decision making, it is wise to assess the attributes, preferences and priorities of those executives who fund and evaluate corporate communication programs. Quantify individual preferences and expectations for activities*

and measures for success, aggregate them and feed the findings back to each executive to help build consensus. Through this dialogue, the corporate communications executive has an opportunity to understand, explore and aggregate the individual conversations into a "master plan." Approvals for the "master plan" should be a much simpler process since its elements have been pre-tested."[37]

To Weiner's point, pretesting messages is becoming increasingly prevalent within organizations that own the budgets for such undertakings. Take Microsoft, for example. To prepare for its May 2006 consumer debut of Windows Live OneCare, Microsoft executives teamed up with PR firm Waggener Edstrom to shape messaging around the product launch. Having secured a retail partnership with Best Buy, the team created two separate brand message campaigns and tested each to see which would get the most traction with the media. The two messages—"OneCare is like a 'pit crew' for the PC" and "OneCare is the all-in-one PC care service"—took very different approaches; the former played up the pit crew theme via a OneCare-branded NASCAR car, whereas the latter appealed to more traditional psychographic preferences.

Both messages were tested in terms of brand message and awareness in the media over the three-month period that straddled the launch—two months leading up to the product's debut and one month following. Using Waggener Edstrom's proprietary measurement system, the team collected metrics that analyzed the volume, tone, depth, and key message pickup of each brand message within media coverage prior to and following the retail launch. Surprisingly (perhaps), the metrics revealed that the all-in-one message was by far the most successful, having been picked up 77 times in media mentions, compared with the pit-crew message's 24 mentions. Ultimately, media gravitated toward terms such as *service*, *care*, and *help*, thus giving the more traditional brand message a higher value. Subsequently, the team abandoned the pit-crew campaign—based on message testing.

However, while the Microsoft example is salient to the point of media analysis and measurement, it predates social media measurement to a large extent. According to Mike Daniels of Report International:

There is no doubt that corporate/product reputation is being driven more and more by online discussion, but the current tools do not provide any accurate form of predictive analysis or discrimination of one discussed issue against any another (at least until after the event—which is way too late, of course). Providing predictive tools that measure the intensity of digital conversations is what is needed.

The majority of social media and consumer-generated media analysis programs are simply providing roadmaps to clients—who is saying what, where and in what volume. Even when aiming to provide a more refined measure of impact by reference to various "authority" measurement algorithms, in the end we see virtually no connection to what companies' critical audiences are actually consuming media wise, or indeed at what point would their perception and behaviors change.[38]

While social media measurement still may be a proverbial Wild West, rapid advancements are being made by many communications mavericks, thanks in part to the wealth of digital tools and applications that track everything from Web-site traffic to message pickup among bloggers (see sidebar below). But the intangibles—loyalty and engagement, for example—still remain. Both these elements are integral to a company's digital integrated marketing efforts' successes; more important, while specific metrics for measuring the level of brand loyalty and engagement are still nebulous, the impressionist picture these attributes paint is very telling.

SOCIAL MEDIA MEASUREMENT RESOURCES

Measuring the impact of brand marketing in the digital media space may seem overwhelming, but the following (noncomprehensive) list of tools, vendors, and services that track conversations on social networks, blogs, microblogs, widgets, message boards, and/or community forums will get you started.

- Technorati: *www.technorati.com*
- Collective Intellect: *blog.collectiveintellect.com/*
- Dow Jones/Factiva Insight: *solutions.dowjones.com/insight/4064/*
- Nielsen BuzzMetrics: *www.nielsenbuzzmetrics.com*
- Cymfony: *www.cymfony.com*
- Techrigy: *www.techrigy.com*
- BuzzLogic: *www.buzzlogic.com*
- Radian6: *www.radian6.com*

- BoardTracker: *www.boardtracker.com*
- Linqia: *www.linqia.com*
- Twing: *www.twing.com*
- BrandIntel: *www.brandintel.com*
- Trucast by VisibleTechnologies: *www.visibletechnologies.com/solutions/ trucast.php*
- KDPaine & Partners: *www.measuresofsuccess.com*
- Clearspring: *www.clearspring.com*
- Gigya: *www.gigya.com*
- Widgetbox's Widget Syndication Metrics: *docs.widgetbox.com/ developers/metrics/*
- Mixercast: *www.mixercast.com*
- MuseStorm: *www.musestorm.com*
- Tweeterboard: *www.tweeterboard.com*

Conclusion

Marketing has been the age-old competitor of PR and communications in terms of budgets and senior executive mindshare. As the business environment evolved and bore witness to a massive shift in power from organizations to their stakeholders, however, the corporate communication function inherited tremendous responsibility, thanks to its intrinsic ability to build relationships and manage intangible business assets. As this business evolution occurred, companies' brands and reputations became more vulnerable and, in turn, more dependent on internal ambassadors to communicate key messages to influential stakeholder groups. From viral marketing to microblogging sites, this new dynamic has redefined the role of corporate communications in organizations, establishing a new discipline—digital integrated marketing communications—and redefining the way companies connect with their various audiences to positively affect their brands, reputations, and bottom lines.

Chapter 4

COUP de REPORTAGE
New Media Relations
in the Conversational Age

Marketing isn't the only organizational function that had to adapt to meet the demands of empowered stakeholders. Media relations—the founding tenet of public relations (PR) and corporate communications—has experienced a seismic shift as the Internet's ubiquity permeated every facet of business. The weight traditional media always carried in making or breaking brands and reputations lessened with the emergence of every new digital platform. Likewise, journalism's romanticized standards, built up by Algonquin Round Table-esque meetings of the minds and immortalized by the investigative, live-the-story styles of the Thompsons, Woodwards, and Wolfes of the profession, are unrecognizable in a time when an opinion and an Internet connection are all it takes to be a reporter.

"Today, after two centuries of institutionalized media, content creation has been democratized," said Sir Martin Sorrell, group chief executive of WPP. "The voice of ordinary people is increasingly as loud as that of mainstream media. Now everyone has the potential to influence a company's reputation—whether peer-to-peer, word-of-mouth, or through online comparison and product recommendation sites. Conversation is in. For brands to have influence, they must be talking—not just mindless chatter, but serious information presented in an authentic way."[1]

This chapter will dissect media relations in the context of a three-dimensional media landscape governed by impulse above logic, chaos above order. The growing role of digital media in defining corporate brands and reputations initially put many business leaders on the defensive, but many now are finding that they don't have the choice when it comes to joining the conversation. When the fight-or-flight instinct kicks in, it's step up or step aside. With the corporate communication function at the helm, organizations are modifying their media strategies accordingly. The following sections will detail the new media relations environment that corporate executives now face, as well as the challenges and opportunities that are present in communicating with the media both as a stakeholder group and as a vehicle for reaching consumer audiences. They also will offer strategies for understanding the nuances of communicating news and information effectively to the "press"—an entity made profoundly nebulous by consumer-generated media, digital platforms, and the emergence of citizen journalists.

Digital Soapbox: Online Platforms Turn Citizens Into Journalists

The media's influence over the successes and failures of companies is not a recent phenomenon; what is recent, however, are the increasing difficulties defining who—and what—the media are. Traditional media—newspapers, magazines, television, radio—have served as a conduit of information between companies and their stakeholders for ages, but these platforms have always acted more as a mouthpiece for corporate news rather than as a channel for two-way communications. Now, blogs, social media outlets, and online communities have empowered anyone to act as a journalist of sorts—hence the term *citizen journalism*—and to engage various audiences in conversations that have acute effects on the reputations of companies. As online interaction media became more prominent, in fact, the general public's opinion of the "most essential medium" changed radically; in the first decade of the twenty-first century, the public's choice of the Internet as the most essential medium has increased by 39 percent, whereas newspapers and radio decreased by 10 and 53 percent, respectively. Meanwhile, television held its ground with a mild 8 percent increase.[2]

Whether out of the spirit of innovation or the fear of being left in the dust, traditional media outlets made the transition online as the public's consumption habits became more digitally inclined. Plus, the rise of online news from nontraditional sources in the form of bloggers lends further support to corporations developing a thoughtful approach to their media relations with both traditional and nontraditional media; the 2008 Edelman Trust Barometer (which focuses on influentials) indicated that 86 percent of Internet users rank reading news as the top activity they engage in online, and social media as a source for corporate information is gaining credibility, especially among younger influentials.[3]

This monumental change in the public's media consumption habits, coupled with the explosion in relevance of consumer-generated media, affects both businesses and media organizations. For starters, one could argue, as the former president of CBS News did, that "every company is a media company" to some extent because businesses now create content that goes directly to their stakeholders without the filter of traditional media's editorial standards. The quality-control responsibilities still lie with the corporate communication function in almost all cases, but now these responsibilities have very little to do simply with crafting press releases and sending them out on the newswires. Rather, building relationships with influential media both online and offline is the crux of the success or failure of media relations campaigns.

Now and Then: Traditional Tactics Give Way to Digital Devices

As mentioned previously, media relations' backroom iteration within corporate organizations was based primarily on primitive tactics meant to inspire reporters to give a company positive coverage: writing press releases, coordinating news conferences, planning events, announcing new-product launches, etc. In the days before e-mail communications were ubiquitous, these outreach efforts came in the form of cold calling reporters and mailing or faxing releases, event invitations, or announcements. The girth of a PR professional's Rolodex was one of the best judgments of success, as was the "thump factor"—that is, the loudness of the thump when the book of press clips mentioning the company hit the desk.

Today, the convergence of old and new media outlets online makes these tactics archaic, if only because they don't facilitate relationship-building, engaging conversations, or targeted outreach. However, while the media are still a conduit for message dissemination via these channels, they also have become a stakeholder group, setting their own preferences and acting on their own whims. In fact, many of the most influential media representatives live and work solely in the online space, sparking an argument about whether traditional media have been felled at the hands of the "digerati." Arianna Huffington is one example of a journalist who created an online empire: the "Huffington Post," a left-wing online news and commentary Web site and aggregated blog. When confronted with the traditional versus new media debate, her response embodies the rough-and-tumble, 24/7 characteristics of today's news cycle that bloggers are so well equipped to handle:

> *Traditional media have ADD [attention-deficit disorder]: They are far too quick to drop a story. Online journalists, meanwhile, tend to have OCD [obsessive-compulsive disorder]—we chomp down on a story, refusing to move until we've gotten down to the marrow.*[4]

This obsessive behavior is more than a little overwhelming for business leaders, and understandably so. In the same *BusinessWeek* cover story that ran Huffington's commentary, Jeff Jarvis, the "BuzzMachine" blogger whose missive against Dell prompted the company's forced foray into the blogosphere, offered this insight into the twisted world of new media relations:

> *Three years ago, blogs were still a curiosity to a business audience—new enough to warrant a cover story, strange enough to require explaining. Now blogs and social media are not only better understood and accepted, but they are coming to be seen as a necessity in media and, more and more, in business. ... Social media are changing [business'] fundamental relationship with customers to be less about serving and more about collaborating. No, I don't mean that every product will be the product of a committee. But customers who want to talk will, and smart companies will not just listen but will engage them in decisions. This will have an impact not just on PR and image but [also] on product design, marketing, sales, customer service—the whole company.*[5]

Both these bloggers' comments set the stage for what will be discussed in the following section: how companies can define *media* in the context of their stakeholders' interests and, in turn, how they can identify the influential "journalists"—whether traditional, citizen, or some hybrid—that can deliver their messages to the *right* masses.

DNA Testing May Be Required: Differentiating Influential Journalists From Inflamed Commentators

In late August of 2008, bloggers descended on Denver, Colorado, by the hundreds. There were stay-at-home moms, retirees, teachers, and even cattle ranchers, all of whom arrived with laptops in hand for none other than the Democratic National Convention (DNC). Approximately 120 bloggers were given full press credentials for the 2008 presidential election's democratic showing—a number more than three times greater than that of the Boston DNC in 2004—and hundreds more showed up on their own accord to blog the days away. According to Jose Antonio Vargas, a reporter and blogger for the *Washington Post*, "Here in Confab City, you can't swing a messenger bag without hitting a blogger; the place is lousy with them."[6]

As for the Republican National Convention (RNC) held in St. Paul, Minnesota, nearly 200 credentialed bloggers set up shop, up from the mere 12 who were granted access four years earlier.[7] And, as the numbers of bloggers in DNC and RNC attendance skyrocketed between 2004 and 2008, traditional news outlets—specifically, newspapers—reportedly reduced their convention staffing by up to 20 percent[8] (for more on the use of digital communications in the 2008 presidential election, see Chapter 8).

This anecdotal evidence is perhaps the most blatant example that media as we know it has morphed into an unrecognizable organism and that it is no longer governed by formal training, long-established standards, or official affiliations. Given this disconcerting reality, then, how can communications executives go about engaging the media (old and new) that are most influential to their organizations and their other stakeholders in the content of digital tools?

"The real power of these tools is to engage in conversation and collaboration—what you call engagement. That's easy to say, but it's a real change for communicators to go from message creation and dissemination to actual dialogue," according to Jon Iwata, senior vice president of marketing and communications at IBM. "You have to be prepared to respond when others speak, challenge and inquire. Most challenging is that you have to be willing to allow others in the company—I'd say everyone in the company, eventually—to engage with each other and the external world without continuous monitoring and oversight by authorized spokespeople."[9]

This idea of dialogues and conversations with influential media is most pertinent to bloggers, who comment on everything from politics to business, from entertainment to the environment. While some of these bloggers are simply exercising their right to free speech, others offer insightful commentary about issues and, in turn, have influence over large audiences, raising a critical question for many executives: Are bloggers really legitimate members of the media? Or, perhaps more important, does it really matter?

"Social media is changing the way we communicate," said George Wright, vice president of sales and marketing for Blendtec. "If you're caught up in the argument of 'Is a blogger a journalist?' then you've missed the boat."[10]

True, dismissing bloggers as unemployed basement dwellers is a mistake, but most organizations have outgrown this perspective after learning that one may be the loneliest number, but it's certainly not the weakest. Take Starbucks. Until recently, the coffee retailer seemed to be unstoppable as its stores popped up in villages and cities around the world. However, when the chain set up shop in Beijing, China's Forbidden City Palace in 2000—at the invitation of palace managers, no less—even the behemoth brand couldn't overcome the negative sentiments that percolated online, led primarily by blogger Rui Chenggang. The store ultimately would survive seven years within the city's hallowed walls, finally closing its doors on July 13, 2007. Chairman and CEO Howard Schultz had this to say in response:

> *We were invited to open up a store [in the Forbidden City], we did very well, and then all of a sudden it was reported by a local blogger that perhaps we were being disrespectful of the history and culture of China. As soon as that occurred, we took a step back and said, 'We don't want to do anything that would dilute the integrity of the heritage and culture of the Chinese people. If they want us to leave, we will leave.' We did that very respectfully and walked away. I think many other companies would have fought it, but we didn't. We don't want to do anything that would be inconsistent with how people would view an outsider.*[11]

This is just one example of why reaching bloggers is becoming increasingly essential to successful media relations efforts while remaining a task-riddled with sand traps that the corporate communication function is best equipped to handle. Doing so involves three skill sets, to be discussed in the following sections: identifying influential bloggers, building relationships with them, and ultimately, engaging them with the intent of receiving positive coverage.

Positive Identification: Understanding Which Bloggers Are Influential to Your Stakeholders

Identifying the bloggers whose audiences influence your organization is similar to the process of vetting potential mates on an online dating site. Initially, it involves a great deal of looking, listening, and learning to recognize synergies between both parties' interests. But just as there are laws of attraction, there are basic strategies for identifying the bloggers who influence an organization's target audiences; for the most part, they come in the form of—what else—online monitoring and tracking devices (for more on social media tracking and measurement, see Chapter 3) such as

- *Technorati (www.technorati.com)*—searchable site that tracks more than 100 million blogs.
- *Google Alerts (www.google.com/alerts)*—sends registered users an e-mail each time a specific company name is mentioned in a blog or online news item.
- *BlogPulse (www.blogpulse.com)*—tracks the volume of chatter on the Web about a company or topic.
- *Compete (www.compete.com)*—provides site, search, and referral analytics and ranks online traffic.

These are just a few of an ever-growing number of free applications on Web sites that help corporate executives to wrap their arms around the massive volume of online conversations that could affect their brands or reputations. But more than being reactive simply by waiting for a blogger to praise—or pummel—their company, corporate communications executives must court bloggers proactively for coverage or simply serve as a conduit for reaching a target audience. In this light, then, the debate over whether or not a blogger is a journalist becomes moot; many of these new media mavens have far more influence than celebrity C-suite executives with big brands, thick Rolodexes, and deep pockets for traditional ad spend.

Case in point: In September 2008, computer behemoth Hewlett-Packard (HP) announced that it increased personal computer sales by 10 percent the previous May simply by leveraging the blogging community to promote its recently released HDX Dragon computer system.[12] Skeptics immediately assumed that the company paid off bloggers to build buzz around the product, but according to HP's vice president and general manager for the Personal Systems Group, Scott Ballantyne, bloggers weren't given a cent. All HP executives did was send 31 new computer systems to 31 influential bloggers in the tech space, offering to let them give them away in competitions among their readers.

The offer instigated a massive participatory online conversation in which the bloggers and their readers generated so much impromptu publicity around the competitions that the subsequent sales numbers spoke volumes. In fact, the HDX Dragon had been on the market for nine months prior to May 2008, and sales were languishing. Then, during May, sales skyrocketed 85 percent compared with average monthly sales leading up to the blogger outreach effort. What's more, overall HP PC sales surpassed forecasts for the United States by 10 percent as a result of increased publicity online, and traffic to *HP.com* jumped 15 percent—the company's only investment was the cost of the 31 computer systems themselves. According to Ballantyne, "This was for the community, by the community, with the community."[13]

These percentages, all supported by HP executives, verify the incredible influence bloggers have over target audiences; HP's skill in identifying the ones who would create the biggest "bang for their buck" (or lack thereof) illustrates the value in digital media relations. That said, the HP example could be viewed by naysayers as a combination of luck, a well-known brand, and a blogger community that is very active and easy to locate. All these points are valid, but by going beyond merely identifying influential bloggers and actually engaging them through formal media relations campaigns, corporate communications executives will generate even more supporting evidence that this new breed of journalist (or whatever label you would prefer) may become the greatest sales rep you never had on your payroll.

Listen Up: Putting Your Ear to the Computer Screen to Target Influential Bloggers Effectively

HP executives successfully identified the bloggers who exercise significant influence over HP stakeholders by having a stable of employees charged with actively surveying cyberspace (the company has more than 50 corporate blogs alone). But this doesn't mean that blogger outreach is only for the biggest, most tech-savvy corporate players; on the contrary, organizations of any size and budget can identify influential blogger communities through free applications such as those mentioned in the preceding section and then effectively target them by adapting media outreach strategies for a digital audience.

The first thing that any communications executive must do is resist the urge to send press releases and pitches to the bloggers they identify as audience influencers because this is one of the main ingredients in the recipe for failure. True to almost all "digerati," bloggers—especially those who have a significant following—are extremely conscious of maintaining authenticity, which means that communications executives must learn to speak new dialects if they have any hope of targeting bloggers successfully with media messages—in other words, executives must learn to listen.

Common blogger etiquette suggests that communications executives should read at least 20 of the blogger's posts along with the comment threads before ever reaching out and pitching a story. Some communications industry leaders, such as Katie Paine, CEO of KDPaine & Partners, recommend reading as much as six months' worth of posts before ever engaging the blogger. Listen until you understand the tone and nature of the conversation," Paine said. "Just as you wouldn't barge into a cocktail party and start bloviating, you need to treat the blogosphere as you would a cocktail party. Make the rounds, understand who might have something in common with you and engage in a conversation if appropriate."[14] In theory, this reconnaissance gives the executive a thorough understanding of the blogger's tone and interests, as well as of the audience's level of engagement with the blog.

If you thought you had to be pitch-perfect with traditional media, then you might be surprised to learn that these journalists are tone-deaf in comparison with their digital counterparts. Because online media are so much about customization and individual engagement, bloggers can be flippant with communications executives who "corrupt" the code of authenticity with generic press releases and media pitches that land in bloggers' inboxes. So, beyond making sure that you approach a blogger only with information that is completely germane to his or her audience, the pitch itself must be as concise as possible—some would even argue in favor of Twitter-esque pitches that consist of keywords and ideas and little else.

"You certainly can't spin your way to a blogger's heart," WPP's Sir Martin Sorrell said. "Respect and engagement are essential. Handing product over to bloggers would not be enough. If, however, you invite bloggers in to get their ideas on a brand, you might succeed. Get them involved; give them something of value. The prize for getting it right? The stakeholder becomes a brand loyalist and tells other people."[15]

Sticks and Stones May Break My Bones, but Words Will Never Hurt Me: Responding to Negative Blog Posts

It's as close to a guarantee as you can get: Ask a roomful of senior corporate executives how they feel about reaching out to bloggers for coverage, and a majority of them will say, "What happens if they write something negative/inaccurate/untrue?" Given the likelihood of this happening, executives must (1) have a strategy prepared in anticipation, and (2) know how to execute it if and when the need arises. After all, the entire concept of stakeholder empowerment implies a loss of control, and its ubiquity in the modern business environment means that corporate reputations increasingly depend on what is said about a brand online.

"This willingness to surrender control is essential, because in digital and social media there is an inverse relationship between credibility and control," according to WPP's Sorrell. "The more control you keep over the message, the less credible it is. And vice versa."[16] Thus digital media relations—more specifically, blogger relations—require new strategies and tactics that never would apply in a traditional media setting.

Beyond taking the previously mentioned steps to ensure that you identify, target, and engage bloggers effectively in the first place, there is often little that can be done about the negative conversations about corporate brands that percolate online. The corporate communication function must monitor digital channels to become aware of any rogue commentary; then it is a matter of deciding which comments actually have the potential to damage the corporate brand and reputation and which ones are purely off-the-cuff remarks that will burn out on their own.

"First of all, only respond if it makes a difference to your business," said Katie Paine. "We have a client that has what I would consider a 'stalker'—someone who is consistently negative to the point of being threatening. But his blog has no authority and very few comments, and it doesn't come up in a Google search. While it may be personally annoying, he's not having any impact on the business, in which case it's not worth engaging."[17]

It's important to note the difference between authority and size, but because a blogger has a small audience, his or her authority over that audience—and that audience's authority over your brand—may have more tangible influence over reputation than coverage in a top-tier news source. According to Paine, "[Smaller blogs] ... can have links, videos and photos that get picked up by other blogs. But, more important, find out if the negative conversations online are true. You can't put lipstick on a pig—or a bad product. If you have cockroaches in your kitchen, get rid of them before you engage."[18]

Finally, don't be antagonistic or defensive in your response. "When we respond to complaints, we don't take the attitude of 'You're wrong because....' We apologize, or we send them to our customer relations department, or we shed light on our reasoning," said Paula Berg, manager of emerging media for Southwest Airlines. "We will try a number of responses, depending on the situation. We have even considered policy changes based on feedback. Southwest is well known for its pen-pal nature, and social media has proven to be one more venue for us to create relationships and meet our [stakeholders'] needs."[19]

Own It: Taking a Proactive Communications Approach by Creating and Maintaining a Corporate Blog

Monitoring and engaging influential bloggers are important measures for every corporate communication executive, but such a stance is increasingly becoming only one piece of the digital media relations puzzle. The other piece, albeit more time-consuming and, some might argue, more inviting to risk, is maintaining a corporate blog that opens the organization up to conversations with all stakeholders, media included.

Corporate blogs, regardless of the bylined author, are most often managed—or at least vetted—by the corporate communication function. While some behemoth companies were at the forefront of the business blogging phenomenon, launching their own blogs even before knowing the medium's complete capabilities and pitfalls, other corporate leaders balked at the idea of opening their organizations up to the freewheeling commentary of stakeholders. However, by late 2008, it was hard not to resign oneself to the reality that those digital media platforms—especially blogs—weren't going to fizzle out.

According to the Fortune 500 Business Blogging Wiki, which was created by *Wired* magazine Editor-in-Chief Chris Anderson and Socialtext cofounder Ross Mayfield, 61 of the Fortune 500 companies were blogging as of October 2, 2008—that's 12.2 percent.[20] While this is by no means a majority, it represents a marked improvement in multinational corporations' willingness to embrace (or at least tentatively accept) the blogosphere. Plus, the percentage doesn't take into account the Fortune 500 companies that have more than one corporate blog: Hitachi has six, HP has 55, IBM has 125, and Sun Microsystems has more than 4,600 blogs that are Sun-related.[21]

But what is the specific argument for using a corporate blog as a media relations tool? "To be effective, we all have to adapt and try new things," said Bob Lutz, vice chairman of global product development for General Motors. "[Corporate blogging] … is an opportunity to have a real dialogue with our customers and potential customers, and an opportunity to put our message out there that's totally unfiltered. It's also immediate. If I were a journalist, I would really hate the pompous, self-congratulatory big shot stuffed shirts who they often have to interview, especially when all they can get from the interview is little tidbits of the predigested corporate line doled out with heaping side helpings of corporate arrogance."[22]

When done effectively, corporate blogs convey executive voice in the unfiltered, immediate style Lutz referred to; plus, research reveals a growing trend of journalists turning to the Web to find information about stories. According to the 2008 *PR Week*/PR Newswire Media survey, nearly 73 percent of responding journalists sometimes or always use blogs when researching stories.[23] This means that the vast majority of journalists are searching the blogosphere for information about companies, and it would behoove those companies to have control over at least some of the content these journalists find. This reality alone makes a very compelling argument.

For those seeking a more official reason to accept corporate blogs as legitimate media relations tools, consider this: On July 30, 2008, the U.S. Securities and Exchange Commission (SEC) announced its move to recognize corporate blogs (and corporate Web sites in general) as public disclosure under Regulation Fair Disclosure (Reg FD). (For more on the SEC announcement and Reg FD, see Chapter 6.) In other words, by acknowledging that corporate Web sites and blogs were legitimate forums for providing information to investors in compliance with federal securities laws, the SEC legitimized this content as valid source material for the media.

So the argument for having a corporate blog has been made. How, then, can executives ensure that this platform is used to the organization's greatest advantage? (*Hint*: Read next section.)

Nuts about a Blog: Creating a Corporate Blog That is Authentic and Reflective of the Organization's Brand and Culture

Anyone looking for a best-in-class example of a corporate blog worth emulating needn't look any further than Southwest Airlines. The company's corporate blog, "Nuts About Southwest," has been a digital darling ever since its 2006 launch; since then, it has collected a laundry list of accolades for its textbook method of integrating social media components into the blog, all while staying true to the Southwest brand, maintaining a completely transparent front, and engaging all stakeholders along the way.

The internal aspects of Southwest's blog will be discussed in Chapter 5, but its approach of having employees from across the organization contribute content makes it a dynamic media-facing property as well. Employees refresh content daily, using "Nuts About Southwest" as a platform for providing simple explanations of complex industry issues, from bankruptcies to fuel hedging to overbooking, in turn making it a valuable resource for reporters. The company's corporate communications team pitches the blog's content to the media, and it's usually very well received because the voice is authentic, transparent, and nonpromotional—characteristics that Southwest executives cultivated since the blog's launch.

"We wanted the blog to have a grassroots feel to it, so our publicity was minimal," Paula Berg said. "We did a soft launch on April 27, 2006, and waited. About a week into it, we pitched it to one of our reporters and let him roll with it. Aside from that, we let people find their way to it."[24]

Another factor that contributes to the blog's authenticity is its openness to commentary, whether it's positive or negative. According to Berg, "The blog is completely moderated, so no comment is posted without someone on my team reading it first. That said, there are very few comments that do not make it past the screening process. We do not post anything vulgar, racist, or otherwise offensive. Whenever we decide not to post a comment, we respond thanking the author for participating and explaining our decision. If possible, we invite them to make the necessary edits and re-post, but we never edit comments ourselves."[25]

The company's receptiveness to honest, sometimes-negative commentary from media and customers alike has had positive effects on its corporate reputation and business strategies. Case in point: On March 6, 2008, the Federal Aviation Administration fined Southwest Airlines $10.2 million for alleged missed aircraft inspections—potentially the biggest crisis the company had faced in its 37-year history. Over the course of the next eight days, executives posted a total of five messages on the blog, which collectively generated approximately 450 comments. Most were negative. But the team's decision to allow negative comments helped it gauge public sentiment, and stakeholders were grateful for a forum in which to voice their concerns. Southwest's brand managed to weather the proverbial storm with minimal damage to the company's reputation, further supporting the theory that open dialogue—even when it's inflammatory—can be a means that justifies the end as long as stakeholders' messages are heard *and* taken into consideration (for corporate blogging dos and don'ts, see Table 4.1).

More recently, Southwest executives upped their blogging standards once again, incorporating additional social media elements to enhance users' engagement levels. The new features, which include a video blog, reader polls, news feed, and sharing and rating options, also enable visitors to personalize their experience—a big advantage for reporters who can customize the blog's content to display information that's most relevant to them and to notify them only when news of interest is posted.

Southwest Airlines' corporate communications executives may have mastered the recipe for corporate blogging success, but it's safe to say that the number of companies that meet the same standards is dismal. According to a June 2008 report by Forrester Research, which looked at 90 blogs from Fortune 500 companies, most are "dull, drab, and don't stimulate

Table 4.1: Corporate blog dos and don'ts

Don't	Do
Blog for the sake of blogging.	Evaluate your company's identity and stakeholder preferences to ensure that a blog is an appropriate platform for engaging key stakeholder groups.
Adopt a blog tone that doesn't match the corporate identity.	Make the blog's tone consistent with the identity and corporate culture. A blog doesn't have to be funny or offbeat to be successful.
Ghost-blog.	Ensure that the stated author of the blog is indeed the true author. This doesn't mean the corporate communication function shouldn't vet/edit posts; rather, it should make sure that messages are on point with all other communications outreach.
Blog only when the spirit moves you.	Blog early and often; most blogging connoisseurs agree that a blog with fewer than three posts per week is a blog not worth reading.
Use a corporate blog as a place to post press releases.	Blog about corporate news, but only in a way that is authentic and speaks to stakeholders. Say why they should care, point out an industry trend—anything to separate the blog content from that of the online newsroom.

discussion."[26] Approximately 66 percent of the blogs rarely get comments, 70 percent only contain commentary on business topics, and 56 percent republish press releases or summarize news that is already public.[27]

So what's wrong with these three measures of success?

- *Approximately 66 percent of the blogs rarely get comments.* This is a tell-tale sign that the blog's content isn't engaging, and it is the primary objective of any blog—corporate or otherwise—to engage audiences.
- *Seventy percent only contain commentary on business topics.* There are too many other places where corporations "talk business," including the corporate Web site, press releases, and the online newsroom. To be successful, the corporate blog should be the "business casual" version of your identity; for a buttoned-up, strictly business organization, this may just be akin to loosening the necktie. For a creative, innovation-driven company, it may mean that flip-flops are appropriate (see Figure 4.1). Regardless, it is essential to make sure that the general tone is in line with the company's identity and its core audiences.

- *Fifty-six percent republish press releases or summarize news that is already public.* A corporate blog is not a breaking-news feed or a newswire service, and the media will not treat it as such. If the only content on your corporate blog is press releases or old news, cut your losses and shut the blog down now.

Speaking of taking down corporate blogs, in April 2008, amid a reputation and communications crisis that stemmed from the grounding of its fleet of MD-80 planes, American Airlines quietly launched a blog at the domain *http://aaconversation.blogspot.com/.* It was the company's first foray into corporate blogging, and according to comments made by the airline's spokesperson to media, it was done hastily to provide a place for customers and media to get information about the cancellations.[28] The problem?

First, hosting the corporate blog on Blogspot chipped away at its credibility right out of the gate. Second, there was no American Airlines branding to speak of, making it difficult to discern who actually "owned" the blog. Third, if the purpose was to provide information to stakeholders in an interactive forum, the effort failed horribly: The blog was taken down after just a handful of posts went up, making it fodder for media ridicule rather than a source for information.

This example of what not to do speaks to a number of points that are critical to using corporate blogs effectively as media relations tools: (1) They must be authentic and transparent, (2) they must offer content that is up-to-date and useful now, not five minutes ago, and (3) they must be easy to find by being somehow connected to the company's site.

American Airlines is one example of a company that launched a corporate blog in the wake of a crisis, but to bad effect. At the other end of the spectrum is Sony Electronics, which created a self-inflicted blog crisis and then used the same medium to turn it around. The trouble began in December 2006 with a blog by the name of "All I Want for Xmas Is a PSP." The blog, which allegedly was written by "Charlie" and incorporated YouTube videos of his hip-hop singing cousin, "Pete," told the story of the duo's attempt to get one of their parents to buy them a PlayStation for Christmas. Humorous and seemingly homemade, the blog developed a following and acted as consumer-driven marketing for the product—only it wasn't consumer-driven at all.

On December 12, 2006, news broke that the blog wasn't authentic at all when the domain registration was traced back to Sony's then ad agency Zipatoni, the apparent mastermind behind the effort. Sony's corporate communications department didn't have its hand in the ploy, but it hardly mattered. According to Patrick Seybold, director of corporate communications and social media at Sony PlayStation, "The PR department wasn't involved at all [in the fake PSP blog], which I think was mistake number one. I think [those involved] thought it would be a good way to drum up some pre-holiday momentum, but I think we all know now it probably did everything but that."[29]

Not exactly—the tactic definitely drummed up momentum, but in an entirely wrong direction. When online media and consumers caught wind of the marketing ploy, all hell broke loose, and the Sony brand took the ultimate beating in the blogosphere. Visitors to the blog spit fire, crucifying the company for trying to dupe consumers into purchasing the gaming unit by impersonating two average Joes. On December 15, 2006, before the "flog" (fake blog) was taken down, Sony executives posted this *mea culpa*:

> *Busted. Nailed. Snagged. As many of you have figured out (maybe our speech was a little too funky fresh???), Peter isn't a real hip-hop maven and this site was actually developed by Sony. Guess we were trying to be just a little too clever. From this point forward, we will just stick to making cool products, and use this site to give you nothing but the facts on the PSP. Sony Computer Entertainment America.*

Sony execs were clearly at fault and had no choice but to accept blame. Instead of letting the fire simmer and die out, though, the corporate communications team used the experience as an impetus for rebuilding brand loyalty and trust through dialogue—that is, via the same digital communications platform that got them into trouble in the first place: a blog. Over the course of the next few months, Patrick Seybold, Sony's director of corporation communications and social media, collaborated with Kazuo Hirai, president and group CEO of Sony Computer Entertainment, Jack Tretton, president and CEO of Sony Computer Entertainment America, and Peter Dille, senior vice president of marketing, to get approval for an official Sony PlayStation blog. In cooperation with executives from every corner of the company, including corporate, legal, information technology (IT), human resources (HR), sales, and marketing, the team launched *http://blog.us.playstation.com* on June 11, 2007. Seybold wrote the debut post, which stated:

> *Now, what we've learned, perhaps the hard way, is that a blog like this is really about you and the things you want to hear, share and discuss with*

us. With that in mind, you'll notice that comments are enabled—and encouraged—so tell us what you want to see here and we'll do our best to make it happen.[30]

The PlayStation blog steadily gained traction, with some commentators expressing skepticism, but few specifically referenced the fake blog incident. The communications team made a concerted effort to ensure that this blog exceeded expectations in terms of transparency and authenticity, even hiring former *Orlando Sentinel* reporter and blogger Jeff Rubenstein to oversee its development. "Sony appeared to be amid a turnaround," he said. "It really looked like it was turning a corner from a difficult launch [of PlayStation 3]. People were excited about the brand again. The blog had started off on the right foot. It was a more humble, here-for-you approach."[31]

A year later, sales data proved the blog's success. When PAIN, a comedy video game, was featured on the blog, it received substantial pickup on gaming sites, and one executive attributed its first-week sales numbers to the PlayStation blog. Then, in July 2008, NPD Market Research reported that PlayStation sales forecasts were on an upswing, with PS3 sales up 311 percent from June of 2007.

All told, the initial hit to Sony's reputation proved to be worthwhile based on the initiative borne from it. Other companies, once helpless to negative blog coverage (whether deserved or not), have taken back some control by launching their own corporate blogs to bring the conversation onto their own turf—an approach to be illustrated in Chapter 9 by Dell's transition to digital dominance.

Tweet on This: Looking Beyond Blogs to Engage Media Online

Blogs may be the most common denominator of digital media relations because bloggers have influence over target audiences, thus making them de facto media representatives. However, more and more corporations are learning about the other nooks and crannies in cyberspace where many journalists go to get story ideas, bond with their fellow media brethren, find sources, and even post coverage.

Twitter, the microblogging platform discussed in Chapter 3, crawls with media at any given time, day or night; and why not? It's an efficient way to break news, especially if you know that many of your audience members are avid "Tweeters." There are a growing number of free services and applications created specifically for finding Tweeters based on interest, as well as their followers (for a list of related resources, see the sidebar "Resources for Finding Tweeters" below). And if you think only fringe citizen-journalist types occupy real estate on Twitter, think again: *The Financial Times*, the *New York Times*, *USA Today*, CNN, Fox News, and NPR are just a handful of many mainstream media outlets that monitor conversations on Twitter. Beyond monitoring the microblog for breaking news and story ideas, these journalists also actively engage in the exchange of information among readers and other journalists. Consider the following examples:

- *Journalists stay connected.* During Steve Jobs' much-anticipated keynote speech at the 2008 MacWorld Expo, so many journalists and techophiles were Twittering about his presentation in real time that the site crashed. Users around the world expressed frustration because many stayed awake and Twittered into the wee hours of the morning in their local time zones to get constant updates on Jobs' announcements from those in attendance.
- *Twitter announces poll results.* During the January 3, 2008, Iowa caucuses for the U.S. presidential election, political strategist Patrick Ruffini asked those participating to send him results directly via Twitter. Ruffini aggregated the results and distributed them through a Twitter channel, in turn revealing the results far earlier than any other news source. The next day, Ruffini blogged about the experience, saying, "This exercise in citizen journalism foretold the result far more quickly than dispatching two dozen stringers to caucus locations throughout Iowa. Post-macaca, predictions abounded of citizens armed with camera phones bringing us live coverage of everything. It hasn't happened … yet, … but we saw a glimpse of the future tonight in Iowa."[32]
- *A new generation of press conferences.* On August 13, 2008, Dell executives held a press conference in San Francisco to introduce its new generation of mobility products. Local media appeared to cover the event, and a Webcast broadcast online enabled journalists in other locations to tune in. Dell went even further to allow for ultimate media interaction: Twitter users could tweet questions about the new products, and Dell representatives would tweet back with

answers. The company crossed into a new digital frontier as one of the first to give media and consumers the opportunity to ask questions via Twitter during a live news conference.

Corporate communications executives looking to expand their media relations efforts to microblogging platforms like Twitter must remember that as is the case with blogs, there is a very specific etiquette for initiating conversations, and there is also a very specific benefit.

"The difference between microblogging sites and more traditional media is that [the former] allows a company to identify smaller trends," according to Heidi Sullivan, director of electronic media at Cision North America. "Additionally, Twitter allows users to have conversations. Relationship-building is key. Your company's social media representative(s) must have a personality and independent thoughts to get noticed on Twitter. Companies like Pandora and the ChicagoTribune.com have Twitter personas with character. They ask questions, make jokes and respond to comments. This has allowed them an authenticity within their community that they would not receive from just posting news stories and being solely self-serving."[33]

RESOURCES FOR FINDING TWEETERS

- *TwitDir*—finds everything from most-followed users, to top posters, to the top 100 followers.
- *Twubble*—finds popular Tweeters who your friends are following.
- *TwitterWhere and TwitterLocal*—finds local Tweeters within a certain distance of any given location.
- *Twits Like Me*—finds Tweeters with similar interests to yours.
- *TwitterWho*—finds Tweeters by e-mail address.
- *TwitterSearch*—finds out who is tweeting about what based on search terms.
- *Twittervision*—tracks tweets worldwide in real time.

Twitter and like-minded microblogs have proven to be useful channels for connecting with stakeholders, whether customers (as discussed in Chapter 3) or media, but there are many others. Social networks, for example, facilitate the connections between individual executives and their colleagues (past and present), clients, and even acquaintances. Facebook and MySpace are among the most popular social networks, but they still maintain an air that's more casual than professional. LinkedIn, on the other hand, was launched in May 2003 as a "grown-up" version of Facebook and MySpace, appealing to a more business-minded audience by focusing on professional—not personal—relationships. Five years later, membership exceeded 25 million users from more than 150 industries.

LinkedIn also gives executives the ability to form groups, as well as to follow work- and news-related Web activity among members of their own organizations, competitors, and their industries as a whole via a widget that can be downloaded to the LinkedIn user's home page. This widget aggregates the links, news stories, and media sources that are most relevant to the user's profile automatically, allowing individuals to track the news that their connections are consuming (for more on LinkedIn and using social networks to gauge internal stakeholder activities, see Chapter 5).

Digital Media Toolbox: Everything You Need to Build and Execute Modern Media Relations Campaigns

The ability to dexterously socialize with bloggers and other digitally inclined media is important, but it's only as good as is the home base you lure these digital influencers back to once the relationship is solidified or the press release you send them to tease a story once you've caught their attention. In other words, the corporate Web site and all its media-related components must be humming with interactive elements, dynamic content, and frequent updates to create an engaging experience for each individual user.

Press Release2.0: Social Media Applications Revolutionize Traditional Text Announcements

Press releases are arguably as old as the PR profession itself. Ivy Lee, the executive retained by the Rockefeller family to provide PR counsel for Standard Oil, is considered to be one of the founding fathers of the PR profession. When a Pennsylvania Railroad train crashed on October 8,

1906, killing more than 50 people, he penned what is now recognized as the first press release. The media reacted kindly to the innovative communications approach, and the *New York Times* even printed Lee's release verbatim on October 30, 1906, as a "Statement from the Road."[34]

More than 100 years later—even as distribution channels evolved from "snail mail" to fax to e-mail and beyond—the traditional press release model of text-heavy promotional news announcements sparks everything from criticism to ennui among media recipients, not to mention corporate executives. According to Bob Lutz, vice chairman of global product development for General Motors, "Instead of being a weapon for putting out the truth, [a press release] ... becomes a method of risk avoidance. It focuses on making sure no one says the wrong thing. By focusing on not saying the wrong thing, you're essentially saying nothing."[35]

This approach to communications via press releases certainly falls flat in the new dimensions of cyberspace. Even members of journalism's old guard are becoming less and less responsive to the static "PR speak" that usually dominates press releases, instead looking to dynamic online platforms to find an authentic take on what's really going on. However, if you consider the most archaic form of press releases in the Internet age—those distributed as text within e-mails or as attachments—to be Web 1.0, then the Web 2.0 version of this communications platform is the social media press release. In short, social media press releases take the traditional release concept and "digitize" it with new media components, including Web video, links to audio files/podcasts, Technorati/Digg/Facebook tags, embedded live links, and custom Real Simple Syndication (RSS) feeds.

The social media release was borne out of an article written on February 27, 2006, by Tom Foremski, then a reporter for the *Financial Times*. Titled, "Die! Press release! Die! Die! Die!" the article damned press releases as useless, delete-on-receipt documents with too much spin, pat-on-the-back phrases, and meaningless quotes.[36] Foremski's diatribe prompted Todd Defren, principal at SHIFT Communications, to create a template for a social media news release that would replace meaningless puff and jargon with interactive digital components that tell the company's story to the media more effectively (see Figure 4.1). Since then, organizations are jumping on the social media release bandwagon in droves, adapting templates and content to meet their own needs.

Social media releases certainly are becoming more prevalent, but some communications professionals argue that their value is overwrought. According to Greg Jarboe, president and cofounder of

Figure 4.1: Template for social media press releases

SOCIAL MEDIA PRESS RELEASE
TEMPLATE, VERSION 1.0

CONTACT INFORMATION:	Client contact	Spokesperson	Agency contact
	Phone #/skype	Phone #/skype	Phone #/skype
	Email	Email	Email
	IM address	IM address	IM address
	Web site	Blog/relevant post	Web site

NEWS RELEASE HEADLINE
Subhead

CORE NEWS FACTS
▪ Bullet-points preferable

 LINK & RSS FEED TO PURPOSE-BUILT DEL.ICIO.US PAGE
The purpose-built del.icio.us page offers hyperlinks (*and PR annotation in "notes" fields*) to relevant historical, trend, market, product & competitive content sources, providing context as-needed, and, on-going updates.

PHOTO	MP3 FILE OR PODCAST LINK	GRAPHIC	VIDEO
e.g., product picture, exec headshot, etc.	e.g., sound bytes by various stakeholders	e.g., product schematic; market size graphs; logos	e.g., brief product demo by in-house expert

MORE MULTIMEDIA AVAILABLE BY REQUEST
e.g., "download white paper"

PRE-APPROVED QUOTES FROM CORPORATE EXECUTIVES, ANALYSTS, CUSTOMERS AND/OR PARTNERS
Recommendation: no more than 2 quotes per contact. The PR agency should have additional quotes at-the-ready, "upon request," for journalists who desire exclusive content. This provides opportunity for Agency to add further value to interested media.

LINKS TO RELEVANT COVERAGE TO-DATE (OPTIONAL)
This empowers journalist to "take a different angle," etc.
These links would also be cross-posted to the custom del.icio.us site.

BOILERPLATE STATEMENTS

 RSS FEED TO CLIENT'S NEWS RELEASES

"ADD TO DEL.ICIO.US"
Allows readers to use the release as a standalone portal to this news

 TECHNORATI TAGS/"DIGG THIS"

SEO-PR, "The social media press release is an unfortunate mix of two good ideas. Adding Technorati tags to your social media releases doesn't get them into Technorati. Submitting press releases to social news sites like Digg is social media suicide. Using a jazzy new format that features bullet points and del.icio.us links isn't going to make bloggers care about your product."[37]

While some critics share this view of social media releases, others believe that the open access to corporate information online, as well as the SEC's decision to recognize the disclosure of financial information on corporate blogs and Web sites, makes them even more relevant in media relations efforts.

"The SEC is taking the right steps to embrace the new tools and services that reach people in addition to wire services," Brian Solis, principal of FutureWorks, wrote on the TechCrunch blog (*www.techcrunch.com*) on July 31, 2008. "With the recognition of blogs as a viable form of disclosure, under certain circumstances, of course, the SEC is officially recognizing Social Media, and in a sense, socializing the rules associated with Reg FD. Perhaps, the most significant change stemming from the new SEC guidance is that Web-based disclosure does not have to appear in a format comparable to paper-based information, unless the Commission's rules explicitly require it. This is music to my ears as it finally opens the door for the Social Media Release."[38]

Regardless of which side of the argument corporate communications executives fall on, it's important that every professional realizes the importance of adapting their old-school strategies to function in today's stakeholder-centric environment. For some brands and their audiences, high-octane social media releases may be the best bet for securing media coverage, whereas other organizations and their targeted stakeholders will experience greater return with more traditional releases. It's just a matter of identifying the objective you want to achieve with the release, understanding the preferred consumption habits of the release's target audience, considering the brand's identity, and crafting messages.

"I see press releases having an important role in a few areas," said Steve Rubel, director of insights for Edelman Digital and host of the widely read "Micro Persuasion" blog (*www.micropersuasion.com*). "First of all, they communicate a message very quickly to the press, which is something that a blog or a feed really can't do. And they reach a large number of people, particularly investors. Also, they can have a high impact on search engines, and I think that's important to look at."[39]

Figure 4.2: Ford social media press releases have live links to additional digital components, including photo galleries, YouTube videos, and RSS feeds

Ford Motors has been a pioneer in adopting the social media press release (SMPR) and adapting it to its specific media audience (see Figure 4.2). The company has a Web site (*www.ford.digitalsnippets.com*) dedicated to housing social media press releases for product and corporate news. Within these two categories, releases are subcategorized to make it easy for media to find exactly what they are looking for (product SMPR categories include Ford Mustang, Ford Flex, Ford Trucks, etc.; Corporate SMPR categories include safety, quality, environment, technology, etc.). Visitors to the "Digital Snippets" site can subscribe to RSS feeds for any category; the press releases themselves, then, have digital features embedded, ranging from YouTube videos and Flickr photos to media kits and community forums. Of course, each release contains the necessary news/product details, albeit abbreviated for quick consumption.

Bringing Home the Bacon: Online Newsrooms Become 24/7 Press Junkets

Digital media outreach efforts via blogger relations, social media news releases, and the monitoring of online news outlets is only part of the overall media relations picture. In addition to these efforts, the corporate communication function must create a home base to serve as the go-to spot for media in search of corporate news and information. Given the previously mentioned statistics describing journalists' use of the Web for finding, researching and writing news stories, there is a strong business case for doing so.

Online newsrooms are one-stop shops for all media relations needs. They host dynamic content—Web videos, news feeds, widgets, podcasts, searchable archives, etc.—and they give journalists access to information they want, when they want it (for a roadmap outlining the process of building an online newsroom, see the sidebar "Roadmap for Online Newsroom Development" below). Plus, multimedia platforms like these are catalysts for increasing traffic to the corporate Web site, and their content is completely in the control of the company rather than its stakeholders.

ROADMAP FOR ONLINE NEWSROOM DEVELOPMENT

With all the opportunities presented by online newsrooms come challenges to creating and maintaining them effectively. For example, there is an initial Web development expense; content must be dynamic, interactive, and constantly updated; and too many layers of information can make navigation difficult. To avoid these pitfalls and seize the digital media relations opportunities presented by well-conceived newsrooms, take the following steps:

1. *Sketch out a root outline and infrastructure.* Initially, corporate communications executives should meet to develop a list of the materials and applications that should be on the site. Then it's essential to organize the components on paper to visualize the structure that is intuitive and easy to navigate. What elements should be on the main page? How many subpages should there be, and what content fits within each? Once these questions have been considered, make sure that the corporate Web site has the bandwidth to support the desired applications.

2. *Actualize the layout.* This is the part of the newsroom development that can be costly and time-consuming because it requires collaboration with the IT department or an outside vendor. The communications team should be prepared to give the IT department/vendor a wire frame, or an outline that details the number of pages and subpages that must be created, as well as where each resides in relation to the opening page. Specific attention also must be paid to branding; the font size, background colors, and logos should be consistent with the main corporate Web site and reflect the company's identity.

3. *Add content.* Once the infrastructure has been built, add media relations content with consideration to the journalists' points of view. Intuitive navigation is essential, as are clearly marked tabs that lead to contact information (specific names, phone numbers, and e-mail addresses—no switchboards, addresses for general inboxes, or forms to be filled out), news releases, multimedia content, and executive bios/corporate information.

4. *Prepare to go live.* Before the newsroom is visible to media and the general public, the corporate communications team must beta-test the site by assigning employee focus groups a list of items to find and then testing the time it takes them to do so. The newsroom also should be searched for any broken links. Then, if possible, give the newsroom its own URL as opposed to one that is buried within the main corporate site.

5. *Launch.* Once the newsroom has been built (or, if it already existed, reno- vated), inform the media of its existence via a multimedia press release. Then give them a means to offer feedback, make comments, ask questions, or request additional information.

However, it's critical for organizations to customize their Web offerings with their specific targeted media in mind. One thing remains consistent for all successful online newsrooms, though—nav- igability. No matter the number of bells and whistles, media will unan- imously find a site to be worthless if the design isn't user-friendly. Beyond that, any combination of the following features can enhance the user experience:

- *Image library*—should include high-resolution, downloadable images of executive photos, company logos, product images, etc. Apple's online newsroom (*www.apple.com/pr*) is strategic in its approach to offering downloadable images to media; the site offers two types of photographs—high resolution at a minimum of 300 dots per inch (dpi) and low resolution at 72 dpi—to appeal to users with both fast and slow Internet connections.
- *News feeds*—give media the opportunity to opt in to receive updates of company news. Nike's media center (*www.nikebiz.com/media*) addresses news updates from several angles. Media can subscribe to an RSS feed to receive updates, view individual releases, either print or e-mail them, and search the news archives by category, year, or month.
- *Web video*—functions include product demonstrations, executive interviews, clips of news conferences, commercials, etc. Southwest Airlines' newsroom (*www.swamedia.com*) has a user-friendly video gallery with thumbnail screenshots of clips, a preview option, the size of each video, and the ability to download.
- *Blog roll*—link to corporate blogs to give media the opportunity to see what corporate executives are saying about issues involving the

company/industry as a whole. This offers a more candid view of the organization and often will spark story ideas. Sun Microsystems' news center (*www.sun.com/aboutsun/media*) has a section on the site's home page called "BlogCentral," which gives a snapshot of the most recent posts on the company's many blogs.

- *Twitter links*—show media another place they can find corporate executives. AT&T's newsroom has a running tab called "Recent Tweets" that shows the tweet along with the date and time it was posted. At the bottom of the section, a live link invites media to "Go to *Twitter.com* to follow us."
- *Interactive calendars*—lists upcoming events, conferences, product launches, milestones, etc. in a visual way.
- *Thought leadership*—compiles thought-leadership pieces authored by corporate executives, from white papers to research to op-ed columns, in a central location.

Ford Motors sets a high standard for online newsrooms, just as it does for social media news releases. In addition to its media room (*www.media.ford.com*), its "Digital Snippets" site builds out media relations content to host an array of digital components, from social media press releases to photo galleries and YouTube videos.

Indeed, if the traditional press release was given a social media makeover, so too was the Web 1.0 version of an online newsroom. All the digital components now required to make newsrooms viable media relations tools have precipitated a social media newsroom concept, much like that of social media press releases (see Figure 4.3). The social media newsroom template, also developed by SHIFT Communications' Todd Defren, is a loose interpretation of what this platform should resemble, but it offers a strategic roadmap that can be adapted for your organization.

For companies that don't have the infrastructure or financial resources to build a truly effective digital newsroom, there are alternative publishing platforms that offer starter templates, which then can be built out and customized. WordPress (*www.wordpress.org*), for example, is a downloadable software script that acts as a self-hosted blogging tool—but that's not to say it only creates blogs. According to Todd Andrlik, director of marketing and public relations at Leopardo Construction:

> *Instead of building a social media newsroom from scratch, why not build it from a WordPress template and almost immediately gain RSS, search*

Figure 4.3: Template for a social media newsroom

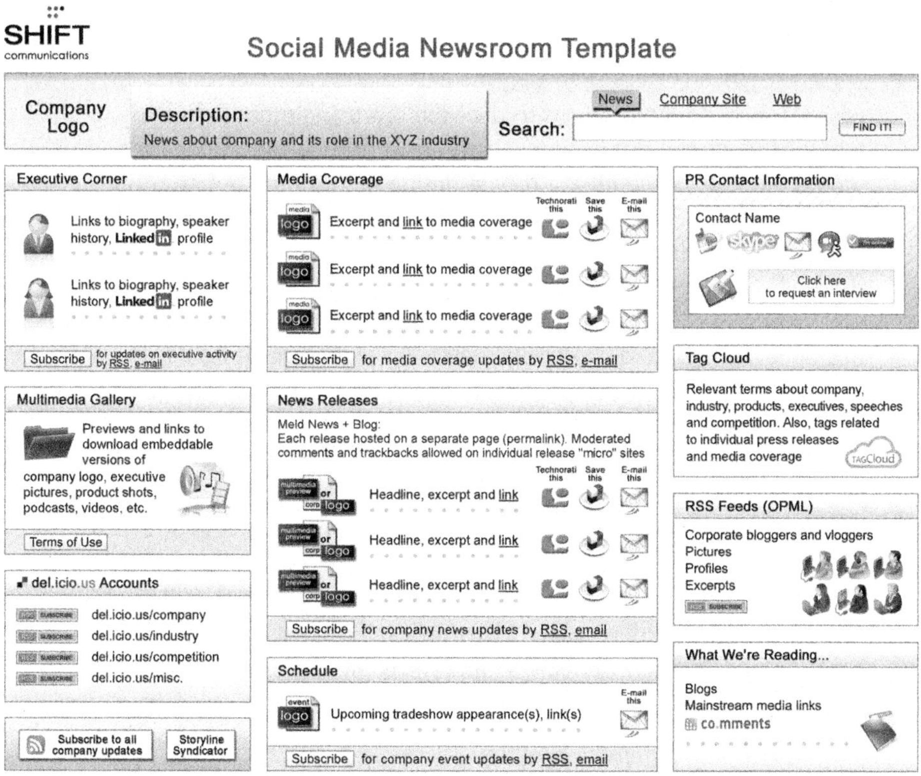

functionality, categories, comments, archives, easy video integration and
a menu of cool widget options? Every release, or post, that you publish
is instantly a social media release. And, better yet, you're engaging in
the conversation at your corporate site instead of a third-party
newswire.[40]

Andrlik adapted the WordPress template to create a dynamic social
media newsroom for Leopardo Construction, disabling the feature that
allows comments to make it more of a monologue (direct dialogues with
media are best left for blogs). The WordPress platform proved to be a
perfect solution for Leopardo, as it could be for any company that wants
to convert a static newsroom into a social media playground without
breaking the bank or overloading the company server.

Connective Tissue: Search Engine Optimization Brings Digital Media Relations Full Circle

It's already been established that media—and every other stakeholder group, for that matter—turns to the Web more and more frequently to find information about a company. In terms of media relations, having strong outreach strategies, a robust online newsroom, and attention-grabbing press releases is required to garner positive (and squash negative) coverage. However, if Google is most Internet users' first stop on the Web—and research indicates that it is—then true media relations success begins with the ability of communicators to control the content that appears highest up in search queries for their companies.

This is the concept of *search engine optimization* (SEO), or the process of increasing the amount of visitors to a Web site by ranking high in the search results of a search engine such as Google or Yahoo!. Because corporate reputations increasingly are defined by search engines, in terms of both media coverage and public perception, SEO strategies are vital to the ability of organizations to control messaging and, in turn, affect the public's perception of their brands. According to Andrew Barnett, digital strategist at Fleishman-Hillard, "Search increases brands' exposure of assets online, connects with key stakeholders, drives conversations, improves branding and manages reputation."[41] Just one or two of these actions is reason enough to commit to optimizing all online content; when considered as a whole, the argument becomes indisputable.

The Key to SEO Success: Tagging Key Terms to Boost Search Ranking

Search engines are based on algorithms that automatically "crawl" through the ever-growing number of Web pages that make up the World Wide Web to find those that most closely match a search term. These crawlers then return that information to a central depository, where the data are indexed and frequently updated. Thus, when Web users perform a search query, the search engine actually is looking through these data indices rather than every single Web page on the Internet.[42]

If this sounds very technical, that's because it is, but these programming and algorithmic nuances have virtually no bearing on what executives need to know to optimize their company's content (on Web sites, in newsrooms, in Web videos, in press releases, etc.) for search. You just need to understand what drives results in layperson's terms—the keywords users type into search queries when looking for information.

Keywords are the crux of optimized content because stakeholders conceive of them based on the information needs that drove them to the Web in the first place. It's up to corporate communications executives to anticipate the keywords and phrases that are most likely to be used in specific search queries that relate to their brands because doing so enables them to intercept stakeholders at their moment of interest and to drive their actions accordingly (e.g., shift a perception, drive sales, etc.). This is why SEO isn't just a media relations tool but also a marketing strategy, a measurement technique, a means of managing crises, and a way to connect with stakeholders.

Choosing keywords to optimize content, then, is as much an art as it is a science. While many terms are used in all corporate Web content (the company name, for example), others are very specific to the individual message being released (i.e., a new-product announcement, a promotion, a response to a crisis, a blog post, etc.) and may not be instinctive. Alternatively, the keywords that seem obvious have pitfalls of their own, including being among exponentially more indexed pages that the search engine will return and competing with unrelated content for higher search rankings.

To manage the balancing act, the first step in any keyword strategy is to identify the objective of the message relative to the target audience. Then the communications team must identify the universe of potential keywords or phrases that stakeholders might use when searching for a related product, service, or news item. This list should be comprehensive, but by no means will it be the final collection of keywords that will be tagged in the content; ultimately, only two or three will be used in the final optimized product. Luckily, the process of narrowing down the list of possible terms to a handful of high-impact ones is manageable, thanks to the availability of free keyword research tools online (see the sidebar "Free Online Keyword Research Tools" below).

FREE ONLINE KEYWORD RESEARCH TOOLS

- Google AdWords Keyword Tool: *https://adwords.google.com/select/Key word-ToolExternal*
- Wordtracker Keywords: *http://freekeywords.wordtracker.com/*

- Microsoft adCenter Labs Keyword Forecast: *http://adlab.msn.com/Keyword-Forecast/*
- Trellian Search Term Suggestion Tool: *www.keyworddiscovery.com/search. html*
- Google Suggest: *www.google.com/support/bin/answer.py?answer=106230 &hl=en*
- Google Trends: *www.google.com/trends*

Southwest Airlines realized the importance of researching keywords for use in corporate communications efforts when its executives faced unsatisfactory search results for their press releases and wanted to conclusively link their PR efforts to ticket sales. The company teamed up with SEO-focused PR firm SEO-PR to conduct in-depth research on the search terms that, when integrated into press release headlines and subheads, would get better traction in search engines. The team's most compelling finding also was perhaps the most obvious—so obvious that it had been overlooked in all past communications strategies: Assuming that users would search for the company's abbreviated name, executives had always used *Southwest* as a primary keyword in news releases. Leaving out the word *Airlines* lumped the company's content with exponentially more Web pages, meaning that its news releases didn't appear as high in search results. Simply tagging the airline's full name as a key phrase made it stand out more prominently.

But that wasn't the team's only keyword discovery. Well known as a low-cost carrier, research suggested that Southwest Airlines would benefit immensely from incorporating *low fares* into its word bank of key terms. With this information now in its arsenal, the corporate communications department had a strong foundation for taking its SEO efforts to the next step, which it did with four press releases that definitively tied the PR efforts to sales (for more, see the next section).

Tag, You're It: Imbedding Keywords into Content to Optimize Search Results

Once the keywords for the communication element have been identified, executives must create or revise its content to incorporate these words in terms of priority. For a press release, this means having the *most likely to be searched* term in the headline and the rest of the key terms in the first few sentences of the release's body. By this point, these keywords will have been *tagged*, which is the programming equivalent to giving a parolee a tracking device that makes him or her "findable" as long as it's attached. These tags can be assigned via simple HTML codes, but it is increasingly common for digital channels such as blogs, video-sharing platforms, and corporate Web sites to have preestablished fields labeled "Tags," into which executives can type each keyword, separated by commas (WordPress, for example, makes tagging keywords a piece of cake). The site's content management system (CMS) takes care of the rest. But don't think that peppering a press release—or any content—with multiples of the same keyword will boost its search results; search engines are smarter than that, having been programmed to disregard repetition as spam. No keyword should be used more than six times in any optimized material. It's also important to note that search engine crawlers only read the first few lines of text in any given site, so burying important content/keywords at the end of a release won't do any good.

For even greater optimization, executives can imbed live hyperlinks into online content because these URLs will catch the attention of search engines if placed strategically. Ideally, links will appear early on in the text, and they will contain one of the keywords (e.g., *www.companyname.com*). Plus, as an added bonus, unique URLs imbedded into Web content double as built-in measurement devices. When Southwest Airlines executives optimized four press releases for search in 2004–2005 to announce one-way bargain tickets to select destinations, they placed live URLs in each release that took users directly to a unique landing page that provided more information and linked them to the point of sale. This strategy made it possible for the company to determine conclusively that viewers of these press releases ultimately generated $2.5 million in ticket sales.[43] From a media relations perspective, the same technique could be used to find out how many journalists clicked for more information compared with the number who covered the company's news.

Optimizing Social Media: A Little Strategy Goes a Long Way

Press releases may be the most commonly optimized communications vehicle, but that's the beauty of the Web—virtually everything is searchable, which means that virtually everything can be optimized for search. The corporate communication function can help to increase visibility and brand awareness by optimizing all its company's digital assets.

Figure 4.4: Technorati: State of the blogosphere in 2008
*(http://technorati.com/blogging/state-of-the-blogosphere/
the-how-of-blogging/; downloaded December 15, 2008.)*

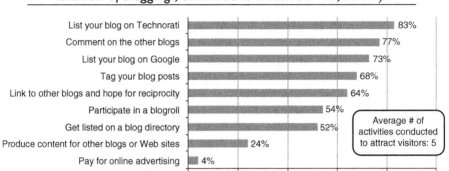

According to WPP Group Chief Executive Sir Martin Sorrell, "Search is everything in influencing a decision to buy. A good Web site is no longer enough. Content of all types—video, graphics, networks, conversation—needs to be searchable from every direction."[44]

Ford's online properties are completely optimized for search based on their strategic use and placement of keywords, including brand names, industry buzzwords such as *safety, environment*, and *quality*. Social media components such as tagged videos and hyperlinks with keywords help their SEO cause.

AT&T, with the help of PR agency Fleishman-Hillard, executed a campaign centered on increasing the visibility of the media-focused assets in its online newsroom. By conducting keyword research, establishing a style guide for writing press releases, and then optimizing the releases by using keywords and embedded links, the company saw more than a 1,000 percent increase in traffic from the use of targeted keywords, as well as a 50 percent increase in search volume from 2007 to 2008.[45]

Another way to think of SEO is to look at ways in which top bloggers attract visitors to their sites—in other words, how they optimize their content to be highly ranked in search results. The 2008 Technorati State of the Blogosphere Report revealed that, on average, bloggers participate in five activities specifically intended to attract visitors, including participating in blog rolls, tagging blog posts, and commenting on other blogs (see Figure 4.4), all of which can (and should) be done by executives to enhance the visibility of their own corporate content.

Conclusion

Since the day Ivy Lee distributed his press release for Standard Oil in 1906, the media relations discipline has been transformed into an unrecognizable rendition of its former self. The media, once a powerful conduit of information exchange between businesses and stakeholders, now finds itself competing not with other news outlets, but with companies and stakeholders themselves. The ability to create content has been democratized by emerging digital communications channels, thus redefining the true meaning of journalism.

This new media reality doesn't just challenge news outlets; corporations that once depended on their outbound press releases to be interpreted (hopefully accurately) by reporters and then communicated to stakeholders now are forced to engage directly with audiences in two-way conversations rather than one-sided monologues. The corporate communication function, already programmed to handle messaging and media relations based on its PR background, has taken the lead in adapting its organization's online presence to identify and engage a new breed of digital media professionals. Whether its blogger relations, online newsroom development, or search engine optimization, these modern media relations activities define a company's ability to control its brand and reputation in this cutthroat, blog-eat-blog world.

CHAPTER 5

THE WATER COOLER GOES TO CYBERSPACE

INTERNAL COMMUNICATIONS IN A DIGITAL WORLD

A company is only as strong as its weakest link or, in the spirit of the corporate Darwinism theory introduced in Chapter 2, its weakest employee. For as long as businesses have existed, a derelict employee could do fairly significant damage, but his or her means of doing so were fairly limited to theft, fraud, and other litigious matters—actions whose effects often were short-lived once the employee was terminated.

Now, the tables have turned, and senior executives find themselves at the mercy of their staffs in more ways than they'd care to believe. According to the "Eleventh Annual Global CEO Survey" conducted by PricewaterhouseCoopers, the war for talent remains a key concern among CEOs worldwide. What's more, 89 percent of respondents to the same survey said that "the people agenda is one of my top priorities" when asked, "To what extent do you agree or disagree with each of the statements regarding people issues within your organization?"[1]

Recruiting top talent—especially when it comes to members of generation Y—requires innovative techniques that surpass the typical job-application-submission cum interview cum offer sequence of events. Once a job candidate does become an official employee, the challenges don't stop; keeping talent is as difficult as finding it, so employees' benefits, growth opportunities, and morale all must be catered to on a near-individual basis. Then there are the employee relations and internal communications considerations, which were once relegated to the human resources (HR) department but now require multifunction collaboration to foster strong corporate cultures and to connect employees who are scattered in offices around the globe. Accordingly, the idea that organizations must understand what it means to act as a single enterprise has changed—no longer can a company rule its employees and publics with a top-down approach, just as a multinational conglomerate can no longer expect to get the most out of its towering empire by applying different rules to different regional offices around the world.

The thing that defines a company today has to be whatever common thread exists between a company and its employees—this is the tie that binds the *one-company philosophy*. At its core, a one-company philosophy is an attempt to increase synergy and, consequently, better enable orchestration across all of a company's departments by ensuring that the values and beliefs of its core businesses reside within its employees rather than on a piece of paper in a strategic plan.

This chapter will identify the specific factors that introduced modern intraorganizational challenges into the fold. It then will define the intertwined practices of talent management, employee relations, and internal communications in the context of the corporate communication function's increasingly strategic role in each. Finally, it will highlight the ways in which corporate executives can use digital platforms to enhance internal communications initiatives and combat the talent management issues head on.

Conflicts of Interest: A Challenging Business Climate makes Corporate Culture the Panacea During Change

Among all the factors that sparked the modern business juggernaut—stakeholder empowerment, globalization, emerging digital channels, a turbulent economy, globalization, etc.—external communications isn't the only thing challenging corporate institutions. In fact, most business leaders would agree that their most important stakeholder is employees, making strategic internal communications a primary concern. According to Matt Gonring, a consultant with Gagen MacDonald:

> *The most significant thing that has happened in my experience over the last five years is that, in spite of the economy, the function of employee and internal communication has become an established management discipline in the companies where I have worked. We came from a time when employee communication was a bit of an afterthought, and a bit one-way. Now it's a dynamic two-way process that is recognized by senior management as a critical dimension of managing the enterprise, engaging the workforce in being a part of change and the overall strategic direction of the company. The focus of the internal communication function has shifted from pursuing outputs to achieving outcomes—and that is a significant step forward.*[2]

The corporate communication function shoulders more and more of this burden because its collaboration with HR draws it further into the employee relations vortex (for more on the integration of corporate communications and HR, see the next section). At the center of this proverbial employee relations vortex is the organization's corporate culture. The significance of a strong corporate culture was introduced in Chapter 2, but it is central to the discussion of internal communications because its tentacles touch everything from talent management to employee relations, from change management to professional development.

Corporate culture is much like the internal version of a brand, in which specific identities, images, and values contribute to an individual's feelings about and attitudes toward the company. In this case, the "individual" is not just any stakeholder but an employee—someone who has a uniquely vested interest in the organization and who has the ability to drive the perceptions of those outside the company. Highly productive businesses invariably have high-performing corporate cultures that align well internally and externally to support the overall business; culture shapes the employee experience, which, in turn, affects the customer experience, business partner relationships, and ultimately, shareholder value. A 2007 report from Towers Perrin and the Human Capital Institute[3] identified the following important dimensions of a corporate culture, which include an organization's

- Criteria for employee recruitment, promotion, retirement, and exit
- Formal and informal ways of socialization

- Recurrent systems and procedures
- Organizational design and structure
- Design of physical spaces
- Stories and myths about key people and events
- Formal statements, charters, creeds, and codes of ethics

With these dimensions as a backdrop for understanding corporate culture, the following sections describe how executives can leverage digital communications platforms to enhance corporate cultures relative to change management, rebranding, and employee morale.

Culture Shock: Strong Corporate Cultures Ease Anxiety Around Organizational Change

Talent management and internal communications challenges to some organizations in the relatively young twenty-first century are akin to finding the ideal hired help in a busy (albeit economically endowed) family; screening is necessary, but due diligence almost always will result in a good match—at least for the time being. But imagine if this was taking place in an extended family that was joined recently by marriage, complete with stepchildren and half-siblings, mothers-once-removed, and ex-husbands and wives in the wings. These circumstances are symbolic of those that face organizations in the midst of a massive organizational change related to a merger, acquisition, leadership change, or otherwise.

"Any large multinational organization struggles with change, and people are often naturally resistant to change," said Rafael del Pino, chairman of Ferrovial Group. "That's why communications is so important. People need to understand what needs to change and why and their role in the process, while the company itself needs to be prepared to help people take on new roles in the organization, as the company adapts to a constantly changing world."[4]

Indeed, the corporate communication function plays a compelling role in change-management issues that organizations face internally regardless of the catalysts for the change. A primary catalyst, though, is the high level of mergers and acquisitions (M&A) activity. As mentioned in Chapter 2, the number of cross-border M&As owing to globalization is on the rise, economic downturn or not. This trend's implications for business models, organizational structures, and integration strategies have been discussed already, but the internal communications/employee relations components of these changes are most integral to the subsequent success of any change-oriented venture such as M&As.

As globalization has spurred cross-border deals, strategies for aligning corporate cultures have become increasingly dependent on digital communications platforms. How else can corporate leaders effectively reach employees scattered around the world to communicate new policies, keep them aware of changes, and implement training to integrate processes? A number of strategies that address each of these challenges will be discussed later in this chapter; in the context of M&As, though, it's important to focus on targeting employees, identifying their needs, building a communications strategy around those needs, and charging management to execute the strategy (see Figure 5.1).

Digital communications channels can facilitate cultural alignment among employees, whether via announcements on intranets, connections on internal social networks, or executive statements presented virtually through Web casts. For more on effectively implementing all these platforms to enhance internal communication strategies, read on because each is considered in the context of branding, corporate culture, employee engagement, training, recruiting, and retaining top talent.

Figure 5.1: Four elements of cultural integration. (*From "Mastering Post-Merger Integration," Roland Berger Strategy Consultants, Hamburg, Germany, November 2006.*)

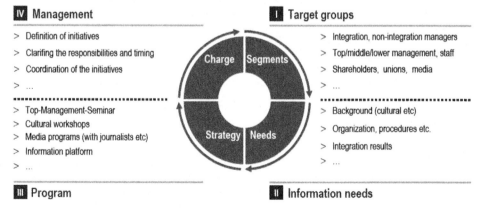

IV Management

> Definition of initiatives
> Clarifing the responsibilities and timing
> Coordination of the initiatives
> ...

> Top-Management-Seminar
> Cultural workshops
> Media programs (with journalists etc)
> Information platform
> ...

III Program

I Target groups

> Integration, non-integration managers
> Top/middle/lower management, staff
> Shareholders, unions, media
> ...

> Background (cultural etc)
> Organization, procedures etc.
> Integration results
> ...

II Information needs

Charge | Segments

Strategy | Needs

Mirror Image: External Rebranding Initiatives Reflect the Importance of Cohesive Internal Cultures

Mergers and acquisitions present significant internal communications challenges, and digital communications platforms, in turn, offer opportunities to overcome said challenges. But M&As aren't the only change-management issue that require attention to corporate culture and a healthy communication strategy; rebranding initiatives, from corporate name changes to product relaunches, require employees to be completely onboard internally before any external successes will be won. Of course, not only is corporate culture critical to rebranding efforts, so too are the digital platforms that communicate efforts to employees and that act as an adhesive as messaging evolves to accommodate change.

Rebranding around a corporate name change isn't as uncommon as one might think. Some of today's most iconic companies weren't born with the names they currently bear. Google, the world's number one search engine, was launched as BackRub in 1996 and didn't adopt its current moniker until 1998. Tobacco giant Philip Morris became Altria in 2001 to disassociate itself from the negative perceptions of cigarettes. AOL has undergone multiple iterations before settling on its current identity; founded as Quantum Computer Services in 1985, it was renamed America Online in 1991 and finally made the AOL abbreviation official in 2006.

For Philips, the process to honing the internal culture was almost a direct inverse of Panasonic's. Instead of rebranding the company externally to match the feelings employees had for years, Philips launched a new brand identity, "Sense & Simplicity," to the marketplace in 2004 to great success, but its internal brand understanding and commitment scores remained low. According to Jules Prast, then-executive vice president of corporate communication for Royal Philips Electronics, "The internal brand score-card revealed stubborn pockets of resistance. The challenge was identifying these across a widespread organization."[5]

Recognizing that internal alignment with "Sense & Simplicity" would be necessary to driving a sustainable competitive advantage, Philips executives initiated an internal communications strategy that hinged on facilitating an intranet-based dialogue through which corporate leaders could capture insights and ideas exchanged among individual employees. These online dialogues acted as a barometer to gauge internal brand alignment progress throughout the entire initiative.[6]

Key to engaging employees in this online forum was senior-executive participation. Direct access to senior executives prompted employees to get involved initially, and executive facilitators helped employees to overcome their fear of exposing their opinions by setting a candid tone for a dialogue about roadblocks to brand behavior adoption. Through this open exchange of ideas came potential solutions to identified problems, which executives captured and prioritized on a "Simplicity Hitlist."[7]

The approach of going straight to the source—employees—to uncover reasons behind the disconnect between the company's internal culture and its external brand proved to be successful. The dialogue led to a robust "hitlist" of strategies, from debureaucratizing to reducing e-mail volume to mobilizing employees. Results of Philips' internal brand survey also indicated success: From 2005 to 2006, positive response frequency increased across all categories. According to Prast, "Participants delivered a much-needed wake-up call. It was a bold examination of the brand promise from a 'family' perspective and it helped us troubleshoot and plan new initiatives to further embed Sense & Simplicity."[8]

One of those new initiatives born from the online dialogue with employees leveraged multiple facets of Web communications to connect staffers with the Philips brand: Simplicity Showdown, an online video game that fused the company's heritage with its refined vision moving forward. The game, introduced in the summer of 2006, tackled two internal culture challenges: employees' lack of connection with the "Sense & Simplicity" brand and with their managers (because internal surveys indicated that North American managers weren't communicating effectively with their teams). Using the interactive technology staged on the company intranet, the corporate communications team helped to develop a virtual narrative to meet the initiative's goals. The video game would roll out in phases over the course of a one-month competition in which managers would lead their teams in a virtual treasure hunt through famous landmarks around the world that had a Philips connection. Before they could move to the next level, the teams had to answer questions related to the brand and its strategic objectives. The motivation for playing? The winning team would be sent to the Bahamas for the annual strategy meeting that otherwise would be held in their hometown.

Once the online game's storyline was intact, the communications team built buzz around its release to ensure high levels of participation and engagement. This was an essential step because the nontraditional approach of encouraging managers to play games with their staffs didn't set well with many employees at first. After some coaxing (and after receiving promotional postcards at their home addresses to get their attention), however, managers logged on and registered their teams in droves. Approximately 4,000 of the company's 12,000 North America employees participated, and 94 percent of managers held discussion sessions with their teams over the four-week period; 58 percent did so more than was required. A post–"Simplicity Showdown" employee engagement survey showed that 72 percent of managers were seen as active role models for company values (compared with 50 percent in 2005), 85 percent of employees said that they believed that Philips has an outstanding future, up from 66 percent in 2005, and 65 percent of employees said that they trusted the company's leadership, compared with just 49 percent a year earlier (for a list of best practices in using online games to build corporate cultures, see the following sidebar).

ONLINE GAMING CHECKLIST

- *Make sure that you have the infrastructure to support the gaming technology.* Bandwidth limitations will cause the application to crash, rendering the entire effort pointless.
- *Identify objectives up front.* These objectives will guide the development of the game's narrative. If you don't have a solid roadmap from the beginning, it's easy to end up with a virtual storyline that doesn't address any of the challenges it was meant to overcome.
- *Set benchmarks.* Survey employees before launching the game to establish a baseline against which you can measure success after the initiative's completion.
- *Make friends with the information technology (IT) department.* Two downsides to online gaming technology are cost and a time-intensive development process. For large companies, much of the legwork can be done internally by IT executives or Web developers, but outside vendors often are required to build out features and applications. On the backend, make sure to have IT executives on hand to troubleshoot any technical glitches.
- *Align the game with the brand.* Inspiration may come from memories of Atari and Nintendo games of yore, but every aspect of the corporate online game—from its theme to its look and feel—should reflect the corporate identity and culture. Online games present tremendous branding opportunities, so pay attention to every detail, and customize as much content as possible.

- *Encourage competition.* It's basic human nature to be driven by competition, and online gaming initiatives shouldn't be any exception. Offer incentives for participation, and reward the best performers.

The success of this effort, from its early move to start online dialogues between employees and senior executives to the launch of "Simplicity Showdown," highlights a number of points critical to internal brand building in the digital age. First, external brand achievements start with the emotional connection of employees to the corporate culture. Second, senior leaders can't get away with a closed-door mind-set anymore. And finally, interactivity is the key to engagement.

Happy Days: Employee Engagement Fuels Loyalty and Resilience

Conventional wisdom dictates that happy employees are more productive, motivated, and loyal, not to mention more likely to act as de facto ambassadors for the brand by recommending the company's products/services to their family and friends. This naturally improves corporate reputation and, in turn, a company's ability to weather crises, endure change, and succeed financially. The preceding two sections addressed the change-management component of internal communications and corporate culture, but what about organizations that are in a period of relative stability? Corporate culture by no means becomes less important; on the contrary, fostering an ironclad corporate culture during quiet times makes the organization more resilient during turbulent periods and more adept at taking on risks.

As Sam Palmisano, CEO of IBM put it:

It's about culture and how decisions are made. For IBM today, being [one company] . . . means figuring out ways for 370,000 IBMers, expert in virtually every industry and working in 170 countries across the globe, as well as literally millions of business partners and other members of IBM's global ecosystem, to exercise their own judgment and imagination . . . but at the same time produce work that is consistently and recognizably "IBM."[9]

There are an ever-growing number of ways that the leading innovative corporations like IBM are using digital channels to nurture their corporate cultures during healthy phases via proactive employee engagement efforts. As for IBM's own methods, the company's intranet, which was more than two decades old by the new millennium, had already proven to be a valuable tool for disseminating changes in policy and management announcements. Out of that vehicle, IBM was able to develop "jam sessions," which have become an often-emulated means of connecting employees around the world and empowering them to voice their ideas. The first-ever IBM jam session, "WorldJam," took place in 2001 after an IBM employee survey revealed that employees saw the company intranet as the most credible, useful, and preferred information resource.[10] Palmisano said that while the jams began as pragmatic efforts aimed at capturing and socializing best practices in IBM's day-to-day operations and in its culture, the technology was never really the important part.

"Our jams were, at their core, all about trust," he said. "They said to everybody in the place, 'We believe you have the information and the ideas. We believe that you know what's happening with our clients, what's happening with the technology, what's happening out there in the market and the world at large. Let's get together and figure out what to do about it.' "[11]

Thus the executives implemented "WorldJam" as a 72-hour global event in which all employees could participate virtually through the corporate intranet. The event's success precipitated effusive praise from employees and external stakeholders alike, as well as a series of subsequent jam sessions, including "InnovationJam" and "ManagerJam" (for a step-by-step guide to starting a jam session in your own organization, see the following sidebar).

HOW TO START A JAM SESSION

I.   *Understand the objectives.* As with most large projects, jams begin with a clear set of objectives. Stakeholders need to consider what they expect to change as a result of the jam. For "ManagerJam," there were five objectives: (a) Begin nonhierarchical dialogue among managers, (b) begin the behavior change (i.e., collaboration, networking, and open sharing of ideas), (c) begin to build a sense of community among managers based on management issues, (d) get managers to think differently about solving company-wide management issues, and (e) build a knowledge library based on manager insights.

2. *Select engaging topics.* The best results seem to come from including a number of varied topics rather than a few focused ones. Employee surveys, executive strategies, focus groups, and other communications vehicles can help to shape the jam topics. Crafting the topic statements with care is key; the statements need to be both engaging and provocative.

3. *Conduct topic research.* Once the topics have been selected, each one needs to be researched to fully understand what the organization already knows about it. The research can take as long as a month to compile depending on the number of topics selected.

4. *Select facilitator teams.* Facilitator teams are a combination of people with prior jam experience, those who are subject-matter experts, and people who in some way embody the desired jam results. Facilitators are not "announced" in the jam as the moderators are. In this role, facilitators have the freedom to guide the dialogue as participants. A facilitator team supports each moderator, who is the more formal discussion leader. For global jams, facilitators should be located around the world.

5. *Engage the moderators.* Moderators are selected based on their recognized expertise or leadership in the topic area. These tend to be busy individuals who are fully engaged in their day-to-day work, and their time can be difficult to schedule. To ease this problem, a lead facilitator may be assigned to each moderator. This person, who has jam experience, acts as right-hand person for the moderator, coordinating the facilitator team and providing focused communication to the moderator during the jam event.

6. *Transfer skills and build the facilitator teams.* About one month before the jam event, facilitators and moderators meet for a day to be briefed on the jam's objectives and to be trained on jam best practices. In this meeting, they also clarify roles and begin building the facilitation teams. Globally dispersed facilitator-moderator teams also launch a collaborative space in which they continue the jam preparation. The collaborative space is also used along with instant messaging and telephones for communication during the jam event.

7. *Prepare to Jam.* During the month prior to the event, facilitator teams review research materials for their topic, develop work processes for the jam event, discuss possible directions the dialogue on their topic may take, and align on possible facilitator actions.

    The jam research teams begin to design the research to be conducted at the conclusion of the jam. Communications teams develop campaigns designed to pull participants into the jam and to sustain participation throughout the event. Time is scheduled on the calendars of key executives who will participate in the jam event.

8. *Jam!* During the jam itself, the well-prepared team executes its plan. Topic-facilitation teams stay in constant contact via instant messaging and occasional telephone calls. Cross-topic discussions and geographic hand-offs occur in collaborative space.

9. *Mine the knowledge.* Since the entire jam transcript is preserved, all the work done during the event becomes part of the organization's knowledge library. Throughout the months following the jam, the event continues to inform the organization.

Source: Lynn Dorsett, Michael A. Fontaine, and Tony O'Driscoll, "Redefining Manager Interaction at IBM," IBM Institute for Business Value, 2002.

According to Mike Wing, vice president of world wide intranet strategy and programs for IBM:

> *ManagerJam was an innovation at the intersection of two distinct trajectories: the changing role of the manager and the emergence of a new form of corporate interaction. It's neither top-down, nor bottom-up; it's horizontal—what we call employee-to-employee communications. Rather than being some kind of giant cyber-suggestion system, it's a radically democratic environment designed to help managers help each other.*[12]

IBM's 2006 "InnovationJam" pushed the collaboration needle even further by allowing IBM clients to join the online conversation, thus potentially giving competitors a sneak peak at future strategies—but such is the spirit of innovation. Ten new businesses alone were borne of this single jam session. Palmisano subsequently announced the company's $100 million investment to incubate the new businesses; he spoke to stakeholders in a town hall–style meeting hosted in Beijing in 2006 and simultaneously broadcast in the virtual world Second Life for all those who wanted to tune in.

Jam sessions have proven to be an effective way to start and maintain conversations, generate ideas, and engage employees, but their value is best achieved by organizations with deep pockets and the infrastructure to support such a robust technological system. For companies looking for a more self-sustaining engagement method, internal social networks give executives the ability to customize the online experience (via branding, company-specific features, etc.) and then turn it over to employees to create content.

Much like Facebook, LinkedIn, and MySpace, internal social networks allow users to create personal profiles, post messages, and add other digital features. The main differentiating factor is that internal networks are just that—internal. The beauty of these platforms: They don't have to "live" on the company's intranet, so they don't suck up bandwidth or cripple IT infrastructures. Plus, thanks to services such a Ning (*www.ning.com*), executives can create customized social networks for free. These networks can be password-protected so that only employees can access the content.

BlueShirt Nation is a prime example of an internal social network that succeeds on many levels. It was created by two Best Buy employees, Gary Koelling and Steve Bendt, who worked in the company's advertising department and needed information about the customer experience to better their campaigns. Their first order of business was to connect with Best Buy sales associates, who interact directly with customers daily. This effort evolved into the development of an internal communications initiative that spread across the entire company; thus BlueShirt Nation (*www.blueshirtnation.com*) was born.

"It started with an idea—an idea that we couldn't get sponsored," said Steve Bendt. "The idea was to create a place where employees could talk to each other. The hope was that we could learn more about what our customers were going through in the stores so [that] we could create better marketing. People loved the idea; they talked about it, supported it, but no one would fund it. So in June of 2006 *blueshirtnation.com* went online—funded by Gary Koelling. For the domain name and a year of hosting, it cost a hundred dollars. The software that built the site was free. There was one user, the administrator. After Gary's hacked version was live and there was a usable prototype, people started to take notice. Management shifted and our new CMO heard what we were doing. He decided to give us some time, some cover and a little money to see if this thing could grow."[13]

Koelling and Bendt started small by gathering 20 volunteers from Best Buy stores around the country to meet and brainstorm about the network. "We held what we called Hack Slams," Koelling said. "We sat in a room, talked politely about what it is and then went bowling.

We went bowling to get to know each other. We took cameras. We ate pizza. We came back and got honest. We talked about what really sucked about the current site. We took the pictures and videos from bowling and posted them to the site. We talked about what it would take for them to use the site. We made changes to BSN right there in the room. Then we talked about those changes. We talked about things like trust and anonymity on the site. We talked about things that would ruin the experience for them and make them never come back. We talked about the things that would make them want to tell others to join."[14]

After the focus group, the duo took the show on the road, visiting 130 stores around the country and introducing employees to BlueShirt Nation. "We brought stickers and T-shirts," Koelling said. "We met with thousands of employees and told them a simple message: 'We built a site that's kind of like MySpace, Facebook, YouTube, and Digg. It's just for Best Buy employees. Will you check it out? If you like it, tell others. If you think it sucks—go ahead and post it on the site.' They did both. While all of this was going on, we tried to stick to a few key principals. Build the site fast, be able to adapt quickly, listen closely. We focused on winning the trust of the most skeptical audience, which were our store employees. We did that by talking one-on-one with them, promoting the site in ways that were frankly counterculture. We tried to address the main problem they told us: 'My opinion doesn't matter.' "[15]

Since then, BlueShirt Nation's membership has grown to more than 20,000 Best Buy staffers nationwide. Two-thirds are actively engaged in the community, logging on at least once a month, and in a company with a 60 percent turnover rate, the internal social network's members represent fewer than 10 percent of those who depart. The network, open only to Best Buy employees with active employee identification numbers, fosters the open exchange of ideas surrounding everything from productivity issues, to benefits enrollment, to personal news about new additions to staffers' families. Beyond minimizing turnover among employee members, the BlueShirt Nation also was the driving force behind the "401(k) Challenge," a video contest hosted on the internal network to encourage employees to sign up for the company's 401(k) program, which resulted in a 30 percent increase in enrollment.

Koelling and Bendt attribute BlueShirt Nation's continued success to a number of factors, and chance is one of them. According to Koelling, "BlueShirt Nation is a fluke. The Best Buy culture wasn't set up to take on something like this. That's why it's built outside of the IT network, that's why a couple ad guys run it. At every minute of every day, we still face the challenges that you'll face in your organization." Based on their experience, Koelling has made the following recommendations to build an internal social network that engages employees and cultivates a strong corporate culture[16]:

- *Resist senior management's urge to control the network.* "The top will want to control it, because things like this look dangerous. It flattens the org chart, redistributes responsibility and rewrites the leader/follower contract. Legal hates things like social networks. Too many outliers. They'll try to crush the spirit before it ever leaves planning phase. They'll want to measure its success. The truth is, you can't measure success because you don't know what success is in a social network. We still don't. We see the benefits outweigh the costs, so we're still alive."
- *Make development an ongoing process, not a preliminary process.* "They'll want to plan it, build it, launch it when its perfect. If it's done right, though, it'll never be perfect—it'll always be changing."
- *Find a few ambassadors who will grow the network organically.* "There'll be pressure to build the community fast—bad idea. There'll be a temptation to throw money at it—doesn't work. There'll be talk of scale, [that] big is better. If we were to give advice, it would be to start small. Find the people that are passionate about it. Give them freedom, give them cover when they need it, give them a small budget, and most of all, give them time. Let them learn, let the idea grow, and encourage them to fail. The truth is, you're at the mercy of the people that you're trying to influence. If you try to force it, its not real and will feel contrived—it'll backfire."

Lost in Translation: HR and Corporate Communications Integrate to Overcome Talent-Management Challenges

Thus far, one theme remains consistent among the business functions discussed in this book: Traditional roles within siloed departments are no longer effective, let alone possible. Building relationships with stakeholders, whose influence over corporations and bottom lines has grown exponentially, is of paramount importance. This has long been communicators' bread and butter, so the need for their skill sets has permeated almost every aspect of corporations.

The same is true for the human resources (HR) department, which was created to oversee administrative functions, including the processes surrounding hiring new employees and explaining/processing benefits packages, evaluating performances, handling personnel issues, and when the need arose, administering pink slips. But times have changed, in turn creating new needs and placing new demands on a function that isn't traditionally equipped to manage certain challenges. Key issues HR leaders grapple with include the effect of globalization, outsourcing, and the need for new kinds of change management as the percentage of a company's employees based outside its country of origin continues to grow.[17]

According to the "Eleventh Annual Global CEO Survey":

> *Our findings suggest that CEOs recognize the strategic importance of people and the need for agility. But they do not believe that their companies can manage change adequately.... The evidence suggests that new organizational structures are necessary to facilitate collaboration; that more effort should be devoted to developing the leadership skills of middle and senior management; and that CEOs must empower their HR functions to a more pivotal role. They will need both to task HR professionals with making their contribution more relevant to the current business environment and to encourage them to become more innovative in competing for talent and driving organizational change.*[18]

Talent Wars: Generation Y Should I Listen to You Collides with a Because-I-Said-So Corporate Mind-set

The corporate communication function has become a stopgap for unmet HR needs, specifically those involving recruiting top talent, facilitating internal communications among employees in disparate locations, leading change-management initiatives, and positioning the corporate culture as a brand that can be marketed to potential employees. The former need is particularly relevant in the context of attracting millennial employees, which comprise a growing percentage of the workforce, as well as possessing finicky professional wants and needs that befuddle senior corporate executives. After all, this is a group whose members hand out their Facebook URLs before ever reciting their phone number, who haven't had a land-line telephone since moving out of their parents' houses, who text faster than most nonmillennials can type, whose idea of a commercial is something they saw on YouTube, who are inclined to turn up the volume on their iPods if they don't like what their "superiors" are saying, whose ideas are revolutionizing the business landscape—and who are going to run the world's most profitable companies sooner than anyone could predict.

The book-ending years that define generation Y differ slightly depending on the source (1976–1982 to anywhere from 1989–2001), but a few things are certain: Generation Y-ers, also known as *millennials*, make up more than 20 percent of the U.S. population, and the oldest members of this demographic are now entering the workforce with very distinguishing characteristics that are rattling traditional corporate norms and hierarchies. According to "Generation Y: The Millennials: Ready or Not, Here They Come," a study conducted by NAS Insights, "There are three major characteristics of the millennial group: (1) They are racially and ethnically diverse, (2) they are extremely independent because of divorce, day care, single parents, latchkey parenting, and the technological revolution that they are growing up alongside, and (3) they feel empowered."[19]

This feeling of empowerment, exacerbated by the fact that they learned the digital technologies that are changing the business landscape as they learned to walk and talk, puts millennials in a unique position on graduating from college (not coincidentally, this generation is one of the most educated of all time; 64 percent of women and 60 percent of men go to college after graduating high school, and 85 percent attend full time[20]): They have training and technological expertise that belies their age and that often exceeds that of their senior managers. This creates a rift between management and their millennial subordinates, who have come to be widely stereotyped as insubordinate based on their high expectations for rapid growth, frequent praise, and substantial responsibility and flexibility.

These characteristics present management challenges internally once millennials are hired into the company, but getting them there in the first place proves to be an even more daunting task—especially considering the ubiquitous agreement that people, whether or not they are millennials, are a top priority for business leaders in today's business environment.

Enter corporate communications professionals, who have been forced to develop outside-the-box recruiting techniques as a survival mechanism for their companies, if nothing else. And this doesn't mean that they are collaborating with HR executives to post job openings on *Craigslist.com* or *Monster.com;* rather, it's become a full-fledged free-for-all to catch the attention of the alleged attention deficit disorder–stricken, Adderall-treated generation of twenty-somethings. But, perhaps ironically, those organizations that have adapted to the demanding courting needs of the millennials instead of ignoring them out of principle have enjoyed a great deal of success. The greatest professional aphrodisiac? Digital outreach.

Recent College Grad ISO Career: Digital Platforms Woo Millennial Job Candidates

Generation Y is the most unanimously digitally savvy, having been raised alongside such technologies as instant messenging, mobile messaging, e-mail, blogging, and social networking. It's no surprise, then, that these are the very channels through which this generation's members are most comfortable exchanging information. Thus recruitment efforts have been ramped up in industries across the board to appeal to this generation's consumption preferences. The majority of these new efforts hinge on connecting with millennials via the platforms with which they are most accustomed to communicating—digital ones, of course.

The companies and industries that perhaps seemed most unlikely to adopt digital means of recruiting millennials actually were among the leaders of the pack. Take professional services firms, typically known for being stodgy, corporate, and unbending to a fault. But the "Big 4" accounting firms, for example, have implemented innovative strategies in their own rights, all of which leveraged digital communications platforms to seduce recent college graduates. For example, in early 2007, executives at Deloitte & Touche USA came together to brainstorm ideas for connecting with potential millennial employees. Drawing from the Society for Human Resource Management's "2007 Job Satisfaction Survey," which reported that overall corporate culture is "very important" to more than one-third of respondents, the team realized that its own strong corporate identity and culture could be a huge selling point for millennials.

"We thought [that] creating [a digital] program would give Gen Y-ers the opportunity to apply the same things they're interested in doing extracurricular-wise to what they can do in the work environment," said Dana Muldrow, manager of public relations for Deloitte & Touche. "We knew about their strong digital media expertise."[21]

Joining forces with MWW Group, Deloitte executives initiated a program that used Web videos, all created by current employees, to convey the positive work environment and corporate culture to job candidates. The video project called for employees to submit their own videos based on the "What's Your Deloitte?" theme, and the best would be made available to the public on video-sharing platforms in a film festival of sorts.

By inviting reporters to participate in judging the videos (and by sending out a multimedia press release about the festival), Deloitte garnered significant coverage for the video competition, and millennials inevitably caught wind of the surprisingly quirky culture that came along with a job that their parents would definitely approve of. Traditional media did, too; in the fall of 2007, *BusinessWeek* named Deloitte the number one place to launch a career, having considered the Deloitte Film Festival when making its determination.

McKinsey & Company's German management team launched its own gaming recruitment tool, CEO of the Future, based loosely on Donald Trump's reality show *The Apprentice*. Originally distributed via CD-ROM, by 2007, nearly 5,000 managers and students between the ages of 22 and 32 participated in Web-based challenges from around the world, completing tasks including starting a European insurance company in Korea and developing a research and development (R&D) strategy for a make-believe pharmaceutical.[22] The name of the game is to increase the value of their companies, and finalists are rewarded with a final-round presentation in which they deliver their solutions to McKinsey partners and the CEOs of the year's sponsors, including Bayer and Siemens. McKinsey has hired several past winners based on their performance in the online challenge.[23]

Online video games and film competitions don't match the DNA of all organizations, but these examples do illustrate the point that many organizations and industries are moving away from stilted stereotypes to embrace innovation amid a changing talent-management landscape. And millennials aren't the only targets of digital recruitment techniques: Demographics all the way up the corporate chain of command can expect to be contacted through untraditional methods—that is, if they haven't been already (see the following sidebar).

MONKEY IN THE MIDDLE: USING DIGITAL CHANNELS TO TAP SEASONED TALENT

Millennials may comprise an increasingly significant portion of the talent pool for corporations, but they certainly aren't the only demographic courted by senior leadership, nor are digital channels lost on them. Thus digital recruitment strategies aren't confined to filling junior positions with recent graduates, which might explain why, when asked what technologies would be most effective in their firms' recruiting efforts in the next three years, the highest percentage (62 percent) of surveyed executives cited professional networking sites such as LinkedIn, followed by social networking sites such as Facebook and LinkedIn (35 percent).[24]

But executives can only use these channels to recruit top talent if they participate in the first place. Those who have a profile on LinkedIn, for example, can send a message out to all the contacts in their network announcing the available position. Applicants, then, come with a built-in recommendation of sorts because they heard about the opening through connections of the hiring manager.

Likewise, corporate managers increasingly research job candidates on these networking sites, looking at their personal profiles (if they exist), their friends/connections, and their commentary. It's not uncommon for a manager to Google a candidate and find unbecoming information about him or her on a social networking site or personal blog—something both parties should consider before putting personal information online for the entire world to see.

Boot Camp: Digital Platforms Facilitate Professional Development and Enforce Transparent Communications

Change- and talent-management challenges are one piece of the modern internal communications puzzle, but once job candidates become actual employees, the next management phase begins: training. According to the "Fifth Annual Deloitte Volunteer IMPACT Survey," 87 percent of surveyed HR managers agree that their company's training and development programs are under pressure to develop the next generation of leaders. The American Society for Training and Development reveals that businesses already invest an average of $955 annually per employee on training, or 2.3 percent of payroll costs, with employees spending an average of 32 hours per year in formal training programs.

Training new employees and developing the skills of veterans is clearly a big investment for organizational leaders, but exploding costs, geographic barriers, and generational differences make the traditional crash course over coffee and donuts anachronistic. According to the Arthur W. Page Society's 2007 "The Authentic Enterprise" report:

> *Our surveyed CEOs identified a highly permeable membrane today between what is "internal" and "external" to a corporation. It is in the corporation's best interests to empower more and more of its work-force with new collaborative tools, training know-how—and trust—so they can responsibly and strategically interact with the external world. Corporate communications must acquire and spread mastery of these capabilities, while at the same time helping the corporation to develop the appropriate policies and guidelines to ensure responsible use of social media.*

These observations have a number of implications for the corporate communication function, from the implementation of specific training measures to the formation of internal policies that govern employees' use of digital media in a professional capacity, both of which will be discussed in subsequent sections.

Removing the Training Wheels: Digital Communication Channels Equal Professional Development without Borders

"I put much emphasis on staff training," said Yang Chao, chairman of China Life Insurance Company. "Every year, we send staff and managers to study overseas. At the same time, we have our own internal insurance school and our staff receive annual on-the-job training so that their overall competencies will be constantly raised. You must first build a strong staff before you can build a good business."[25]

Chao's statement about the importance of his staff's strength speaks for a majority of his peers, 93 percent of whom cited "investing in training and development" when asked, "How valuable are each of the following methods in addressing skills or talent shortages in your organization?"[26] In the same vein as using online gaming technologies to recruit talent, some companies are implementing them to train new hires and update the skills of veterans. The pharmaceutical R&D division of Johnson & Johnson (J&J), for example, uses a Second Life–like application called "3DU" to indoctrinate newbies into its HR-related features, from benefits to ethics policies. Another program, "Mission Possible," gave 1,500 employees a crash course in each other's roles in the drug-development process in 2006. Key elements of the virtual programs' interactivity quotient include[27]:

- *Management participation.* In 3DU, J&J President Garry Neil has his own virtual likeness that greets users with a video message and introduces other board members and senior executives. This gives new employees a feeling of comfort and familiarity just knowing they would recognize company leaders.
- *Camaraderie.* Participants of 3DU have their own avatars, which they guide through the training program while having the opportunity to meet other trainees virtually, regardless of their location. Once their training has been completed, their 3DU accounts remain active so that they can use the platform to connect with other employees if they have a question about a project, etc.
- *Authenticity.* Mission Possible participants are brought up to speed on industry developments by engaging with virtual characters, including "Virgil Vigilance" and "Regina Regulatory," all while taking on challenges that incorporate questions to test them on the material being presented.

Another university-style training program is that of JetBlue Airlines, although the distribution platform is very different from J&J 3DU platform. Founded in 2004, JetBlue University (JBU) has hundreds of faculty members stationed in locations across the country for the purpose of training everyone from operations and technical crews, to flight crews, to customer-services representatives. In early 2008, JBU went digital by powering its trainers with a Web 2.0 toolkit for sharing strategies and best practices despite their geographic dispersion. Using blog-based collaboration software, JBU executives built a platform for faculty to exchange ideas and discuss process improvements. The platform, in turn, became a training tool in and of itself, allowing employees to experiment with digital communications channels such as blogs and online video without the risk of public humiliation.

As Murry Christensen, JBU's director of learning technologies, put it:

Our basic intention was to foster collaboration and communication among the JBU faculty. In doing that, we were interested in understanding and working in the spirit of social media. For us, that meant not making top-down decisions about structure and architecture, but rather letting those bubble up from underneath in the same spirit as user-driven content. We didn't want to impose structure any more than we really needed to in order for people in the various colleges and on the various campus to be able to effectively communicate with each other.[28]

The Cyber-Grapevine: Setting Employee Blogging Policies to Enforce Transparency and Enhance the Brand

In January 2005, then-22-year-old Mark Jen started a new job as an associate product manager at Google, a company known as much for its casual corporate culture and decadent campus headquarters as for its leading-edge Web applications. January 17 marked his first day on the job and the first post on his new blog, *99zeros.blogspot.com*, which he set up to chronicle his experiences on the job. The missive began innocently enough: "in the ever increasing chaos known as the blogosphere, i've decided to add yet another random stream. if nothing else, this blog will serve as a personal journal of my life at google. maybe one day, a collection of these postings and comments will compile into a book...."[29]

Jen's cyber commentary didn't exactly make it into a book, but it did land him in headlines of top-tier media outlets around the country. Two weeks after his Google/99zeros debut, he was unceremoniously let go when corporate management caught wind of his musings. And not that they were derogatory or compromising—his commentary mentioned everything from HR orientation, to the company ski trip, to the company's global sales conference: "all in all, the conference is done really well. the logistics are coordinated well, the equipment is top notch, and of course, there's tons of food and drink to be had. the content is quite interesting, but i'm not allowed to share most of it (sorry: p)," he wrote on January 18, 2005.

Jen did mildly criticize Google's benefits package (which "actually seem to be thinly veiled timesavers to keep you at work"), for example, and he alluded to Google's competitive advantages over his former employer, Microsoft, by complimenting his newfound ability to "spend my 20% time exploring new ideas to my heart's content and there are tons of possible improvements in the system—more work than our current team can handle. Every improvement we make has the potential to help out tons of customers and the people here are focused on getting these solutions out to customers as soon as possible."

After apparently being chastised by Google executives (and having already gained a following of readers), he posted this: "Hi everyone, sorry my site has been down for the past day or so. I goofed and put some stuff up on my blog that's not supposed to be there. Nothing serious and they didn't ask me to take anything down (even the stuff where i'm critical about the company). I'm learning that google is understandably careful about disclosing sensitive information, even vague financial-related things. The quickest way for me to fix the situation at the time was to take it all down. Now i'm back up. Just so you know, google was pretty cool about all this. Thanks for and sorry for the frenzy of speculation."

Jen posted that on January 26. Two days later, he was fired. He later posted the following explanation:

> *on january 28th, 2005, i was terminated from google. either directly or indirectly, my blog was the reason. This came as a great shock to me because two days ago we had looked at my blog and removed all inappropriate content—the comments on financial performance and future products. For my next entries, i was very cognizant of my blogging content, making sure to stay away from these topics. I mean, as much as i like to be open and honest about communicating to users and customers, i'm not insubordinate. If i was told to shut down this blog, i would have.*[30]

Mark Jen is one of many employees who have been terminated for keeping a personal blog that either directly or indirectly discussed company information. But Jen's case is ideal for analysis because it falls somewhere in the no man's land between right and wrong: His posts were largely benign, often praising the company and sometimes reflecting on his qualms with almost internal dialogue–like contemplation. The rest was uninteresting to anyone aside from his close friends and family. Trips to Ikea and tales of his morning commute made up the remainder of the blog's content. It could even be argued that had he not been working for one of the most visible and therefore monitored corporations in the world, his no-name blog never would have been discovered by anyone, let alone his employer. But that is now the world in which we live and in which businesses operate. Employees from companies including Delta, Microsoft, Wells Fargo, and Starbucks also have been fired allegedly for maintaining personal blogs that spilled professional (or unprofessional, depending on how you look at it) details.

That said, many of the highest-profile blog-related firings took place between 2003 and 2006 when the vast majority of companies were still wrapping their arms around the concept of blogging as a legitimate means of reaching shareholders. The perceived lack of control—a sticking point for many corporate leaders to this day—was seen as a risk that outweighed any possible benefit, so management teams would cut their losses by firing the "rogue" employee. However, as the number of employee bloggers reached groundswell numbers, senior executives began to catch on, introducing corporate blogging policies to protect their brands and reputations, and to set limitations that, if employees stayed within them, would give them back some of the freedom to blog their minds.

Ever the innovator, IBM was among the first organizations to introduce guidelines for blogging. In the spring of 2005, the company created a wiki and implored employees to contribute what they believed were practical advice and fair restrictions in terms of authoring blogs. This wiki became the first iteration of the company's blogging policy, and its benefits were manifold: It set guidelines to protect IBM and staffers, and because it was authored by the employees themselves, they believed it to be fair and viewed it with a since of ownership. Plus, IBM's decision to use a social platform to encourage collaboration affirmed the company's commitment to embracing innovation, dialogue, and the exchange of ideas.

Today, these guidelines aren't just limited to blogging; they have been revised and renamed "IBM Social Computing Guidelines." According to the official guidelines posted on IBM's Web site, "Since [2005] ..., many new forms of social media have emerged. So we turned to IBMers again to re-examine our guidelines and determine what needed to be modified. The effort has broadened the scope of the existing guidelines to include all forms of social computing."[31]

Blogging and general social media use policies have assuaged the concern of some management teams over allowing their employees to speak openly about their companies and brands on personal blogs. Southwest Airlines, for example, encourages it, as long as the employees follow the guidelines established by the company (for more on "Nuts About Southwest," see Chapter 4).

"We do not have a problem with employee ambassadors from other parts of the company getting involved in the conversation, provided they know the company well enough to represent it accurately," said Paula Berg, manager of emerging media for Southwest. "We do have many employees with their own blogs who are very involved in social media. We have some guidelines that basically say employees should abide by the same standards as any other time they represent our company. Part of being in the travel industry is that people always want to hear about your job. This is just one of many ways that our employees are involved in the buzz surrounding Southwest, so nothing has changed in terms of our expectations about their behavior."[32]

Like Southwest Airlines, many other companies have gone so far as to encourage, if not require, this stakeholder group to contribute to official company-sponsored blogs with the specific purpose of communicating the organization's brand identity and internal culture to external stakeholder groups. Southwest's "Nuts About Southwest" blog, for example, is written by employees from every department, and each contributor has his or her own unique tone and unique audience.

Whether a company supports one blog with multiple employee contributors or multiple blogs each with its own employee contributor, it's important to take the appropriate measures to ensure that the digital channel reflects the organization's brand and culture (for best practices in employee blogging, see the following sidebar). The strategies discussed in Chapter 4 regarding corporate blogs that address external stakeholder groups remain constant from an internal perspective; it's just key that each employee maintains an authentic voice while accurately representing the company's mission and goals.

TIPS FOR EMPLOYEE BLOGGERS

1. *Read other blogs.* To better understand the tone and style of blogs, research other blogs. Blog search engine Technorati provides a ranking of the most popular blogs. It is helpful to read and post on other blogs that have similar content to yours.

2. *Set expectations.* Blog readers expect regular postings, open two-way dialogue, and hyperlinked, networked content. Thus blog authors and corporate communicators must/should clearly define the blog purpose and operating guidelines at the blog's launch.

3. *Before launching a blog, determine expectations in the following categories:*
    - *Blog purpose.* Blog readers may have different ideas of what a blog and its content should contain; to eliminate confusion or misconceptions, it is helpful to introduce the blog's objectives up front.
    - *Frequency of postings.* While many bloggers post frequently, even daily, this is not necessary for a corporate blog to be successful. Indeed, employees do not expect a senior-level leader to spend time crafting blog messaging every single day. However, to ensure that the blog remains "sticky," give readers an idea of the blog's expected cadence, ideally posting at least every other week.
    - *Response to comments.* Companies vary in their decision on whether to censor incoming comments and whether to respond directly to comments. For example, General Motors Vice Chairman Bob Lutz does not respond directly to any comments on his "Fastlane" blog; if he responds at all, he does so in subsequent posts. Other blog authors, however, respond directly to reader comments. In either case, explaining the process for receiving, displaying, and responding to comments helps to prevent negative stakeholder reactions.

4. *Write candidly.* Blogs usually take a slightly more informal and personal tone than more traditional corporate communications.

5. *Post about familiar topics.* To make the blog more valuable and authentic, write about topics you know well.

6. *Link to other content.* Most blogs link to content on other blogs and Web sites. Links should be included within the blog content itself, as well as a list on the sidebar(s).

7. *Pick a topic for each blog.* While there is no "right" length for a blog posting, each entry should have a focused topic. Keep it simple. For example, Bob Lutz's posts to his blog "Fastlane" average 500 words. For longer posts, it can be helpful to show only a portion of the text (i.e., 150 words) on the homepage with a link to "Full Text" for interested viewers to continue reading. This enables visitors to skim a list of your most recent entries rather than be confronted with a daunting block of text.

Source: Communications Executive Council research.

Sun Microsystems' CEO Jonathan Schwartz has his own corporate blog (*blogs.sun.com/jonathan*), which he began in 2004, two years before being promoted from president to CEO of the company. With his promotion, Schwartz's blog became one of the most high-profile blogs for a CEO of a major company, and he chose to continue maintaining it—not to mention allowing readers to post comments that are screened only for profanity and spam. Like any highly visible CEO, Schwartz does have his detractors, and his blog gives them a public forum for criticism. Largely, though, his gesture to complete openness and transparency has generated positive fanfare for the organization, and it has set an example for Sun's other employee bloggers (of which there are thousands). True to his self-described unconventional personality (evidenced by his now-infamous ponytail), Schwartz's blogging style and tone are casual, conversational, and not at all corporate. Members of Sun's general counsel—all avid readers of the blog—admit to occasionally recommending that Schwartz add the safe-harbor provision, a boilerplate statement aimed at protecting companies from shareholder lawsuits by investors who feel shortchanged by unfulfilled promises, to certain posts.[33]

When developing employee bloggers, according to Sun Vice President of Worldwide Public Relations Karen Kahn, "Blogs are great, but they don't work for everyone. You can't write the CEO's blog [for him or her]. You can offer ideas, but as soon as it's inauthentic, it's over."[34]

Conclusion

Companies' competitive advantages were, in the past, most often relegated to factors such as product price, speed of service, or availability. Staffs' compilation of skills was more a matter of learned processes than raw talent, meaning that those who rose to the top—senior managers—had the proverbial pick of the litter when it came to hiring. However, just as the media discussed in Chapter 4 have become a fragmented but empowered stakeholder group, employees have a sense of ownership in companies based on their newfound ability to directly influence brands and reputations. Couple this influence with business trends that have caused intraorganizational relationships and responsibilities to mutate (e.g., an increase in M&As, an influx of millennials into the talent pool, etc.), and corporate leaders now find themselves directing more and more time, energy, and money into overcoming talent-management and internal communications challenges. In short, a cohesive corporate culture—the ability to operate as "one company" in front of all external stakeholders—is now a defining (if not the most definitive) characteristic of a successful organization.

Web technologies make these cohesive corporate cultures attainable, even for companies whose staff is dispersed across different continents, but they also introduce challenges. If not managed properly, these technologies can turn discontented employees into the most dangerous threats to a company's brand, reputation, and even bottom line. Avoiding this ill-conceived fate requires a strategic implementation of digital channels for internal use and attention to the necessary synergies among employees, managers, and brands. According to IBM's Sam Palmisano:

> *[Becoming "one company"] ... is accomplished through the common sense of empowering the population. And then producing consistency and turning ideas into value. It's not about what we own. But what we can co-create.... The way you achieve consistency is through openness and transparency. It's embedded in the values. It's not through process and structure, but a shared understanding.*[35]

CHAPTER 6

TRADING VIRTUAL SPACES

SHAREHOLDERS TAKE INVESTOR RELATIONS TO THE WEB

The chapters thus far have identified the instigators for the drastically changing business climate; they also have discussed the increasing integration of corporate communications subfunctions within the organization, including marketing and human resources (HR). But just as digital platforms are prompting the integration of these functions with that of corporate communications, so too are they requiring that the corporate communication and investor relations (IR) functions work in tandem with each other.

According to the National Investor Relations Institute (NIRI), *investor relations* is

A strategic management responsibility that integrates finance, communication, marketing and securities law compliance to enable the most effective two-way communication between a company, the financial community and other constituencies, which ultimately contributes to a company's securities achieving fair valuation.[1]

This nod to integration is consistent with the theory that the evolving business environment necessitates corporate functions to work cooperatively to manage stakeholder empowerment. Specifically, the IR function manages the investor/shareholder and analyst stakeholder groups, with the digital communications phenomenon by no means passed over either. Rather, studies show that shareholders are going online with greater frequency, and shareholder activism has reached new heights as institutional investors look at corporate management with greater scrutiny. Another complicating factor: Revised financial reporting guidelines and regulations set a significantly higher standard for transparency, and stakeholders other than investors—namely, consumers and media—have begun to watch companies' activities more closely, critically, and skeptically.

"We live in a skeptical age. If there is one defining mood among consumers, voters and investors, it is lack of trust," according to Sir Martin Sorrell, chief group executive of WPP. "Companies—especially financial institutions—and governments face an uphill struggle over the next few years to convince their customers and electorates that they are competent—and, more importantly, above reproach. Of course, mistrust of large corporations began during the last downturn with the Enron and WorldCom accounting scandals. It has been amplified by the current banking crisis."[2] Because of this, companies must respond by communicating their IR efforts more transparently and in more accessible ways—namely, via the Web.

"Social media can only multiply that mistrust," Sorrell said. "Every toxic story about a bank's inefficiency or unfairness will chime with the horror of the credit crunch. If they can't handle my account properly, is it any surprise they can't run their own affairs without bringing the world economy down? The solution should be to communicate more, not less."[3]

This chapter will address this solution by offering a brief description of the modern IR function, explaining how IR is closely tied to corporate reputation and therefore integral to business success, identifying strategies for integrating the IR and corporate communication functions by leveraging digital channels, and offering case studies of organizations that are at the forefront of taking IR to the Web. It will address these issues in the context of the economic downturn that reached critical mass in the fall of 2008, thus making the investing climate all the more turbulent and forcing corporations to take extreme measures to reassure shareholders that their brands are financially viable, no matter the business backdrop.

Diversifying Portfolios: As Business Evolves, Investor Stakeholder Groups Proliferate—and Gain Power

Traditionally, the IR function always has had one primary objective: position the company to compete effectively for investors' capital. In the early twentieth century, this task wasn't complicated by as many regulations and scrutinizing stakeholders as it is today; in fact, practicing secrecy—not transparency—was the rule, not the exception. Disclosure of any kind was seen as potentially harmful to the interests of the organization and therefore was discouraged. But this all changed in the 1930s with the passage of two federal securities acts that required public companies to file periodic disclosures with the U.S. Securities and Exchange Commission (SEC): the Securities Act of 1933 and the Securities Exchange Act of 1934. Despite these new reporting requirements, executives only practiced mandatory disclosure, thus embodying the archetypal one-way messaging structure that dominated communications with stakeholders for so long.

In fact, the *investor relations* moniker didn't even exist until 1953, when the then Chairman Ralph Cordiner of General Electric made the first systematic effort to formalize the corporation's relationship with shareholders by creating a new department and coining the term *investor relations*. This initiative prompted the first in-depth investigation of the company's shareholders, their needs, and their preferred means of communication.[4]

As forward-thinking as they were, Cordiner's actions weren't taken on a whim; rather, they were in response to the economic boom of the 1950s, during which time the number of individual shareholders increased dramatically; 4.5 million families—4.2 percent of the total U.S. population—owned a total of 6.49 million shares in 1952, according to a study commissioned by then New York Stock Exchange Chairman G. Keith Funston, conducted in collaboration with Lewis H. Kimmel and the Brookings Institute.[5]

This spike in stock owners challenged corporate leaders, who were accustomed to managing only a small number of wealthy investors who, for the most part, remained passive. Now, companies had more reason to engage these individual shareholders based on their purchasing power and subsequent potential to affect an organization's financial success.

Incidentally, the means for doing so came directly from their public relations (PR) functions, out of which IR grew. At the time (and still to this day), it was a natural extension of PR. This function's executives had established relationships with stakeholders and understood the concept of messaging. Not surprisingly, though, this primary iteration of IR more closely resembled publicity. Thus Cordiner's move to create a separate function for dealings with shareholders was well informed because it paved the way for IR's evolution alongside that of changing business demands.

Reaching Maturation: The Investor Relations Function Adopts a Definitive Role within Organizations

In 1969, the National Investor Relations Institute (NIRI) was established as a professional association of corporate officers and IR consultants who were responsible for communicating with corporate management, the investing public, and the financial community. Around the same time, the Chicago-based Financial Relations Board (FRB), now a unit of the Interpublic Group, became the first PR firm dedicated to helping its clients develop relationships with investors.

In the 1980s, state and local laws enabled pension funds to increase the equity allocation in their portfolios. That share rose to 36 percent in 1989 from 22 percent in 1982, making institutional investors an even more important constituency for the IR departments of corporations. At the same time, inflation caused many individual investors to flee the stock market, and by the end of the 1980s, institutional investors represented 85 percent of all public trading volume.

The first conference calls were held for hundreds of institutional investors at a time in the 1980s. Soon thereafter, quarterly conference calls were standard practice at many companies. A decade later, the Internet provided yet another channel for communicating company financials to large numbers of investors. Organizations began to create IR areas within their corporate Web sites to post information such as news releases, annual reports, 10-Ks (SEC-required annual filing) and 10-Qs (SEC-required quarterly filing), and stock charts. The digital components of IR will be discussed in subsequent sections; first, though, it's important to understand the various types of financial stakeholders and the ways in which they affect the communications strategies of companies.

Diversifying Portfolios: As Business Evolves, Investor Stakeholder Groups Proliferate

The IR function's original target audiences were twofold: individual shareholders and financial media. Like everything else in business, though, this changed dramatically over time. Now, a company's IR strategy must address individual shareholders and financial media, as well as institutional investors, credit-rating agencies, activist shareholders, and buy- and sell-side analysts (for information on each investor stakeholder group, see the following sidebar). Each of these specific stakeholder groups places different demands on the IR function in terms of messaging, depth of information required, and consumption habits. Thus consistent communications—especially in the context of digital channels—becomes more critical than ever. And while each group has its own effect on brands, reputations, and bottom lines, one in particular most embodies the shift in power over these assets in the age of digital communications—activist shareholders.

BREAKDOWN OF INVESTOR STAKEHOLDER GROUPS

- *Activist shareholders.* These are investors who demand to take an active role in the management of the companies in which they invest, as opposed to acting as passive bystanders (for more information, see "Activist Shareholders Become the Investor Community's—And Corporate America's—MVPs" on page 146).
- *Buy-side analysts.* These analysts typically work for money-management firms (mutual funds or pension funds) and research companies for their own institutions' investment portfolios. Many perform proprietary analysis, including company visits and their own review of company financials.
- *Corporate governance intermediaries.* These are organizations that assist investors with improving the corporate governance of the companies in which they invest. Organizations such as the CFA Institute Center and intermediators such as Investor Shareholder Services (ISS) help to rally investors around an issue, provide research on public-policy issues, make proxy voting recommendations, ensure fair voting over the issue, and help to evaluate potential investments.
- *Credit-rating agencies.* These are agencies that evaluate publicly traded companies based on their ability to meet debt obligations. Rating agencies, including Standard and Poor's, Moody's, and Fitch, make the

information available to the public through published reports, which are greatly relied on by buy- and sell-side analysts.

- *Hedge funds.* These are private investment funds that are open to a limited number of investors and that pay performance fees to investment managers.
- *Individual/retail investors.* These are shareholders who own stock directly or through mutual funds, company stock plans, or 401(k) plans. They may actively trade securities to generate trading profits on an intraday basis, apply buy-and-hold strategies to save for retirement, or anything in between.
- *Industry analysts.* These are analysts who conduct market research within particular industry segments to determine market trends, forecasts, and models.
- *Institutional investors.* These are institutions—typically mutual funds, hedge funds, or pension funds—that have larger holdings than individual investors and tend to trade more actively, thus having a greater effect on market volatility. Institutional investors own approximately 55 percent of the U.S. equity market.
- *Sell-side analysts.* These are analysts who cover stocks within certain industries and generate detailed research reports that offer buy, sell, or hold recommendations. This research then is provided to clients of investment banks or retail brokerages. Sell-side analysts act as intermediaries between a company and existing and potential investors.

Activist Shareholders Become the Investor Community's—And Corporate America's—MVPs

Originating in the mid-1980s with the emergence of index tracking, increased government intervention, and weakening takeover strategies, shareholder activism has increased ever since as corporate management teams face more scrutiny of their financial actions. A NIRI survey of activist investors conducted in late 2007 revealed that nearly half of publicly traded companies have had activist investors hold their stock.[6]

Shareholder activism exploded alongside the ubiquity of corporate scandals, from Enron to Tyco International to ImClone Systems, Inc. As financial malfeasance permeated the corporate world, activist investors popped up in droves; when asked what they consider to be the main driver of shareholder activism, 94 percent of surveyed IR professionals cited corporate scandals. Combine this with the digital platforms that aid and abet dynamic conversations and information sharing, and executives find themselves fielding aggressive advances from shareholders demanding transparency of financial reports, changes in management, revised executive compensation policies, attention to environmental/ social concerns, and/or external audits of conflicts of interest.

A 2007 survey of investors revealed that 86 percent believe that the level of activism in the future will increase.[7] What's more, activist campaigns are becoming increasingly public thanks to enhanced communications; 54 percent of 2007 activist campaigns involved "poison pill" tactics, in which publicly disclosed letters to the board or management were used.[8] Of course, some shareholder activism begets negative media coverage, hesitant investors, and skeptical consumers. This stakeholder group is particularly important to integrating IR and corporate communications because, if left to run amok, it can prompt

- Decreases in stock value
- Hits to brand image and corporate reputation
- Regulatory action
- Increases in the amount of time, energy, and money required to conduct business
- Negative media attention

In response to the increase in shareholder activism, a CFO Executive Board survey[9] revealed that companies are using the following strategies to manage pressures:

- Restructuring annual reports and other financial filings for greater transparency (for more on annual reports, see "From Annual to Perennial: Annual Reports Migrate to the Web" on page 155): 64 percent
- Retooling corporate governance structure for greater independence and oversight: 57 percent
- Implementing investor-based finance analysis to predict key investor decision drivers: 21 percent
- Adopting shareholder resolutions that receive majority support: 18 percent
- Lending greater boardroom consideration to shareholder resolutions that receive double-digit support: 11 percent
- Adding potential concerns to the proxy ballot: 7 percent
- Contracting turnaround management consultants: 4 percent

These measures may alleviate some of the tensions between corporations and activist shareholders, but this particular investor stakeholder group often requires huge compromise on the part of the organization's leadership and board of directors. And in the modern business environment, a massive market capitalization is no longer a powerful enough defense against individual activists, some of whom single-handedly attempt (often successfully) to influence the direction of behemoth companies. Time Warner executives became sharply aware of this in 2006 when activist shareholder Carl Icahn pressed the company to increase shareholder value by dividing itself up into four publicly traded companies and buying back approximately $20 billion in stock. Icahn, who owned more than 3 percent of the company, acted as a purported Robin Hood of the investor community, using his substantial influence ultimately to reach a compromise with Time Warner: Icahn and his posse of activist investors, including Lazard Chairman and CEO Bruce Wasserstein, agreed not to contest the reelection of the board members at the 2006 shareholders meeting if the company would increase its share-repurchase program from $12.5 billion to $20 billion, nominate more independent members to the board of directors, and cut $1 billion in costs by 2007.[10]

Time Warner wasn't the first corporation to come into Icahn's crosshairs, nor would it be the last. Motorola and Yahoo! leaders are among the many who have felt his wrath in recent years. Perhaps even more compelling than Icahn's stronghold in the boardrooms of some of the biggest companies, though, is his newest platform for enforcing corporate accountability: a blog. In June 2008 he debuted "The Icahn Report" (*www.icahnreport.com*) to, in his own words, comment on "the desultory state of corporate governance in America."[11] If Icahn's past track record is any indication, his influence in the new media space will be as potent—if not more so—than his influence in boardrooms.

Hedging Your Bets: The IR Function Is Forced To Transform As The Global Economy Tumbles

Between January 2007 and the end of 2008, the U.S. economy—and, by extension, the global economy—experienced one of the wildest rollercoaster rides in history. Things were beginning to look up after the dot-com bubble's burst and the terrorist attacks of 9/11 contributed to a drastically softened economy. On June 25, 2003, the Federal Reserve set the key interest rate at an all-time low of 1 percent, where it would remain for a year. This increased the buying power of many who had never before been capable of purchasing a home or investing in real estate. A crop of subprime lenders popped up, offering these lower-middle-class individuals mortgages at significantly reduced rates. The tangential effects on the economy were noticeable, with a relative boom period extending from 2003 until late 2006.

But markets showed signs of wavering when, on February 7, 2007, HSBC warned Wall Street about declining profits because of bad investments in subprime loans. In turn, news of sharply rising defaults among subprime borrowers led to a plunge in mortgage lenders' shares.[12] This precipitated a 3.29 percent plunge in the Dow Jones Industrial Average on February 27. But the drama didn't end there; in fact, it was a mere prelude to what would soon unfold into a critical economic crisis.

Over the course of the remainder of 2007, mortgage lenders big and small folded under the financial pressures, and stock markets across Europe and Asia tumbled and rebounded accordingly. After a series of rate cuts by the Fed and a President Bush–approved stimulus package, the investor community appeared to rally—or at least to stabilize—as the U.S. government took steps to avert a recession. By the spring of 2008, however, the horizon darkened further. Bear Stearns, the country's fifth-largest investment bank, collapsed and was sold for just $2 a share, signaling that the subprime mortgage crisis of 2007 had much larger implications. As other iconic financial institutions fell, among them Lehman Brothers, Merrill Lynch, Fannie Mae, and Washington Mutual, one thing became very clear: Corporations were about to face drastic shifts in investor and consumer habits, and their communications strategies would have to change accordingly.

The Perfect Storm: Turbulent Economies, Shareholder Activism, and Emerging Digital Platforms Reshape IR

If the IR function exists to act as the liaison between a company and its investors, then imagine the redefined importance of transparent, authentic, and consistent communications in the context of a completely destabilized global economy. Of the organizations polled during the third quarter of 2008, as the economic crisis was beginning to reach critical mass, 32.5 percent said that the greatest IR challenge in the face of the financial crisis was responding to increased demands for information.[13] Couple this with the fact that investors, activist shareholders, and analysts can (and will) turn to the Web to find up-to-date information about a company's financial performance, and you will begin to see the staggering need for revised IR communications strategies, especially via online channels. After all, the IR function's responsibilities largely hinge on internally and externally focused communications in the first place. Research shows that companies that are rated highly by investors tend to systematically lay out and communicate their key messages to investors.[14]

According to Robert Berick, managing director of Dix & Eaton, "Clearly, effective communication plays a significant role in shaping decisions about whether to invest in a company, whether to maintain or add to that investment, and whether to refer others to or away from a particular investment."[15] Specific communications components of IR include:

- Articulating the company's vision, strategy, and potential to investors, analysts, and the media.
- Ensuring that the expectations of the company's stock price are appropriate for its earnings prospects, industry outlook, and economic conditions.
- Reducing stock price volatility. Research shows that corporate IR activity could account for as much as a 25 percent variance in a company's stock price, and 82 percent of surveyed buy-side investment professionals believe that good IR affects a company's valuation.[16]

While these responsibilities have remained consistent over the years, the context in which they are executed has changed dramatically; in addition to volatile global financial markets and the role of digital communications in enabling constant communication among stakeholders, legislative changes, corporate scandals, and a growing demand for sustainability reporting all affect the effectiveness of traditional IR communications strategies.

The obvious implication of this chaotic investor environment is that corporate reputations are as vulnerable as ever, with the greatest detriment in this case coming in the form of financial distress. But before organizations can articulate their external financial communications strategies in the modern business climate, the IR and corporate communication functions must be integrated internally via revised reporting relationships.

The Antisilo Approach: Forming Civil Unions Between the IR and Corporate Communication Functions

Traditionally, the IR function falls under the financial umbrella within organizations, with approximately 75 percent of surveyed corporate IR departments reporting to the company's chief financial officer (CFO).[17] Beyond this general overview, though, IR teams' sizes, structures, and budgets depend on the size of the company. Sixty-two percent of IR departments have two to three full-time employees, and the number of IR staffers increases in proportion to market capitalization. Companies with market capitalizations of less than $5 billion have, on average, a single full-time IR professional, whereas IR departments at companies with $50 billion or more in market capitalization are staffed by an average of four full-time professionals.[18]

In terms of budgets granted to the IR function, the average budget is $1.3 million annually, although this varies greatly based on the level of strategic importance placed on IR. Surveyed investor relations officers (IROs) reported that their IR budgets rose marginally in 2008, increasing by an average of 4 percent over 2007. That said, the largest line-item cost—that of the annual report—decreased by 23 percent from 2007 to 2008, a factor that can be attributed at least in part to the growing trend of producing electronic annual reports. It's also worth noting that the person to whom the IRO reports tends to indicate the size of the IR budget; research reveals that average IR budgets in organizations in which IROs report directly to the CFO are 23 percent higher than those in which IROs report to an executive more junior than the CFO.[19]

But times are changing in terms of reporting relationships, budget allocations, and IR team sizes. Consider FedEx. According to Jeff Smith, investor relations advisor for FedEx Corporation, the company's IR function has a vice president and three managers. But the biggest difference between its structure and that most other companies is that the team reports to the senior vice president for communications, with a dotted line to the CFO.[20] According to Smith, this nuance marks the company's evolution from a reactive to a proactive approach, from management-led meetings to IR-led meetings, and from IR as a rotational position to IR as a career position.[21] This reporting structure automatically dismantles the siloed approach that often separates IR from corporate communications, and it helps to facilitate streamlined communications between the company and its target stakeholders.

Likewise, budget and staff sizes are evolving alongside priorities and risks. Unilever, for example, has a market capitalization of $36.5 billion (as of October 2008) and places a high level of strategic importance on investor relations, and its IR team is large and spread across different geographic regions. Apple, on the other hand, has a market capitalization of $78.5 billion—significantly higher than Unilever's—but the company's IR team consists of only two full-time employees. These examples illustrate the point that organizations are customizing their approaches to IR with relative disregard to a balanced ratio of IR staff size to market capitalization, but one thing remains consistent: The role of corporate communications in any IR strategy is extremely important.

What's Mine Is Ours: The IR and Corporate Communication Functions Merge Over... Marketing?

The high-risk investor climate currently faced by all corporations isn't the only impetus for corporate communications and IR to collaborate. Both functions share inherent synergies based on the role that marketing principles play in each. In fact, marketing is a primary dimension of IR because a key goal of IR teams is to ensure that their companies' stocks are selling at a fair value. To that end, IR executives can increase stock valuation via simple marketing strategies, including

- Targeting the right investors
- Shaping a message that will be attractive to those investors
- Using the most efficient communications channels

Sound familiar? Each of these strategies relates directly back to tenets of communications: targeting stakeholder groups, shaping messaging for them, and choosing the best distribution channels (see Chapter 3 for more in-depth strategies pertaining to these corporate communications components). Then there are the intangible factors that lend themselves to communications skill sets, which are also shared by IR, for what is the value of IR without the strength of a company's shares to back it up? Corporations are complicated by the various characteristics, products, and services that define them, and these elements are often technically sophisticated and difficult to quantify. However, despite measurement challenges, these intangibles can have a significant impact on the value of a company' stock price, but they can't always be assessed via traditional financial statements. The corporate communication function fills in these gaps with its expertise in gauging and managing the intangible factors that contribute to bottom-line business success, including reputation, customer loyalty, brand strength, and stakeholder engagement.

Introducing the ever-expanding number of investor stakeholder groups, from activist shareholders to sell-side analysts, into the mix further contributes to the growing emphasis on providing qualitative—not quantitative—earnings guidance.[22] Nonfinancial factors are so relevant to financial performance that 38 percent of an investor's decision to invest is based on nonfinancial factors, including[23]:

- Execution and quality of corporate strategy
- Management credibility
- Innovativeness
- Ability to attract and retain talented people
- Product-development efficiency
- Brand image

As nonfinancial factors become more important to investors, the number of investor stakeholder groups proliferates, and digital communications channels continue to emerge, the Web becomes a de facto meeting place for shareholders to swap information, conduct research, and connect with their peers. It's only going to become easier for these online relationships to form among investor groups given the August 2008 announcement that Broadridge Financial Solutions, Inc., a behemoth investor communications and brokerage outsourcing firm, would launch a social network to connect every U.S. company and every shareholder. If the proposed social network lives up to Broadridge CEO Rich Daly's expectations, it will validate members as real shareholders through its access to more than 90 million shareowner accounts at more than 850 banks and brokerages. Daly offered the following description of the network during an August 2008 analyst call:

> *The Investor Network is an online electronic forum that will facilitate shareholder-to-shareholder communications with a unique feature that will differentiate it from the chat rooms in existence today. Investors who use our Investor Network will be validated as real shareholders. This feature will not only enhance shareholder-to-shareholder communications, but it will provide a new channel of communication between shareholders and companies.[24]*

The increasing prevalence of these types of communications capabilities among shareholders heightens their influence over companies' brands, reputations, and bottom lines even more. Ultimately, it's IR's responsibility to communicate qualitative and intangible business factors to these investor communities, but with more and more of these stakeholders migrating to the Web to find desired information, the corporate communication function is poised to take shared ownership of these duties.

Wall Street Hits The World Wide Web: Online Communications Redefines IR Responsibilities

Beyond the shared interests that have already been mentioned, the IR and corporate communication functions both have internal- and external-facing stakeholders. The role digital communications channels play in blurring the line between the two presents a Pandora's box of challenges and opportunities. According to the research findings of the Investor Relations Roundtable's 2006 "Measuring and Building the Value of the Investor Relations Function" report, "Investor relations executives have traditionally focused on two primary externally facing activities: communicating the company's strategy to investors and providing updates on the progress and execution of that strategy. These activities form the core of the IR function but also provide insight for IR to play a critical role in internal communications."

As the Internet becomes the focal point for information gathering among all stakeholders, internal and external, the IR and corporate communication functions must collaborate to form a more robust IR presence online. Luckily for both functions, emerging digital communications platforms facilitate integration, as do the new policies that mandate Web usage for IR reporting. Extensible Business Reporting Language (XBRL), for example, is an Internet-centric global standard for business reporting that requires companies to tag information in their financial statements so that investors can easily access data online and compare between companies. This standard was a result of criticism that financial information is too complex for many investors to understand; it serves to enable investors to create their own custom analysis tools based on the business and financial information most relevant to them.

While technological advances and evolving reporting standards are key to broadening the scope of IR, they do come at a price. Reputational risk increases significantly with stakeholder empowerment and shareholder activism, so executives must be diligent in monitoring and managing corporate information online, especially in the channels that they can control—namely, their online annual reports, corporate Web sites, and corporate IR blogs.

From Annual to Perennial: Annual Reports Migrate to the Web

Just as the press release is a founding tenet of PR, the annual report is the IR function's original raison d'être. Annual reports are documents that the SEC requires companies to publish to share the previous year's financial results and to communicate the organizations' visions. These reports are crafted specifically for the investor community, but they are also available to the general public. Because of the importance of these audiences and the regulatory environment that enforces reporting standards, the preparation of these documents is usually the most time-consuming and expensive IR undertaking. But IR executives aren't alone in shouldering this burden; annual reports are also critical to marketing, PR, and branding, requiring the corporate communication function to play a large role in creating the content and ensuring message consistency. In fact, all the most important objectives of annual reports have a communications component. When asked to specify the strategic intent of their company's annual report, 67 percent of surveyed IROs cited complying with SEC regulations, 75 percent cited communicating nonfinancial value drivers, and 86 percent cited communicating corporate strategy.[25]

The corporate communication function's role in creating annual reports becomes even more compelling when considered in the context of the digital platforms on which said reports are now posted. Owing to recent SEC rules and regulations that defined online reporting and usability standards, 2008 was the first year that all U.S. companies were required to post their annual reports and proxy statements online in formats convenient for onscreen reading and printing.[26] Not coincidentally, considering its decision that corporate Web sites and blogs were permissible disclosure vehicles under Regulation Fair Disclosure, 2008 also was the first year that the SEC held its first conference call with bloggers, during which it discussed XBRL policies.[27]

Given all these SEC-imposed standards and regulations surrounding financial reporting online, it's not surprising that most companies are migrating their annual report content to the Web and paying less attention (and money) to printed reports. This isn't to say that these companies are doing so with complete success. IR Web Report's reviews of 2007 annual reports revealed that 90 percent didn't live up to the online usability and interactivity standards, thus implying that online reporting practices still need to be learned by executives before they can be perfected. However, a few companies did stand out from the crowd to illustrate effective use of digital components to communicate financial and nonfinancial information to shareholders.

- *Philips Electronics (www.annualreport2007.philips.com/index.asp)*. On entering the annual report's homepage, users are asked to specify their connection speed (high versus low bandwidth), immediately customizing the experience in terms of loading speed and navigability. Then a Flash video of Philips President and CEO Gerard Kleisterlee introduces visitors to an overview of the previous year's accomplishments in the context of current industry trends and developments. A search feature, a 10-year overview, risk-management strategies, corporate governance, and downloads all round out the report, making it robust in terms of content and user-friendly.
- *Daimler (http://ar2007.daimler.com/)*. There aren't many flashy design features, but the content of this 2007 annual report is dynamic and informative. Financial statements contain notes to highlight key findings, charts expand for easier viewing, and a financial statement "quick analyzer" tool enables individual users to customize the figures/margins/expenditures that they want to see graphed.
- *Coca-Cola (www.thecoca-colacompany.com/ourcompany/ar/)*. The world's best-known brand must bear the responsibility that comes with such a title, especially when it comes to the investor community. This is why the company's 2007 annual review, entitled, "The Language of Refreshment," serves as an umbrella microsite within Coca-Cola's corporate Web site, hosting all reports, overviews, and financial statements in an accessible way. But it's the site's opening display—a Flash video that illustrates its global theme with a display of "refreshing" words in an array of languages—that communicates the company's message and draws in visitors, no matter which stakeholder group they belong to (see Figure 6.1). Then users can click to

Figure 6.1: Coca-Cola's 2007 Annual Review personified a strategic combination of branding, transparent financial reporting and, of course, interactive digital components

view the leadership message, financial overview, company highlights, performance overviews of each operating group, or the full annual report. The Web property extends the brand's story, and stakeholders can customize their experience by downloading PDF, audio, or HTML versions of reports. Pop-up charts that map out financial data round out the review's usability, and commentary about the company's areas in need of improvement underscores a commitment to transparency and authentic reporting.

Supplementing the trend of annual reports moving to the Web is that of interactive video annual reports, which can either supplement or replace standard online content. Companies including California Pizza Kitchen, Ruth's Chris Steakhouse, and Sealy have embraced this platform to communicate with the investor community, using the innovative format to differentiate themselves from industry competitors. Interactive video annual reports have a number of advantages: Standard video content has an indefinite shelf life because only certain sections—quarterly results, for example—need to be updated, it showcases the company's management more effectively, and upfront expenses save money in the long run in terms of time and printing costs. To make the most out of a video annual report, record parts of the presentation that can be viewed online and during IR events, such as analyst days and road shows. These elements, from executive interviews to strategic messaging, supplement data-heavy reports, and their value extends to other facets of IR. According to Patricia Baronowski, director of The Altman Group New York, "Internet video allows a company to detail and personalize their message to investors. [It's] . . . the next evolution of investor communications."[28]

Investing in Bandwidth: IR-Centric Web Properties Enhance Engagement and Boost the Bottom Line

Most corporate Web sites have had sections dedicated to the investor community since Web properties as a whole entered the mainstream; however, in the earliest days of IR Web sites, content was largely static, often encompassing nothing more than a PDF version of the annual report and, for the most innovative organizations, near-real-time stock information. But just as the pressroom portion of these Web sites has evolved to meet changing stakeholder demands, so too has the IR component. As early as 2006, 78 percent of surveyed IROs identified improving IR Web sites as a top priority.[29] That same year, research revealed that IR Web sites were already of major importance to institutional investors; 9 of 10 surveyed investors said that a company's Web site affects their perception of that company.[30]

In terms of corporate IR Web sites that are classified as being among the best, IR Global Rankings, the Investor Relations Society, and *IR Magazine* all present awards for organizations based on content, technology, interactivity, design, and navigability. The Investor Relations Roundtable[31] took these institutions' IR Web site awards into consideration to determine three primary site criteria that define the success of companies' online investor information:

1. *Content:*
   a. The site should provide broad, deep access to current and historical information.
   b. Information should be up to date.

2. *Technology and interactivity:*
   a. The site should provide tools that engage the user in a multimedia experience, facilitate more efficient use of time, and offer two-way communication.

3. *Design and navigability:*
   a. Users should be able to access information quickly and intuitively.
   b. Graphics, text, financial data, sound, video, etc. should be presented in an aesthetically pleasing manner.
   c. All users should have equal access to information and should be able to control font size and navigation.

Based on these criteria, a handful of corporations has led the charge in developing IR Web sites that enhance every stakeholder's experience (see Table 6.1). But, more than content, technology/interactivity, and design/navigation, what specific features combine to create IR-focused Web platforms that leverage the communications power of digital channels? First and foremost, the IR Web site should serve as a means of educating the investor community about the company's performance and strategy, both presently and looking toward the future. Specific components also should include:

- *Segment breakdown of revenue, profits, sales, and costs by product/service.* Kraft is just one example of a company that presents results by product category (i.e., beverages, convenient means, cheese, etc.).
- *Financial and nonfinancial commentary.* Unilever and Cadbury Schweppes both provide nonfinancial commentary about their performance to round out analyses.
- *Investment propositions.* Adidas, Samsung, and Colgate are three companies that offer investment propositions on their IR Web sites, identifying specific reasons to invest and current/future strategies for continued growth.
- *Geographic breakdown of sales, revenues, profits, etc.* Unilever, Cadbury Schweppes, and Toyota all offer this information via charts and tables that illustrate breakdowns by region.
- *Webcasts of IR executives discussing breakdowns.* Nestle, Coca-Cola, and Starbucks are among the companies whose IR Web sites host Webcasts (audio and/or video) to enhance interactivity.
- *Online annual reports.* Annual reports were discussed at length earlier.

Table 6.1: Best-in-Class IR Web Sites

Company	Ticker	Country	Industry	Market Cap (in US$ Billions)	Award(s)
Bayer AG	BAY	Germany	Pharmaceuticals	37.2	Best overall Web site—IR Global rankings
Adidas	ADS	Germany	Consumer products	10.1	Best content—IR Global rankings
Cadbury Schweppes	CSG	United Kingdom	Beverages	20.1	Best Web site in the *Financial Times/London Stock Exchange* (FTSE) 100—IR Society Best Practice Awards
Cisco Systems	CSCO	United States	Communications equipment	45.7	Best Web site—*IR Magazine*
National Express Group	NEX	United Kingdom	Transportation services	2.3	Best Web site FTSE 250—IR Society Best Practice Awards

Along the same lines, IR must be involved in all branding initiatives to make the corporate image one that appeals to all stakeholders, including investors. This factors into all communication-related activities, including the corporate IR Web site (for a list of IR Web site dos and don'ts, see the following sidebar).

IR WEB SITE DOS AND DON'TS

DOS:

- Provide direct contact information for the IR team.
- Make corporate governance documents and information prominently available.
- Provide access information enabling investors to communicate directly with the board of directors.
- If linking to external resources (e.g., call transcripts, stock charts, etc.), be sure to identify them as outside the corporate site. You may wish to provide an intermediate screen that indicates the user will be redirected (see

"Hyperlinks to Third-Party Information" in the SEC's recent revised interpretive guidance on company Web site use).

- Use design elements such as dynamically expanding tree structures (think Windows explorer without the folder icons) that provide the user with a sense of place and preview the content in each section.
- Be careful of features that make too much "noise." For example, a Web site that launches audio or video of the CEO on each visit regardless of the number of previous visits simply will annoy the user. Carefully consider how such "bells and whistles" are implemented by making them user-directed or, as in this example, having the audio/video play only on the initial site visit.
- Use common names for standard pieces of information in order to make them more easily identifiable to users. Such menu items as "Computershare Investment Plan" may be less meaningful to the uninitiated than "Direct Stock Purchase Plan."
- Include a page for fundamentals. While this information is often available, it is generally difficult to find in document files rather than in a more easily accessible format.
- Use the IR Web site not only as a current snapshot but also as a historical record of the company's performance and a roadmap for where the company intends to go (to the extent the company discusses the future).
- Use a linked table of contents at the top of a page if posting a long HTML document.

DON'TS:

- Don't use your frequently asked questions (FAQs) section as an information catchall. Important messages can get buried there. For example, information on shareholder services warrants its own section.
- Avoid having the site launch new windows as a way of accessing content or functionality. This risks both annoying users by cluttering their desktops and creating discontinuity between the content that should be cohesive.
- Avoid the appearance of inactivity by presenting an empty events calendar. An alternative practice is to combine upcoming with past events onto one page.
- Carefully consider requiring users to register for certain aspects of IR sites. This may dissuade users from accessing these areas or cause them to avoid the site altogether.

Source: Jeffrey D. Morgan, "IR Web Sites: Striving to Balance Richness with Ease of Use," National Investor Relations Institute Executive Alert, Vienna, Virginia, September 4, 2008.

Nike is a prime example of a company that incorporates branding efforts into its IR Web site, *www.invest.nike.com*. In addition to ubiquitous branding via the "swoosh" and images of corporate spokespeople, the site features up-to-date investor press releases, video clips of senior management, real-time stock quotes, a simple search function, and the ability for investors to customize their own page based on the specific information they want to see (see Figure 6.2).

As is always the case, customization is key to answering the "What's in it for me?" question that is always top-of-mind for modern stakeholders, and investors are no exception. But there are general best practices that executives can follow to set the foundation for an interactive—and compliant—IR Web site. Ronald Mueller, partner at Gibson, Dunn & Crutcher, identified the following as good building blocks, all of which were given in the context of making an IR Web site compliant with SEC disclosure standards[32]:

Figure 6.2: IR Web sites done right: Nike

- Focus on ways to make the Web site an SEC-recognized channel of distribution by notifying investors that the site will be used for this purpose, by keeping the site up-to-date, and by looking for innovative ways to highlight information.
- Document investors' use of the IR Web site to demonstrate the extent of its usability and value.
- Look for ways to bring traffic to the Web site via Real Simple Syndication (RSS) feeds, media outreach, etc.
- Clearly date information and consider archiving older material; develop standards for when content should be archived/removed.
- Use disclaimers for links and forums.

Put Your Money Where Your Mouth Is: IR Execs Tiptoe into the Blogosphere

Thus far the discussion of the importance of a robust IR Web site has introduced the ways in which IR and corporate communications executives can (and must) work together to engage a rapidly expanding network of investor stakeholder groups, but it hasn't yet addressed truly Web 2.0 channels that these executives can leverage. Direct channels of communications between a company and its stakeholders become increasingly important as reputational risks metastasize and global economic stability breaks down. In this vein, the most forward-thinking companies have adopted a practice that even just a few years ago would be unheard of in the IR space—blogging.

As demonstrated by activist shareholder Carl Icahn's entrée into the blogosphere, investors themselves—even the more "vintage" ones—are using digital communications channels to rally their peers, comment on issues, and put heat on corporate management teams. Blogs aren't just a platform speaking off-the-cuff about investor issues, though; they can have measurable impact on companies' stock prices. Case in point: On Friday, October 3, 2008, CNN's citizen journalism Web site *iReport.com* ran a story claiming that Apple CEO Steve Jobs had a heart attack that morning. Investors immediately caught wind of the story and panicked; before Apple had time to release a statement that the story was completely false, the company's stock price had dropped 9 percent. The following Monday, the SEC launched an investigation into whether the story was an attempt to drive down Apple's stock price, which hit a 52-week low of $85 on October 10.

But rogue bloggers who fail to fact-check (or who blatantly create fictitious accounts just to make investors fumble) aren't the only ones affecting shareholder communities; many of these citizen journalists take proactive approaches to outing companies' malfeasances, as was the case of the Michael Arrington–run "TechCrunch" blog that exposed a scam run by a company that was preparing for its initial public offering (IPO). The post accused the company, Intelius, of funding its growth by tricking consumers into making small recurring credit-card payments via a Web survey. "In other words," Arrington wrote, "without the survey scam, Intelius would have nearly no revenue growth. Companies that aren't growing don't go public."[33]

This instance reflects an outsider looking into an organization to influence its investor stakeholders; the reverse situation proved to be the case for Yahoo! during the attempted hostile takeover attempt by Microsoft in early 2008. During this period, a Yahoo! employee blogged that "Yahoos won't work for Microsoft," citing that "cultural differences" accounted for the fact that an estimated 10 percent of Yahoo! employees would refuse to work for Microsoft.[34]

Four days later, the *New York Times* ran a story that supported the employee blogger's estimate. Ultimately, Microsoft's attempted takeover would fail for a number of reasons, among them a lack of investor support. While this can't be pinned directly to employees' disapproval of the deal, it certainly didn't help; survey after survey reveals that one of the greatest challenges of a merger is to integrate two disparate cultures. The "TechYourWorld" blog post, further supported by coverage from a top-tier news outlet, nurtured the seed of doubt among investors that the merger wouldn't pan out.

The Icahn, Apple, Intelius, and Yahoo! examples are a few of many that illustrate the influence of blogs over investors and their audiences, but that's only one side of the story. IR executives within some corporations are now choosing to fight fire with fire by creating corporate IR blogs to keep these stakeholder groups abreast of financial goings-on, to comment on industry trends, and to bring at least part of the conversation back onto their own turf.

Dell is one of these corporate mavericks currently exploring the "Wild West" of IR blogging. The company introduced its own IR blog, "Dell Shares" (*dellshares.dell.com*), on November 1, 2007. Lynn Tyson, Dell's former vice president of investor relations, penned the first post, in which she said

Michael Dell said to Bloomberg *in July, "We have an enormous opportunity in front of us, but it will require some changes." Dell Shares, our new investor relations blog is among those changes and opportunities. It's an exciting initiative for all of us on the Investor Relations team.*

It is an opportunity for us to go beyond posting information on the investor relations section at dell.com and to be accessible and available, share perspectives and build and maintain relationships with our investors, potential investors and anyone and everyone who is interested in joining the conversations here.

Dell Shares is not just about us and Dell financial information. It is also about you. Relationships are two-way streets with shared benefits and responsibilities. So, we expect to listen and learn from you— our investors and those participating in this journey.[35]

This approach of communicating with the investor community in an authentic and transparent way certainly was revolutionary—and remains so today. After all, corporate executives are hesitant to open themselves up to the uncertainty presented by an IR blog for many of the same reasons they aren't comfortable embracing corporate blogging practices in general—fear of openly critical commentators, lack of time/budget, and a loss of control over messaging—as well as a few new ones—namely, a fear of being compliant with Regulation Fair Disclosure (Reg FD). But with the SEC's 2008 decision to recognize corporate blogs and Web sites as public disclosure under Reg FD, the latter fear becomes moot (see Chapter 4). As for the former concerns, according to Rob Williams, Dell's director of investor relations, "Companies have two choices: Join the conversation, or procrastinate and then join under someone else's terms."[36]

Dell executives joined the conversation in a big way with "Dell Shares," and the investor community has reacted positively. Williams cited the need to democratize information as an impetus for creating "Dell Shares," and the blog now addresses the following topics[37]:

- Earnings announcements
- Acquisitions
- Major programs and initiatives
- Changes to senior leadership
- Capital structure

- Strategy
- Senior management video blogs ("vlogs")
- Analysis of business and inflection points
- Market data releases
- SRI/sustainability
- Analyst meeting coverage
- Notice and access

In less than two years, the blog's readership has more than doubled, and the IR team has used the tool to clarify its position on certain issues and to find and correct misinformation.[38] Completely abandoning all self-consciousness, the blog is open to comments from investors and any other stakeholder. The IR team monitors the site daily and responds to comments, and it also leverages the corporate communications team for conducting blogger outreach.[39] And as for the blogger community's reaction to "Dell Shares," a post on Custom Communications' "Social Media Influence" blog is indicative of the widespread support: "Dell in a few months has managed to create a viable model in corporate transparency with this blog .... Naturally, this triggers an exchange that wouldn't be possible outside of this forum .... Welcome to the future of IR."[40]

Trial By Fire: Using Digital Communications Channels To Manage Investor Crises

In the case of a corporate financial crises, which became increasingly ubiquitous with the economic crash of late 2008, it's especially vital that IR and corporate communications are on the same page with the messages they are crafting in terms of effects on stock value, potential layoffs, safety issues, etc. Most important, with the speed that information travels on the Internet, a presentation to investors, an e-mail to employees, or an announcement to suppliers is immediately made available to the world via the Web. Even inaccurate information posted on a blog can tank a company's stock price, à la the false announcement of Apple CEO Steve Jobs' death and its subsequent stock market fallout. Thus the distinct possibility of financial news going public via the Web demands that companies communicate constantly and transparently or risk losing credibility with stakeholders.

Past strategies for mitigating risk often revolved around staying out of the conversation, especially when it came to IR. However, as this chapter's previous examples have demonstrated, this approach is becoming less and less effective. Actions and reactions take place with or without the input of the corporations in question. Despite this, some companies are taking proactive steps to use digital communications channels to connect directly with stakeholders and impart successful measures. Aflac is just one example.

In 2006, Aflac executives faced a critical situation: Shareholders were feeling their oats with regard to empowerment and, more specifically, questioning the issue of executive compensation—one that had become top-of-mind as it became clear that many senior corporate executives collected massive pay checks while the overall organization faltered financially. In the spirit of true transparency, however, the life insurance company's executives ceded complete control of messaging and opened the issue to stakeholders in the form of an investor election. In short, the communications team needed to convey to shareholders that Aflac's present-day compensation program was fair and that the company's successful financial performance could be liked to its executive compensation policy. Thus, in February 2007, the company developed its "Say on Pay" campaign, where it became the first U.S. public company to allow a shareholder vote on the issue of executive compensation.

The risk was substantial in multiple capacities, including reputation, brand, and bottom line. If shareholders voted against Aflac's executive compensation program, the organization would suffer damage to its reputation, not to mention its stock price. To sidestep the potential landmines, the IR department teamed up with corporate communications executives to craft messaging that would appeal to the business, investor, and activist shareholder communities to subsequently inspire votes in favor of Aflac's effort. The initiative evolved into a media relations program that targeted multiple media shareholders.

"The targeted audience for our message was primarily the business community," said Jon Sullivan, executive publicist/external communications for Aflac. "Secondary audiences [included] . . . potential and current Aflac shareholders and institutions that hold approximately two-thirds stake in Aflac. While the issue of 'Say on Pay' was fairly straightforward, the company was diligent in its efforts in being as concise and clear as possible to deliver the message: Aflac listens to its shareholders."[41]

To convey the message that Alfac listened to shareholders and, in turn, to inspire them to support the "Say on Pay" initiative, the team conducted research to justify the company's fairness in compensation, tested messages in advance of targeting media, referred business reporters to pertinent shareholder activists who would provide a perhaps counterintuitive angle on the story, offered media access to Aflac CEO Dan Amos, and sent out news releases throughout the year in anticipation of the voting to keep the "Say on Pay" issue top-of-mind for shareholders.

"The 'Say on Pay' initiative generated a tremendous amount of media attention for Aflac, as it was a historical first among publicly held companies in the United States," said Sullivan. "Therefore, the PR team was obligated to stay abreast of comparable activities of other major companies, commentary by shareholder advocates, and adjacent business issues—all of which could become part of media interviews. Refreshment of the spokesperson Q&A became almost daily duty, but it was necessary to keep interviews contemporary as well as support to Aflac's reputational agenda."[42]

While Aflac executives didn't rely on digital communications channels more than ordinarily for the time, this entrée into stakeholder ownership of an issue was unprecedented. "The campaign consisted of primary traditional print and electronic earned media; however, we did target the emerging channels of communication, including Web casts at Newsweek.com (*http://feedroom.businessweek.com/?fr_story=8cda 54eba7b5a8a2752a100ba0c31317c892b7eb*), BusinessWeek.com and ABCnews.com," Sullivan said. "These Internet-based mediums provide the ability to reach a variety of audiences, many of whom are more tech-savvy and who desire information in a faster-paced society."[43]

Ultimately, Aflac's "Say on Pay" initiative is an example of an organization that mitigated reputational risk by opening itself up to stakeholder criticism and replying on the strength of its brand and messaging to sway key audiences in the right direction. "The 'Say on Pay' initiative was initiated because it was raised by a shareholder," Sullivan said. "The key to an effective investor relations campaign is to ensure that the investors are party of the solution. Aflac was very careful to include shareholder activists in the communications initiative and, as a result, add third-party credibility to the communication."[44]

This credibility of communication was critical to the success of Aflac's IR initiative, which ended up receiving a 93 percent shareholder vote in favor of its executive compensation practices—proof that ceding control to the "other side" doesn't necessarily guarantee failure. Especially in terms of leveraging digital channels to take the pulse of the investor community's reaction to a potential/realized risk, the following strategies apply[45]:

- *Monitor activist activity online.* Awareness of both activism trends within industries and who owns shares of an organization helps to anticipate potential issues.
- *Enhance online financial communication.* Strategic communications with investors online provides immediate and accurate answers to investors, fosters a relationship between the IR function and investors, and maintains an open line of proactive communications with all shareholders.
- *Use investor behavior analysis.* Proxy services help to analyze investors' behavior patterns and, in turn, create targeted communications to major investor segments.
- *Manage perception and reputation among audiences on the Web.* Tracking conversations among investors online, as well as measuring media coverage and key message pickup, informs executives as to how they are being viewed by all stakeholders, including investors.
- *Employ cross-function responses when critical situations arise*: Cross-functional teams in which IR, PR, finance, and HR executives participate maintain a well-rounded view of issues and aid in building company-wide consensus on issues.

Conclusion

Just as digital platforms are prompting the integration of marketing and HR with the corporate communication function, so too are they requiring communications and IR to work in tandem. After all, the investor stakeholder group has become increasingly fragmented, and one particular subgroup—activist shareholders—has taken on even more power as its members learn to leverage online channels to meet their objectives. Because of this, as well as an increase in public scrutiny and government regulation, companies must communicate their IR efforts more transparently and in more accessible ways—namely, online.

The most successful organizations have embraced this new landscape and abandoned antiquated IR practices in favor of interactive, dynamic, and largely digital approaches to protect their brands and reputations in the face of changing shareholder demands. Whether they are maintaining IR blogs, developing robust IR Web sites, or creating interactive online annual reports, the most forward-thinking corporate leaders recognize modern reputational risks and economic challenges. The line between prosperity and failure has been drawn in sand, and a windstorm is barreling down the coastline. Business executives can either jump on the bandwidth bandwagon or be blown away.

CHAPTER 7

A TREE GROWS IN CYBERSPACE

WEB 2.0 INSPIRES—AND REQUIRES—CORPORATE RESPONSIBILITY EFFORTS TO GO GREEN

Former Vice President Al Gore may have (sort of) lost the 2000 presidential election, but what he would go on to win had a different type of global impact: the 2007 Nobel Peace Prize for his work on climate change, which culminated in the 2006 film *An Inconvenient Truth* (which won two Oscars in 2000, one for best documentary feature and another for best original song). The documentary jump-started a trend that had been gaining momentum slowly for some time—that is, a sharpened focus on environmentalism, sustainability, and corporate responsibility.

Regardless of the specific impact Gore's work had on the increased attention paid to responsible business practices, the level of concern about corporate responsibility most definitely has increased exponentially in the last five years. And unlike the aftermath of the 1989 *Exxon Valdez* oil spill and the 1994 ban on chlorofluorocarbons, heightened interest isn't just a blip that's followed by relative inactivity; rather, it marks changes in policy, participation, and practices on all fronts, from corporate to governmental to consumer. Whether this enduring change was borne out of fear, desperation, or genuine concern, its effects on the way corporate leaders conduct business and communicate results are significant and are made all the more so by the ability of digital platforms to democratize access to information.

This chapter will identify and define the elements of corporate responsibility, often colloquially referred to as *green*, detail strategies for using digital communications platforms to engage individual stakeholder groups in the context of a company's green efforts, and finally, explain the growing prominence and importance of standardized sustainability reporting to organizations' reputations and bottom lines.

Green is the New Black: Idealism Turns to Realism as Corporations are Forced to Practice Business Responsibly

Some cynics may be inclined to dismiss the "greening" of business because they are old enough to remember the *last* green movement. This go-round, though, stakeholders appear to have adopted a new approach to corporate responsibility (CR), paying heed to any number of CR iterations: green marketing, cause marketing, corporate social responsibility (CSR), sustainability, etc. (for a dictionary of CR terms, see the following sidebar). And it's no surprise as to why. All the factors contributing to the changing business environment discussed in previous chapters lend longevity to a movement like this: Digital communications platforms democratize access to information, giving people the power to discover and connect with causes; trust in business is at a low point, making corporate responsibility an easy platform for vocalizing a spectrum of complaints and concerns; and a turbulent global economy makes concepts such as sustainability and alternative energy more fiscally sound than ever. Sam Palmisano, CEO of IBM, summed it up nicely:

> *These collective realizations have reminded us that we are all now connected—economically, technically and socially. But we're also learning that being connected is not sufficient. Yes, the world continues to get "flatter." And yes, it continues to get smaller and more interconnected. But something is happening that holds even greater potential. In a word, our planet is becoming smarter. . . . What this means is that the digital and physical infrastructures of the world are converging. . . . Indeed, almost anything—any person, any object, and process or any service, for any organization, large or small—can become digitally*

aware and networked. But there is another reason we will make our companies, institutions and industries smarter. Because we must. Not just as moments of widespread shock, but integrated into our day-to-day operations. These mundane processes of business, government and life . . . are not smart enough to be sustainable.[1]

In turn, organizational leaders now realize that doing well is increasingly dependent on doing good. Focusing on a triple bottom line—people, planet, and profit—instead of one that's limited to pure dollar value broadens companies' perspective to consider human, natural, and financial capital.

WHAT'S IN A NAME? CORPORATE RESPONSIBILITY DICTIONARY

Cause-related marketing   Marketing that involves collaboration of a for-profit business and a nonprofit organization for mutual benefit. American Express is credited with coining the term in 1983 around the Statue of Liberty restoration project.

Community relations   The act of businesses establishing and maintaining two-way communications with the communities in which they operate.

Corporate citizenship   The concept of corporate institutions conducting business with the interests of all shareholders, as well as those of the environment, in mind.

Corporate social responsibility   Often used interchangeably with *corporate citizenship* or *corporate responsibility*, this is the concept of conducting business responsibly to contribute positively to stakeholder audiences and communities.

ESG   Shorthand for environmental, social (or CR), and corporate governance issues.

Green marketing   As defined by the American Marketing Association, green marketing refers to the promotion of products that are presumed to be safe for the environment.

Philanthropy   The act of donating money, goods, services, or any other resource to support a socially beneficial cause, in which the donor receives no financial or material award for their goodwill.

Sustainability   The concept of minimizing the natural resources used by businesses in terms of processes such as manufacturing, distribution, and production.

But the triple bottom line is a simplistic summary of a collection of multifaceted drivers. Each stakeholder group has its own motivations for and method of requiring companies to operate with attention to their social (i.e., fair trade, human rights, treatment of employees, safety, child labor, etc.) and environmental (i.e., carbon footprint, global warming, renewable energy, conservation, etc.) responsibilities. Stakeholders' belief that corporations have a responsibility to support causes in tangible ways has severe implications for these corporations' brands and reputations. News that an organization isn't living up to social or environmental standards can spread like wildfire, thanks to digital platforms, and it's a near guarantee that it will precipitate a crisis—or, at the very least, some very serious heartburn.

The Business Case: Money Talks, But Does Corporate Responsibility Listen?

Stakeholders' ubiquitous support for conducting business responsibly will be addressed later in this chapter, but the primary concern of corporate leaders is likely to be a bit more self-serving: Does CR/CSR/sustainability/fill-in-the-blank actually pay off? As it turns out, the answer is not black and white but rather a murky shade of . . . green.

According to David Vogel, professor at the University of California Berkeley Haas School of Business:

> *The belief that corporate responsibility "pays" is a seductive one: Who would not want to live in a world in which corporate virtue is rewarded and corporate irresponsibility punished? Unfortunately, the evidence for these rewards and punishment is rather weak. There is a "market for virtue," but it is a very limited one. Nor is it growing.*[2]

Those are certainly fighting words, especially when taken in the context of the fervent believers in CR as a profitable business imperative *and* a moral obligation. However, if you asked Starbucks if "doing good" translates directly into "doing well," most likely you would receive a prickly reply. After all, the company pours a *venti*-sized dose of energy into CR efforts, most notably around its commitment to fair trade and generous employee benefits, but its profit margins experienced a sharp decline throughout 2008. Its stock's dismal performance was linked directly to overexpansion, but cynics also could point out that no amount of fair-trade coffee beans or part-time employee insurance plans would stop the plummeting profits. Good thing Chairman and CEO Howard Schultz is committed to making Starbucks a company that puts "people first and profits last."[3]

While it's tough to dispute Starbucks' dismal earnings, the company has adopted an innovative digital strategy to encourage input from stakeholders—"crowdsourcing." "Crowdsourcing" is one of the neologisms introduced during this age of digital communications, referring to the practice of outsourcing tasks that traditionally would be performed in-house to the general public, usually via a community forum. In Starbucks' case, the company launched *www.mystarbucksidea.com*, where visitors are literally encouraged to submit their ideas on how to make the brand better. The ideas are categorized, and users can vote on the ideas they think should be implemented. The "Involvement" section of the site is dedicated to ideas about community building and social responsibility, where consumers have suggested everything from putting recycling bins in every store, to using energy-saving light bulbs, to canceling its partnership with Product(RED) (for more information on this partnership, see "Sustainable Stakeholder Engagement: Digital Platforms Connect Every Audience with Companies' CR Initiatives" below). Nothing about the "crowdsourcing" effort suggests a direct link to profits, but it is an example of how a company involves consumers in creating new business opportunities and overcoming challenges in the CR space and beyond.

The actual business case for dedicating resources to CR initiatives most likely falls somewhere between profitability and obligation. As hard as some organizations have tried, no one has definitively identified a correlation between environmental, social, and governance (ESG) efforts alone and financial metrics or stock market performance.[4] That said, the perception of CR has been linked to corporate reputation; data collected for the Reputation Institute's 2008 "Global Pulse Study," the Reputation Institute, and the Boston College Center for Corporate Citizenship focused on the three dimensions of corporate citizenship, governance, and workplace practices and determined that these three measures account for more than 40 percent of a company's reputation.[5] Based on the analysis, Google was the top performer, followed by Campbell Soup Company, Johnson & Johnson, Walt Disney, and Kraft Foods, Inc.

According to Jeff Fettig, CEO of Whirlpool Corporation, which ranked number 32 on the Corporate Social Responsibility Index, "We believe the long-term success of Whirlpool is tied in part to the health and well-being of society in general."[6] There are also the periphery benefits of CR: proven employee engagement, increased customer loyalty, and risk avoidance, for example.

If these reasons aren't convincing enough, executives can contemplate the legal ramifications of disregarding standards for responsible business conduct or for executing green marketing campaigns that aren't based on authentic or genuine efforts. A more stringent regulatory environment, not to mention the ever-growing presence (and power) of nongovernment organizations (NGOs), enhances the pressure on companies to implement CR-related practices, profits or no profits (for more on specific government regulations of business, see Chapters 6 and 8). Whether it's standards set to protect employees abroad or the April 2008 Federal Trade Commission's (FTC) move to define government regulation on environmental marketing efforts, strict behavioral guidelines demand the participation of corporate institutions.

Say What? Stakeholder Sleuths Call Out Companies as Disingenuous Do-gooders

The FTC's regulation of green marketing messages points to the palpable influence digital communications channels has over all corporate communications. With the emergence of online platforms coalescing alongside pressures to "be green," many companies enacted surface-level sustainability efforts and then promoted those efforts with messaging that was more fiction than fact. Thus the term *greenwashing*—the perception by audiences that they are being misled by a company regarding the environmental benefits of its practices, products, or services—entered the vocabularies of executives and stakeholders.

Greenwashing is a catch-22 in that its causes and effects perpetuate one another. The results of the 2008 "Green Gap Survey," conducted by Cone, Inc., and the Boston College Center for Corporate Citizenship, effectively articulated this through the following findings:

- 39 percent of those surveyed were preferentially buying products they believe to be "environmentally friendly," whereas 48 percent erroneously believed that products marked as "green" or "environmentally friendly" have positive/beneficial effects on the environment.

- Only 22 percent understood that "green" and "environmentally friendly" products more accurately describe products that have a less negative environmental impact than competing versions.
- 47 percent trusted companies to tell the truth in environmental messaging.
- 45 percent believed that companies were accurately communicating information about their environmental impact.
- 61 percent said that they understand the environmental terms companies use in their advertising.

The same survey also polled Americans on their view of government regulation of environmental marketing messages in light of the FTC's April 30, 2008, public hearing on the subject, finding that

- 59 percent supported a move by the government to ensure the accuracy of environmental messaging by regulating it.
- Responders also believed that certification by third-party organizations (80 percent), review and reporting by watchdog groups (78 percent), regulation by government (76 percent), and self-policing by industry or business groups (75 percent) could play an important oversight role to ensure accuracy in environmental messaging.

These survey findings highlight the confusion that permeates stakeholders' perceptions of green and that is perpetuated by inaccurate green marketing messages. Naturally, the Web has become the go-to place for all stakeholders to research companies' green claims and to criticize or applaud their efforts. SourceWatch (*www.sourcewatch.org*) is just one of many digital platforms that allow visitors to contribute information documenting "the PR and propaganda activities of public relations firms and public relations professionals engaged in managing and manipulating public perception, opinion and policy."[7]

This wiki, developed by the Center for Media and Democracy, is managed by an editor and requires strict referencing, so, unlike some wiki-like channels, it presents information in a more journalistic way. Although its coverage isn't limited to CR and green-type oversights, this topic is a primary focus. It has lambasted such organizations as Ford, Dow Chemical, and General Electric (GE) for greenwashing, drawing attention to the organizations' marketing efforts that are in stark contrast to non-eco-friendly practices. GE, for instance, launched its $90 million "Ecomagination" campaign in May 2005, at which time CEO Jeff Immelt stated, "Ecomagination is GE's commitment to address challenges such as the need for cleaner, more efficient sources of energy, reduced emissions and abundant sources of clean water."[8]

Since then, GE certainly has invested big bucks in the campaign, but detractors point to the company's continued investments in power plants, oil and gas production, and coal-fired steam turbines. Thus, is the goodwill effort inspired more by greenbacks than by green business?

"Green is green as in the color of money," said Judy Hu, global executive director of advertising and branding at GE. "It is about a business opportunity, and we believe we can increase our revenue behind [GE's] Ecomagination products and services."[9]

Sustainable Stakeholder Engagement: Digital Platforms Connect Every Audience With Companies' CR Initiatives

As previous chapters have indicated, the Web 2.0 movement has both enabled and required corporations to engage stakeholders in two-way conversations based on authentic and transparent communications. The same holds true for CR-related efforts, but this messaging has an added dimension because nearly every stakeholder group approaches a company's responsible business practices with his or her own interests in mind; thus the most successful organizations' CR efforts have, for lack of a better phrase, a little bit for everyone.

Consumer Reports: CR-Focused Brands Lure Buyers via Digital Domains

The return on investment (ROI) of CR/green initiatives may be debatable, but one thing seems to be a sure bet: Consumers believe that businesses have a responsibility to help solve pressing social and environmental issues, and the majority of them will switch from one brand to another if the other is associated with a good cause. This makes huge strides in favor of the argument that CR and green business is, in fact, good for the bottom line, but perhaps more important, it presents an opportunity for companies to take advantage of the Web's ability to deliver corporate messages directly to targeted audiences without the bloated budgets required by traditional marketing.

Take, for example, the companies using social networks to expand their philanthropic reach while engaging consumers on a more personal level. Western Union launched the "Our World Gives" Facebook campaign in October 2008, encouraging Facebook users to support charities by having them rally their friends around their favorite causes and associated nonprofits, including the American Red Cross, UNICEF, and Room to Read. The organization that received the largest number of Facebook donations at the end of the campaign was the recipient of $50,000 from Western Union. Not only was the campaign philanthropic in nature, but it also put the Western Union brand in front of consumers who weren't necessarily customers—yet. However, interacting with them on this platform—and, in turn, gaining access to the users' Facebook profiles, because you had to opt-in to visit the "Our World Gives" page—gave the company potential leads to pursue in the future, should it so choose.

Then there's Dell's "Regeneration" campaign, which, with the help of social media marketing agency Federated Media, used Facebook's "Graffiti Wall" application to support a contest in January 2008. The contest centered on participants submitting artwork on the "Graffiti Wall" based on the "What does green mean to you?" theme. The winner received a 22-inch environmentally friendly Dell monitor. The campaign drew more than 7,000 artwork contributions and more than 1 million votes by Facebook members, and most important, it resulted in more than 1,000 ideas being submitted to *ReGeneration.org*, a blog community that supports the global movement to sustain the environment.[10] The brilliance of the campaign was its use of a community and a Web application that already existed, thus making an impact without requiring Dell to shell out large amounts of time and money.

The Timberland Company also jumped online in 2008 with its "Earthkeeper" campaign, although this initiative admittedly (and openly) blurred the lines between advocacy and advertising. The company, which manufactures and sells active lifestyle apparel and footwear, was experiencing a decline in profits when it launched "Earthkeeper" in June 2008. The campaign was both branding for its new Earthkeeper product line and its eponymous green initiative, which set out to recruit one million consumers to "lighten their environmental footprint," according to Timberland President Jeffrey Schwartz.[11]

Needless to say, one way consumers could lighten their environmental footprint was to buy Earthkeeper products, made from recycled and organic materials. But the Web-centric initiative was dedicated to far more than shopping; it used a Web site—*www.earthkeeper.com*—to aggregate all the digital components, including a blog, a Facebook presence, a YouTube Earthkeeper Brand Channel, and a partnership with *Changents.com*. The site acted as a community for individuals wanting to become "Earthkeepers"—those who "believe taking simple steps can help make the world better. Like starting a community garden. Planting a tree, even organizing a rock concert. Yes, a rock concert."[12]

Indeed, Timberland joined forces with Stone Gossard of Pearl Jam to plan day-long events in Boston, New York, Los Angeles, and San Francisco that began with planting trees in local neighborhoods and culminated with a concert in the evening. Those who signed up to participate in the day's green-themed activities received a free ticket to the show. The events took place in early October 2008; on November 5, 2008, Timberland executives announced the launch of a new global television, print, and online advertising campaign around the Earthkeepers brand. "As an outdoor brand we're serious about doing our bit to protect the outdoors, and consumers are increasingly concerned about that too," explained Carol Yang, Timberland's vice president of global marketing. "But they're also weary of being 'told' how to make green choices—so we decided to lighten up and take a tongue-in-cheek approach to communicating the Earthkeepers story."[13]

The ads, which depict two hikers—one wearing Earthkeeper boots and the other not—braving the elements to varying degrees of success, direct viewers to the Earthkeeper Web site, where they can engage with the brand and the cause more intimately. Only time will tell if the campaign helps to reverse the company's sinking profits, but the innovative spirit behind Earthkeeper certainly makes a statement about the power of social media to connect and inspire consumers.

For one more example of social media acting as connective tissue among organizations, their stakeholders, and their CR messages, look no further than Ben & Jerry's. The ice cream maker has been a peace-loving, flower-power-promoting brand since its founding in 1978 by two long-time friends, Ben Cohen and Jerry Greenfield. Between the time the first scoop shop opened its doors and the present day, the company grew into a global franchise before its acquisition by conglomerate Unilever in 2000.

Despite the corporate style of its adopted parent, the Ben & Jerry's brand continues to espouse its "peace, love, and ice cream" mantra through its commitment to helping achieve world peace. In this vein, in April 2008, the company's executives launched a new campaign around their mission. Much like the Timberland "Earthkeeper" initiative, this was a high-calorie blend of brand promotion and philanthropy in that the "Imagine Whirled Peace" campaign coincided with the debut of its namesake ice cream flavor.

The endeavor's goals were twofold: Spread the "whirled peace" message to loyal consumers while broadening the brand's reach to a younger generation. By partnering with nonprofit Peace One Day and gaining permission from the John Lennon estate to use the Beatles icon as a backdrop for the campaign (based on his aptly themed song "Give Peace a Chance"), the Ben & Jerry's team had a strong message, a sturdy brand identity, and an iconic spokesperson of sorts. All it needed was a delivery vehicle.

Naturally, social media was the communication team's first choice; surprisingly, though, the creative brand had little experience with digital media. According to Katie O'Brien, interactive marketing manager for Ben & Jerry's, the "Imagine Whirled Peace" campaign was the company's "first foray into user-generated social media for marketing," but the "social media aspect of the program was really relevant to what we were doing. It was the perfect way to hear from our consumers what they thought about peace, love and ice cream without directly asking them."[14]

To bring social media to life around the philanthropic message, Ben & Jerry's executives teamed up with interactive marketing agency Vitrue to launch the "Imagine Whirled Peace" microsite within the corporate Web site (see Figure 7.1). The consumer-generated crux of the microsite was its peace-sign mosaic, which was comprised of thumbnail images uploaded by individual users, each of which created his or her own message of peace to contribute to the overall mission. By scrolling over the mosaic, visitors to the site can click on each thumbnail to see an expanded view of each contributor and his or her position on peace. The site also contains information about the partnership with Peace One Day, as well as the campaign's annual "bed-in for peace," modeled after Lennon and Yoko Ono's legendary 1969 bed-in.

Ultimately, using social media as a vehicle to connect with consumers about the company's cause helped the brand transition into the digital age and connect with a new generation of ice cream connoisseurs. The numbers speak for themselves. Within the first few month's of the

Figure 7.1: "Imagine Whirled Peace" microsite

microsite's launch, visitors submitted more than 1,200 images pledging their passion for peace, nearly 70,000 people clicked on individual images within the mosaic, and visitors spent an average of 5.5 minutes on the site at a time. Vitrue CEO Reggie Bradford summed it up by saying

> *Giving consumers a voice and outlet to share the brand is becoming a logical and natural extension of every communication initiative, and it will become table stakes for marketers of all sizes. [But] . . . social media initiatives need to tie to the brand's long-term strategy by being tied to the integrated marketing plan, being in the brand's voice and [having] . . . the propensity to become self-sustaining.*[15]

Employee Benefits: Fostering Engagement by Giving to Others

When most people think of corporate responsibility or sustainable business, they likely focus on environmentally friendly causes; however, according to a study conducted by Fleishman-Hillard and the National

Consumers League, the highest percentage of surveyed respondents defined corporate social responsibility as a company's "commitment to employees"[16] (see Figure 7.2). Along the same lines, survey after survey has revealed that employees are far more inclined to take a job with a company that they believe to be socially responsible; for example, 60 percent of respondents to the "Net Impact Member Survey" said that they would be "very likely" to leave their current jobs to work for a company that they believe to be more socially responsible, assuming the benefits and compensation were the same. Thus, as previous chapters have already established, it behooves corporate leaders to make their employees the brand's first line of defense. Now, this means embedding authentic CR objectives and opportunities internally that will positively affect external perceptions.

Gap executives took this to heart with the 2008 employee engagement effort, "Press Play: Be the Change," in which they challenged staffers to create videos of themselves volunteering and then post them to *www.pressplayatgap.com*, a Web site created by the Gap through Memelabs (*www.memelabs.com*), a consumer- and audience-driven platform that drives viral video marketing by hosting content. The Gap drove different stakeholders, from customers and employees to nonprofits, to the Web site to vote on their favorite video; the employee who created the winning video then could identify a charity of his or her choice, to which Gap would donate $10,000. (Second- and third-place winners would receive $7,500 and $5,000 grants, respectively, and the fan

Figure 7.2: Meaning of corporate social responsibility

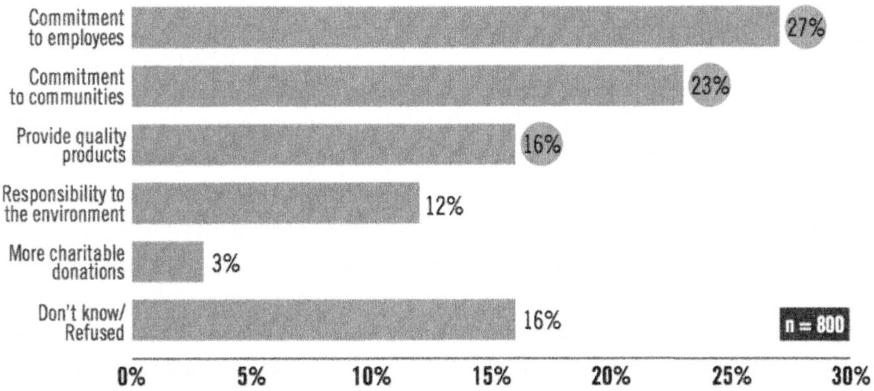

Source: "Rethinking Corporate Social Responsibility," Fleishman-Hillard/National Consumers League Executive Summary, May 2006, p. 4.

favorite would receive $2,500.) Employees uploaded videos ranging from 30 seconds to two minutes in length over the course of three weeks in August 2008. Then, between August 31 and September 6, 2008, visitors to the site could vote for their favorite video.

According to Gail Gershon, director of employee engagement at the Gap Foundation, "We launched an employee video contest to encourage our employees to share the great volunteer work they are doing and highlight the nonprofits they support. We wanted to increase employees' engagement with the community and support nonprofits through both time and money."[17]

The genius of this "Press Play" effort was its attention to capturing multiple stakeholder groups' interest in CR and engaging them at different points of the campaign. Not only were employees encouraged to volunteer, but they also were encouraged to incorporate those efforts into their work lives by translating them into a medium that could be shared with others. "Press Play" also communicated the Gap's commitment to philanthropy in an authentic way by stepping back and letting its employees be the messengers. Stakeholders, in turn, were asked to participate in the contest directly and to interact with the Gap brand indirectly. The winning video and nonprofit were announced on September 15, 2008; Gap employee Toby Goode's "They Will Surf Again" video, which documented a surfing event in Huntington Beach, California, for young people affected by spinal cord injuries, won the grand prize after getting nearly 4,000 votes. His selected charity, Life Rolls On Foundation, received $10,000.

The Gap's CR initiative interpreted social media's power to enable employee engagement very literally. Reuters, on the other hand, took a different approach to corporate citizenship. "[The company] . . . didn't really reach out to a wide variety of people within the organization—it was all quite insular," Reuters' manager of corporate responsibility, Julia Fuller, explained the impetus for evolving the employee engagement initiatives around corporate responsibility.[18] To expand this reach, the company established four employee working streams focusing on community, the environment, the workplace, and the marketplace, respectively.

"These streams include employees from a whole range of job functions and tenure with Reuters," Fuller said. "There are secretaries involved, graduates, senior managers—basically anyone who expressed an interest in CR issues when the opportunity was posted on the intranet."[19]

The company's intranet was the common denominator for each CR group, communicating opportunities and connecting employees throughout a company that is spread across the globe. As opposed to the Gap's campaign, which put social media at the center of the wheel and positioned stakeholder groups as spokes, Reuters leveraged social media to facilitate active citizenship among employees to make their own efforts the driving force.

Regardless of the approach taken by employers to engage employees around CR, philanthropic causes have a strong correlation with positive business effects. According to Cone's 2008 "Cause Evolution Survey," thanks to 24/7 access to information and the increasingly blurred line between work and home, employees now seek more purposeful work. Corporate leaders can take advantage of this trend by offering employees any number of opportunities, including matching donations, paid time off for volunteering, or dollars-for-doers programs (see Figure 7.3).

Figure 7.3: Employee engagement spectrum

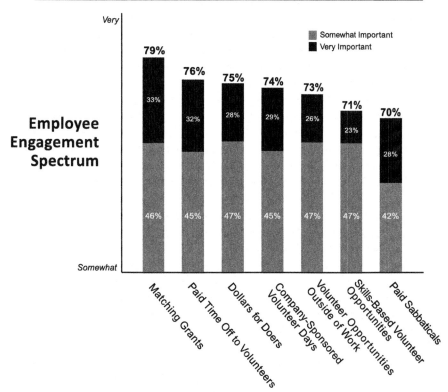

Source: "Past. Present. Future. The 25th Anniversary of Cause Marketing," Cone, Inc., 2008.

Banking on Sustainability: Investors See Big Potential in Green Business Practices

Clearly, opinions differ regarding the tangible ROI of CR efforts, but investors don't seem too divided over their value. In recent years, there has been a dramatic increase in the number of investors incorporating sustainability and ESG factors into their portfolio construction.[20] Various global initiatives, including the United Nations Environment Program Finance Initiative and the United Nations Principles for Responsible Investment, have accelerated this increase by creating global standards for responsible business investments (for more on these and other global investment initiatives, see the following sidebar).

GLOBAL INITIATIVES STANDARDIZE RESPONSIBLE INVESTMENT

United Nations Environment Program Finance Initiative (UNEP FI). A global partnership between the United Nations Environment Program and the financial sector consisting of more than 160 institutions, including banks, insurers, and fund managers, working to develop and promote links between the environment, sustainability, and financial performance.

United Nations Principles for Responsible Investment (UN PRI). A framework developed by an international group of institutional investors to reflect the growing relevance of environmental, social, and corporate governance issues to investment practices. Investors can become PRI signatories voluntarily to work to integrate the principles into mainstream investment decision making and ownership practices.

Enhanced Analytics Initiative (EAI). An international collaboration between asset owners and asset managers aimed at encouraging better investment research, particularly around the effects of extrafinancial issues on long-term investment.

Global Reporting Initiative (GRI). A multistakeholder network that provides guidance for organizations to use as the basis for disclosure about sustainability performance. GRI established a sustainability reporting framework and guidelines for standardized disclosure.

Research also shows a strong correlation between governance and environmental/social performance in the context of investment strength. This trend, best encapsulated by the term *socially responsible investing* (SRI), has prompted the emergence of an even more specific niche within the investor stakeholder group—SRI analysts and SRI fund managers, for example. These groups believe that CR management is a proxy for good management in general, as well as a proactive approach to minimizing risks and maximizing opportunities.

So where do digital communications channels fit into this mix? For starters, research shows that SRI investor stakeholder groups prefer receiving regularly updated information via the Web—a natural propensity considering the environmentally sound qualities of paper-less communications. If you couple this trend of CR-conscious investors with the heightened regulatory environment and financial reporting standards discussed in Chapter 6, then you'll arrive at the next evolution of investor relations—online sustainability reports.

Much like annual reports, sustainability reports communicate financial data, performance metrics, achieved objectives, future goals, and areas for improvement—all in the context of corporate responsibility. Some organizations merge annual and sustainability reports into one, whereas others separate them. Regardless of the approach, this information must be made available to all investor groups for a company to be viable in the tumultuous modern business environment. Of course, digital platforms are conducive to the presentation of this information.

Sustainability reporting began in the 1980s when chemical companies began publishing environmental reports to combat their image problem. It continued to develop into the 1990s as the reports began to address social issues in addition to environmental ones. By the time the Global Reporting Initiative was founded in 1997, it was not uncommon for many companies to include sustainability-related information in annual reports. Now, with the G3 sustainability reporting guidelines and the migration of this information to the Web, companies around the world are beginning to adhere to a uniform standard of principles and indicators based on stakeholder collaboration (for an overview of G3 guidelines, see Table 7.1).

The companies at the forefront of sustainability reporting follow many of the same best practices that apply to online annual reports and investor Web sites: authentic content that is aligned with the brand, transparent communication of opportunities *and* challenges, substantive information that does not sound like marketing "speak," and stated goals that are measurable and attainable. The following examples highlight companies

Table 7.1: Global reporting initiative G3 principles and indicators

Principles	Disclosure Items	Performance Indicators
Materiality	Monitoring and follow-up	Environment
Stakeholder inclusiveness	Certifications	Social
Timeliness	Policy	Human rights
Completeness	Goals and performance	Economic
Accuracy	Disclosure of management issues	Labor
Clarity		Society

that implement these strategies in online sustainability/CR reports to effectively communicate results to investor stakeholder groups:

BP

The energy company has built out an entire section within its corporate Web site that's dedicated to sustainability reporting. The site is broken into categories for easy navigation by topic (e.g., safety, climate change, alternative energy, etc.) and frames content in the context of bigger trends. These trends are positioned with data and financial information, as well as comprehensive interpretations alongside the charts and graphs. Then, to kick the interactivity element up a notch, the platform offers features such as a "Sustainability Worldwide Map" that users can search based on "where we operate," "country and site reports," and case studies, as well as a charting tool that enables investors to analyze, filter, and report on data based on their specific interests (see Figure 7.4).

Nike

The company has come a long way since its reputational crisis sparked by revelations regarding its sweatshop practices in the 1990s; today, the brand has a robust platform for reporting CR and sustainability efforts to investors and other stakeholders. Nike has a Web site (*www.nikeresponsibility.com*) that is dedicated solely to communicating CR initiatives. The opening page on the site greets visitors with one message: "We've evolved how we frame, define and approach corporate responsibility." Visitors then can access a range of information from financial data to business targets. An online forum hosts discussions around core impact areas, giving stakeholders the opportunity to comment on information and offering Nike executives insight into what's on the minds of key audiences. In addition, the company's attention to

Figure 7.4: BP's online charting tool

bp

Contact us | Reports and publications | BP worldwide | Home

Search: [_____] (Go)

About BP | Environment and society | Products and services | Investors | Press | Careers

You are here:
BP Global ▸ Environment and society ▸ Maps, reports and tools ▸ HSE charting tool

◂ **Maps, reports and tools**

HSE charting tool

Sustainability worldwide map

HSE charting tool ▾

Climate change

Health & safety

Environmental

HSE charting tool help

Environmental mapping tool

Case studies

Group sustainability reports

Country sustainability reports

Site reports

Use BP's HSE charting tool to analyse, filter and report on our performance data in the way that suits you best

▸ Climate change   ▸ Health and safety   ▸ Environmental

Our HSE data and reports are categorized into our main business areas: exploration and production

- refining and marketing
- chemicals (Innovene for 2005)
- gas, power and renewables (grouped with 'other business and corporate' where trending data would be misleading)
- other business and corporate

HSE data
Detailed explanations of our HSE performance in key environmental impact areas

▸ Air emissions
▸ Energy efficiency
▸ GHG emissions
▸ Health and safety
▸ Oil spills
▸ Ozone depleting substances
▸ Waste management
▸ Water management

Glossary
Brief explanations of terms used in our sustainability reporting

▸ Glossary

complete transparency is unprecedented, with its 2004 report containing a complete list of Nike suppliers that also was made available online.

Nike executives took CR reporting completely digital with the 2006 report, which was the first to be released in a digital-only format. According to Erin Dobson, Nike's director for corporate responsibility communications:

> *For the first time, we released our report only in a digital format. As we move closer to building a dialogue with our consumer rather than just a stakeholder audience, we must increasingly rely on digital as the primary form of communication. This requires that we build a unique model of communicating Nike's CR initiatives in a form that the majority of our consumers get their information.*[21]

Coca-Cola

Because of the brand's enormous reach, addressing every aspect of CR and sustainability applied to its business would be impossible. This is why the company surveys stakeholders to find out what they are most concerned about and then hones in on those topics in its CR and sustainability report. The CR/sustainability portion of its Web site breaks down information by region, company, bottling partners, and environment. Stakeholders even can get a snapshot of the report's contents by clicking to see operating group highlights (see Figure 7.5).

In addition to making online sustainability reports interactive, it's also essential to investors that you define the organization's goals and then measure success in meeting them. Interactive scorecards are effective ways of communicating this information because they position tracked data against performance. BHP Billiton's scorecard illustrates the company's performance in terms of health, safety, environment, and community targets. The fact that the results openly state that some targets were not achieved also indicates the company's commitment to transparent reporting (see Figure 7.6).

Finally, executives now must consider incorporating another aspect of reporting into their CR/sustainability communications with investors—materiality. Materiality is a concept adapted from financial accounting.

Figure 7.5: Coca-Cola sustainability Web site

Figure 7.6: BHP Billiton's target scorecard

HSEC Targets Scorecard

(Baseline 1 July 2001 to 30 June 2002 for reduction targets except where stated otherwise)

Overall performance against target:

■	Target exceeded or ahead of schedule
■	Target achieved (≥ 95%) or on track
■	Target behind schedule
■	Target not achieved

Performance change since last reporting period:

▷	Performance tracking steadily
◭	Performance has improved
▽	Performance has declined

Zero Harm		**2004/05**
Zero fatalities	■	Three fatalities in controlled activities[1] (FY04:17)
Zero significant environmental incidents (i.e. rated 3 and above on the BHP Billiton Consequence Severity Table)	■	Three Level 3 environmental incidents (FY04: 2)
No transgressions within the Group's activities of the principles embodied within the UN Universal Declaration of Human Rights	■	None identified (FY04: none)
Legal Compliance Zero fines and prosecutions[2]	■	Seven fines greater than US$1000. Total fines paid US$20 836 (FY04: US$209 420)

Management Systems		**2004/05**
All sites to undertake annual self-assessments against the BHP Billiton HSEC Management Standards and have plans to achieve conformance with the Standards by 30 June 2005	▷	100 per cent of required self assessments were completed at operating sites (FY04: 100 per cent)
	◭	An overall conformance of 3.9 out of 5 has been achieved, compared to our conformance target of greater than 4 (FY04: 3.7 out of 5)
All sites[3] to maintain ISO 14001 Certification	▷	All sites requiring ISO 14001 are certified or have been recommended for certification by their ISO auditor
Risk Management Risk registers to be in place and maintained at all sites[3] and within BHP Billiton businesses and Corporate offices	▷	Risk registers are in place and maintained at all required sites, businesses and Corporate offices

Figure 7.7: Ford's materiality matrix *(www.ford.com/ aboutford/microsites/sustainability-report-2006-07/impacts MaterialityMatrix.htm; downloaded November 17, 2008)*

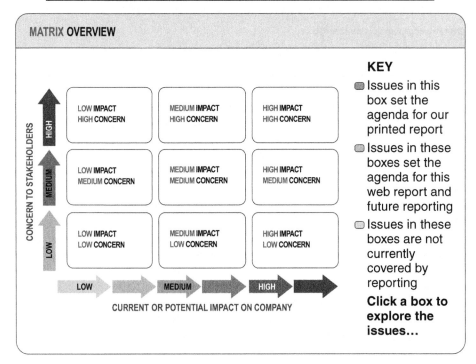

Ford defines *materiality* as "that which is of greatest interest to, and that which has the potential to affect the perception of, those stakeholders who wish to make informed decisions and judgments about the company's commitment to environmental, social and economic progress."[22]

Digital platforms are especially ideal for materiality analyses because they enable investors—or any stakeholder, for that matter—to interact with the information. Many companies, including Ford and Starbucks, present their materiality analyses in the form of a matrix, with one axis representing concern to stakeholders and the other representing current or potential impact on the company (see Figure 7.7).

Minding Your Own Business: NGOs and Nonprofits Become Web Watchdogs

CR/sustainable business has long gone hand-in-hand with NGOs and nonprofits, and understandably so. After all, the latter two categories exist (in theory) not to profit, but to promote causes that benefit various publics. The history of NGOs spans more than 100 years, over which time they have played critical roles in everything from the antislavery movement to women's suffrage. Increased globalization in the twentieth and twenty-first centuries boosted the importance of NGOs, and today they enjoy a prominent role on the global business stage. Thanks to the interconnectivity facilitated by digital technologies, the influence of NGOs over corporations has grown substantially, as has the number of NGOs in consultative status with the United Nations Economic and Social Council (these organizations qualify to serve as experts, advisers, and consultants to governments and the secretariat).[23]

To manage this increased scrutiny and pressure from NGOs and nonprofits, many companies forge partnerships with organizations whose supported causes align with their own. There are a number of benefits to this strategy: Support from a third party lends credibility to CR initiatives, having allies in the nonprofit sector enhances corporate reputation, participating with NGOs often results in positive media coverage, and corporate partnerships provide ways for a company's stakeholders to participate in and support good causes.

Digital channels aren't just a means for NGOs to strengthen their influence over companies; they are also a vehicle for connecting companies, causes, NGOs, and stakeholders to achieve the ultimate participatory environment. Take the Global Fund. This organization was created as a foundation to help finance the fight against AIDS, tuberculosis, and malaria in Africa. It's a unique example of a public-private partnership because it is one fiber of a complex web of companies and organizations, all of whom contribute to the cause in different ways. Established in January 2002, the Global Fund enjoys the support of (RED), an innovative business model created by Bobby Shriver and U2 front man Bono to raise awareness of and money for the foundation. (RED) teams up with corporate brands to create (PRODUCT)[RED]-branded products specific to each individual corporate partner's industry, the proceeds from which go to the Global Fund. For example, the Gap sells a (PRODUCT)[RED] clothing line, Motorola created special (PRODUCT)[RED] editions of three mobile phones, American Express offers a RED Card, and Starbucks announced a 2008 holiday (PRODUCT)[RED] promotion, in which 5 cents of every holiday beverage purchased went to the Global Fund (interestingly, Starbucks' *mystarbucksidea.com* "crowdsourcing" platform discussed earlier hosted comments from some users who didn't support the partnership).

The brand marketing/CR juggernaut created by the collaboration among the Global Fund, (RED), and partner companies is a complex network of participants who can only be brought together via digital means. Indeed, the cause has an active presence on Facebook, with approximately 100,000 fans and frequent news updates, video messages from the likes of Bono, (PRODUCT)^{RED} images, and links to (RED) partner sites. (RED)'s own Web site (*www.joinred.com*) is an interactive platform in its own right, with relevant online videos, product updates, photos, and links to its other social media properties, including a Flickr account, a presence on AOL Instant Messenger, and a MySpace page. All told, the massive effort fuses charity, marketing, branding, and a strategic business model to united multiple stakeholder groups around a good cause.

Leveraging digital platforms to forge positive relationships with NGOs and nonprofits is advantageous, but the alternative—not engaging these organizations at all—can have extremely detrimental effects on companies' reputations and bottom lines. Crises borne out of NGO pressures and raised to prominence via attention online will be discussed in more detail in Chapter 9. For now, suffice it to say that CR efforts always should be executed with the interests of NGO/nonprofits in mind because that can bolster the credibility of such efforts online and offline. Those who choose to conduct business in a bubble do so at their own risk.

Conclusion

Large corporations rarely enjoy a unanimously positive persona of being honest and trustworthy do-gooders—at least as far as the general public is concerned. This reality has reached critical mass in recent years, with trust in business down, public scrutiny up, and scandals rattling companies in industries across the board. Combine this with a sharply honed focus on corporate responsibility and sustainable business, and corporate leaders in all sectors find themselves under pressure from every stakeholder group to make positive contributions to people and the planet—whether or not those contributions are actually profitable for the business.

A growing mountain of research indicates that in addition to being more aware of CR initiatives and to passing judgments based on brands' commitment to good causes, stakeholders turn to the Web more and more frequently to research companies' green activities, be they social, environmental, or governance-related. This has upped the ante for business executives, who now must integrate messaging around legitimate CR efforts into communications with all stakeholders. The business benefits for doing so are immeasurable; the risks of not doing so, on the other hand, could very well be toxic.

CHAPTER 8

A PUBLIC AFFAIR
THE DIGITAL DIMENSION
OF GOVERNMENT RELATIONS

In the wake of the longest presidential campaign in U.S. history—21 months—and the subsequent election of the first African-American President of the United States, the country's political landscape finds itself in the midst of as rapid and drastic an evolution as that experienced by business in recent years. Made even more complex by a heightened regulatory environment, a jump in globalization-inspired cross-border mergers and acquisitions, and the public's often-disparaging perception of government, public affairs and government relations have skyrocketed in importance to both corporations and their stakeholders. These business functions traditionally were relegated to organizations within strictly regulated industries in which lobbying—or at least a relationship with Capitol Hill staffers—was critical to success.

Now, as business and politics become increasingly intertwined, corporate leaders must reconcile a complex challenge: Digital communications empowers stakeholders, mandates transparency, and democratizes access to information, yet politics and government affairs always operated—or at least tried to—under tables, behind closed doors, or at the very least, in highly guarded inner circles that were almost impossible to penetrate.

Unlike the functions described in previous chapters, where embracing and implementing digital communications platforms precipitated from the need to conform to the shifting business environment, government relations and public affairs executives have many masters; therefore, they require a nuanced communications approach that has often prompted many to fall back on tried and tested playbooks. That said, some digital trailblazers in the public arena have found success in harnessing the power of the Internet for governmental relations and, most important, for political campaign organizations.

This chapter explores the nascent digital landscape of government relations, which, by definition, includes the monitoring and analysis of local, state, and federal government policies and legislation. It identifies the hurdles hindering adoption of digital communications strategies by businesses and individuals serving public and private interests, from lobbyists and legislators to advocacy groups and nongovernmental organizations (NGOs). It frames a discussion of public affairs, better known as *lobbying*, in the context of the current political and business environment, drawing connections between the political climate in Washington and its effect on organizations worldwide (namely, in the form of collaborative global business networks), offering strategies for engaging in public affairs projects, and integrating Web 2.0 technologies into these efforts.

Politics Gets a Makeover: Turning Campaigns into Dynamic—and Digital—Brands

The corporate world often deals with established or burgeoning brands by building on successes and minimizing failures. In the Web 2.0 world, doing so requires digital communications platforms and depends on the constant conversations they facilitate. These outlets also have had an immense effect on the inner workings of government relations and public affairs because both necessitate ongoing engagement and the constant monitoring of audiences' conversations online. At the same time, both have been profoundly affected because nearly half of all Americans now get their news from online sources.[1]

Never has this been more important—or more obvious—than during the 2008 U.S. presidential election cycle, where personal and political brands were created and sustained online through continued social engagement. Barack Obama brought digital communications' influence over politics to life over the course of his successful 2008 presidential bid, in which "Obamania" encompassed more than a politician, a political platform, or a traditional campaign strategy—largely thanks to the help of social networking, a Facebook staffer, and a historic digital communications effort unlike any presidential election campaign in the history of the United States.

Author and *New York Times* business columnist David Carr, who also served as a volunteer for the Obama campaign, performed a case-study analysis of the digital strategies employed by the Democratic candidate's camp that significantly shaped the candidate's overall campaign strategy and organizational structure and, in turn, are credited with helping to lead him to his eventual victory.[2] Take-aways from Carr's report, which are summarized below, have major implications for the government relations and public affairs functions within corporations, the effects of which will be discussed later in this chapter. For now, though, consider Carr's digital advice, gleaned from analysis of Obama's storied campaign for the White House[3]:

1. *Keep your digital strategy simple, stupid.* Do not customize and complicate. Create online platforms that enable users to engage with the content. Obama's campaign team launched *my.barackobama.com* ("MyBO") in February 2007, which operated as a social networking site in that it fostered interaction among supporters. Better yet, communicators can use existing platforms such as Facebook (as Obama's camp did with "A Million Strong for Obama"), MySpace, Twitter, MeetUp, or LinkedIn to manage volunteers who, at the core, are a highly decentralized organization. This streamlines communications efficiently and effectively by having built-in applications for blogs, wall posts, group meetings, e-mail, and virtual events. These media create a community where organizational activities are monitored and individuals are able to see results while having both direct and indirect communications with campaign officials.

2. *Hire digital community experts.* Nothing says you're serious like hiring people who know their way around the digital jungle, including the modern-day architects themselves. Obama's campaign hired Chris Hughes, Facebook CEO Mark Zuckerberg's Harvard roommate and one of the original founding members of the online phenomenon. Hughes' ability to craft an online community for the campaign was an essential element of the blueprint for how the Obama campaign would maintain volunteer communications,

coordinate voter outreach and get-out-the-vote (GOTV) efforts, and engage organizers and enthusiasts in the final days leading up to the election via text messaging and sophisticated social media networks.

3. *Grant autonomy and decentralize.* The decentralization of a political campaign is anathema to a traditional campaign strategies' top-down approach. However, by taking the path less traveled, Obama's team established different levels of volunteer membership based on an individual's contribution (both monetary and in terms of donated time); depending on the membership level, volunteers would be granted additional access (e.g., receiving news/announcements via text messages) or receive campaign paraphernalia (e.g., buttons, bumper stickers, etc.). In the same way that consumer-generated efforts embraced by companies give stakeholders a sense of ownership, this approach positioned volunteers as stakeholders in the campaign; in addition, the digital infrastructure organized and connected volunteers in all geographic regions. This unprecedented digital communications effort and decentralized organizational structure gave campaign brass access to critical messaging, as well as feedback that was critical to staying current on changing political winds and crafting messaging and responses almost instantaneously. This approach allowed digital community members to have ownership in their participation over the course of the campaign while also giving them autonomy over their level of engagement and participation.

4. *Use scale of digital conveniences.* The scale of the Internet at first glance may seem overwhelming, but using the conveniences it provides with digital know-how and technology can lead to greater productivity and outreach than were formerly imaginable for any one individual. The Obama camp, for example, used digital technology in its phone bank outreach, keeping volunteers out of dingy basements of local catering halls, community centers, and empty office buildings and instead allowing them to make GOTV calls from the comfort of their own homes. With an Internet connection and a simple software program, volunteers were able to download scripts and call lists. The software's interactive abilities made life even simpler for volunteers by providing scripts that changed based on caller response, putting irritated or rushed individuals at ease and possibly more apt to be engaged.

This isn't to say that with every step forward, there are not stumbles. Obama's database of contacts crashed during the primary's Super Tuesday GOTV effort owing to volunteers entering junk data or Internet connections being too slow to keep pace with calls. Ultimately, the problem was solved quickly, thanks to the online database's "print" function, which gave volunteers access to the lists of phone numbers and scripts. All in all, the digital scale of such a feat, while far from perfect in execution, offers a compelling glimpse into the future role of volunteers' voter outreach efforts and capabilities.

Connecting the Dots: Digital Platforms Bridge Politicos and Their Publics

While 2008 was a historic year in politics, especially in the context of the presidential election, it signaled another shifting paradigm in how people consume information regarding political issues and candidates through digital distribution channels For starters, a research study of millennials conducted by Resource Interactive during the 2008 presidential election revealed that while television remained the dominant medium for building a candidate's public awareness, Web 2.0 channels ranked as high as, if not higher than, television as sources of credible information on a candidate and his or her platforms.[4] In March 2008, a *Fast Company* cover story entitled, "The Brand Called Obama," gave more credence to the effectiveness of digital strategies in spreading political messages, touting Obama's Web campaign efforts as key to his brand-building successes.[5] The article also cited Resource Interactive's OPEN (on-demand, personal, engaging, and networked) plan, providing the following framework for building brands online that applies to any type of organization:

- *On demand.* Have a digital platform that can be customized and is accessible to all Internet users and applications, from search engines and social media sites to e-mail and blogs.
- *Personal.* Craft issue-specific messaging that directly addresses your audience's wants and needs, engages them in a dialogue, and can be adapted to any changes and feedback instantly.
- *Engaging.* Connect with your audience members though live and in-person events that surround and reinforce the brand's message; at the same time, empower audiences to organize and contribute to increasing the brand's reach and scope.

- *Networked.* Gather and retain the audience through continued engagement via multiple digital platforms and media.

Continuing with the Obama campaign case study, the Obama team's unprecedented use of text messaging to personally engage and continually connect with supporters mirrors the OPEN framework for successful brand building. Supporters who opted in via the campaign's Web site received exclusive messages, including the announcement of Senator Joe Biden as Obama's vice presidential running mate to supporters, GOTV reminders, and an election night victory proclamation. This vehicle gave Obama team leaders an instant connection to individual voters, who, in turn, felt a personal tie to the campaign.

This isn't to say that everything went according to plan. The campaign's idea to break the news to supporters that Biden would be Obama's running mate first via text was scooped by the traditional media folks through—what else—a leak. The team had to improvise, sending the text announcement out as quickly as possible. The only problem: Cell phones around the United States rang in unison at 3 a.m. Regardless of the unexpected blip, the approach still marked an undertaking of unprecedented scale, developing sophisticated databases of supporters' contact information for many months in preparation for executing this form of outreach. When it came time to vote, the mobile messaging strategy delivered big time. Text messages reminded registrants to vote and even provided a link to help them find the nearest polling station and, if necessary, to find a ride.

Digitizing for Dollars: Web Platforms Pump up the Volume and Deliver Measurable Results

Fund-raising efforts and outreach are the lifeblood of all political campaigns, and those executed by the Obama camp were unparalleled. Unlike candidates before him, Obama decided to forgo the $85 million in public financing, much to the chagrin of opponent John McCain, who opted for the public financing dollars and, in turn, all the limitations that came along with them.[6] Obama's donations, on the other hand, were largely delivered via digital assets from a total 1.7 million people, of whom about 630,000 were first-time givers.[7] By October 2008, MyBO had 1.5 million registered users and organized more than 150,000 volunteer events.[8] In sum, the Obama campaign had recorded contributions from over 3.1 million individuals—more than twice the number that contributed to George W. Bush's reelection effort in 2004—totaling roughly $600 million, with nearly two-thirds coming from online communities such as MyBO[9] (see Figure 8.1).

Blue State Digital, a market research–news media hybrid company and the same firm behind Obama's phone-banking-from-home effort (see Carr's case study above), also helped build "Obamamania"—the name of the cyber campaign launched from social network sites that played an integral role in boosting the campaign's bottom line.

Having been founded in 2004 by four former members of Howard Dean's failed presidential campaign team, Blue State Digital is by no means new to the political scene. Its mission: To help candidates raise money online. For Candidate Obama, that translated to mission accomplished.

Obama's presidential campaign rival John McCain wasn't without a digital strategy of his own. However, it was, by all counts, too little, too

Figure 8.1: *My.barackobama.com*

late. McCain lagged in both the polls and digital media platforms, having failed to embrace the Web 2.0 culture to engage voters and secure votes. In February 2008, the McCain campaign launched an online community tagged "McCainSpace," almost a year to the day *after* Obama's MyOB digital community had launched.[10] In June 2008, McCainSpace tapped Michael Goldfarb, a blogger for the conservative opinion publication *The Weekly Standard*, to blog regularly on McCain's site.[11] But the McCainSpace site was slow getting out of the gate owing to technical "glitches,"[12] requiring a makeover and relaunch in August— less than three months before Election Day.[13]

The Web metrics were grim, indicating that Web 2.0 was indeed a strong election indicator. According to Web traffic tracking site Hitwise, Obama pulled 67 percent of all traffic to presidential candidate Web sites compared with McCain's 32 percent.[14] Further, an October 21, 2008, snapshot from TechPresident, a site that logs digital election stats, showed Obama tallying more than 84 million YouTube views of his videos—more than four times McCain's 22 million views.[15]

The numbers across all social media and Web 2.0 properties followed the trend. In the six months prior to the election, more than 13,000 MeetUp members used the site's distribution channels to aggregate volunteers and organize live offsite Obama events, whereas the McCain camp tallied a mere 1,472 members on the same platform.[16] According to blogosphere tracker Technorati, in the week ending October 22, 2008, Obama was mentioned 10,291 times in blogs compared with McCain's 3,924 mentions during the same time period.[17]

Video Killed the Radio Star: From Fireside Chats to Viral Videos

Often Web 2.0 campaigns become overnight successes by accident thanks to the unexpected interests of infinite audiences online. Viral videos offer some of the best examples of how little risk can reap huge rewards for a company, brand, or candidate (see Chapter 3 for more on viral marketing).

Election-year politics appeared to catch the viral video bug, too. The Obama campaign used video as one of many digital communications channels; on the flipside, many of his voters followed his lead to vocalize their support via online platforms. Case in point: "I Got a Crush . . . on Obama," a music video performed by the self-proclaimed "Obama

Girl" (born Amber Lee Ettinger) and cowritten/produced by independent music producer Rick Friedrich and advertising executive Ben Relles, was shot over the course of six hours throughout New York City.[18] On June 13, 2007, the video, showing a scantily clad Ettinger seductively singing her love for then Illinois Senator Barack Obama, was posted on YouTube and garnered more than a 1,000 views within the first five hours.[19] By the next day, word of the video spread to traditional media, and it would go on to be nominated in the politics category of the 2007 YouTube Awards.[20]

"Obama Girl" sparked an interest in the Obama campaign that never seemed to lose momentum. Ettinger herself made appearances at the Democratic National Convention, held August 25–28, 2008, in Denver, Colorado, dressed in her signature sexy-superhero regalia. Obama's camp denied any involvement in the making or dissemination of the video, and Kauffman and Ettinger confirmed the statement, explaining that the video was made more for fun than to support Obama's presidential race.[21]

Of course, Obama couldn't go without acknowledging the viral video phenomenon. "It's just one more example of the fertile imagination of the Internet," he said. "More stuff like this will be popping up all the time."[22]

Obama's remark proved to be prescient. Just week's after his winning the election bid, Obama's transition team announced plans to tape a weekly address not just for radio listeners, as presidents have for years, but for Web viewers, too. Nearly 75 years after President Franklin D. Roosevelt introduced fireside chats during the Great Depression,[23] President Obama made YouTube his medium of choice for reaching the masses during the greatest economic recession of the new century.

The four-minute videos were posted on *www.change.gov* on Saturdays during Obama's transition to office. The trend continued into his presidency; when Obama took office in January 2009, the video addresses were transferred to the White House's proverbial corporate Web site (*www.whitehouse.gov*)—the same place President Bush had released podcasts of his weekly radio address.

The presidential weekly Web video series wasn't a one-man show. Obama's cabinet members and other government officials were offered supporting cast roles, thus joining the Web 2.0 world by appearing in choice video segments and making the office of the President the most digitally connected to its constituency in the nation's history.

Transition of Power: Government Affairs and Lobbying go from the Beltway to the Information Superhighway

So far this chapter has detailed the modern political machine's increasing use of digital channels to reach and influence constituents through a case study of the 2008 presidential campaign and election. But there are other key components of the political realm that have major business implications in today's environment: public affairs, government relations, and lobbying (see the following sidebar for definitions of terms).

WHAT'S IN A NAME?

Government relations. Includes the monitoring and analysis of local, state, and federal government policies and legislation on matters of corporate concern working in conjunction with external corporate communications efforts. Government relations (GR) staff and committees typically provide information to various legislative bodies at all levels of government regarding selected legislative initiatives and assist in the development of legislative priorities each year through lobbying and education. GR staff also communicates official policy position holders on specific issues to members and encourages and facilitates advocacy on those issues.

Public affairs. The body of principles that underpin the operation of legal systems in each state. This addresses the social, moral, and economic values that tie a society together: values that vary in different cultures and change over time. Law regulates behavior either to reinforce existing social expectations or to encourage constructive change, and laws are most likely to be effective when they are consistent with the most generally accepted societal norms and reflect the collective morality of society.

Lobbying. The practice of influencing decisions made by government. It includes all attempts to influence legislators and officials, whether by other legislators, constituents, or organized groups. Governments often define and regulate organized group lobbying. Many jurisdictions, in response to concerns about corruption, require the formal registration of lobbyists who come in contact with government representatives. Since 1995, under the federal Lobbying Disclosure Act (2 U.S.C. §1601–1612), most persons who are paid to make direct "lobbying contacts" with members of Congress and officials of the federal executive branch are required to register and file reports twice a year. If lobbyists neglect to register, they are susceptible to criminal charges and harsh penalties.

In fact, the Obama case study bridges politics and government relations/lobbying as demonstratively as it illustrates campaigning opportunities presented by digital communications. Almost immediately after Obama became President-elect, lobbyists scrambled to get insight into his 2009 plans. What's more, his transition team members' connection to various influential lobbying firms emerged—this after he campaigned on a platform promising to end the influence of lobbyists in the executive branch.

To operate within this promise, Obama did impose rules barring transition team officials from working on any policy issues that team members had lobbied on during the previous year and from seeking to influence any of the same agencies during the 12 months following his transition into office. For example, Henry Rivera, a former Democratic commissioner with the Federal Communication Commission (FCC), was originally slated to help plan for that agency's transition, but he was removed from that platform because he had represented clients on communications policy issues during the previous year. Instead, Rivera was placed on the team handling science, technology, space, and the arts because Obama's policy did permit people who have lobbied in one area to join the transition team in another area.[24]

As for bridging politics and lobbying with business, think of it like this: Just as politicians and lobbyists try to reach and influence constituents, businesses do the same with their stakeholders. Combine this with the public's relative distrust of both institutions, and the two practically become mirror images of each other. Now, thanks to all the changes in the political and business areas, public affairs and government relations are becoming more prominent and influential stakeholder groups for corporations.

Getting in on the Ground Floor: Lobbying Emerges to Link Business and Government

A brief explanation of how lobbying, government relations, and public affairs came to play such a prominent role in modern business helps to put these functions' roles within organizations into context. Over time, the ebb and flow of business and government relations has tended to follow two trends: political issues of the day and the economy. While the latter often was a bigger driver than the former, both have been integral to understanding how the conversation between private industries and their government regulator and lawmaker counterparts has evolved (for a timeline on regulations introduced by the government, see the following sidebar).

AN ABBREVIATED HISTORY OF GOVERNMENT RELATIONS

- *Act to Regulate Commerce, 1887.* Established the Interstate Commerce Commission, which was ultimately abolished in 1995.
- *Sherman Antitrust Act, 1890.* Established a legal framework to prevent trusts from restricting trade and reducing competition; remains the main source of antitrust law in the United States.
- *Clayton Antitrust Act, 1914.* Established the Federal Trade Commission (FTC) to promote consumer protection and to eliminate and prevent anti-competitive business practices, such as coercive monopoly.
- *Securities Exchange Act, 1934.* Established the U.S. Securities and Exchange Commission (SEC) to enforce federal securities laws and to regulate the securities industry and stock-option exchanges.
- *Regulation Fair Disclosure, 2000.* Implemented by the SEC to require all publicly traded companies to disclose material information to all investors at the same time, thus fundamentally changing the way companies communicated with their investors by mandating transparency.
- *Sarbanes-Oxley Act, 2002.* Established new and enhanced standards for all U.S. public companies and accounting firms in reaction to a number of corporate scandals, including Enron, Tyco International, and WorldCom.

Historically, business has always fought regulation and government intervention because of the costs associated with implementing often cumbersome or redundant new safeguards and regulatory procedures.

However, over the course of nearly a century of big brother's oversight and intervention into business—which, in turn, raised costs—corporations in the late 1960s and early 1970s started putting their money where their mouths are to make sure that their executive voices were heard from Wall Street to Capitol Hill.[25] Thus the practice of lobbying emerged as a crucial link between the worlds of business and government. By targeting key influential legislators to advocate their positions and protect their interests, corporations were able to continually be a part of the conversation, monitoring government relations among lawmakers, constituents, and regulators.

Because of this, corporations are now key influencers on the political stage. Recent statistics show how much money is flowing into lobbying efforts (see Tables 8.1 and 8.2), with nearly 40 percent of the Fortune 500 companies registered to lobby.[26] Virtually all the top 200 Fortune 500 companies are politically active.[27] More staggering was a study of 565 of Fortune 100 companies published in the *American Political Science Review* in December 2000 that revealed that 72.6 percent engage in some form of measurable political interaction with the federal government, 56.4 percent of domestic Fortune 500 firms engage in lobbying activities, and 54.6 percent have political action committees (PACs), which are committees formed by business, labor, or other

Table 8.1: Lobbying by the Dollars

Total Lobbying Spending	
1998	$1.45 Billion
1999	$1.44 Billion
2000	$1.54 Billion
2001	$1.63 Billion
2002	$1.81 Billion
2003	$2.04 Billion
2004	$2.17 Billion
2005	$2.41 Billion
2006	$2.60 Billion
2007	$2.82 Billion
2008	$1.97 Billion

Source: Center for Responsive Politics.

Table 8.2: Lobbying by the Numbers

Number of Lobbyists	
1998	10,693
1999	13,444
2000	12,760
2001	12,078
2002	12,347
2003	13,171
2004	13,418
2005	14,508
2006	15,249
2007	15,498
2008	15,966

Source: Center for Responsive Politics.

special-interest groups to raise money and make contributions to the campaigns of political candidates whom they support.[28]

Corporate Communications and Public Affairs in the Twenty-first Century: Making the Marriage Work in the Digital Age

To enhance their reputations, many corporations partner with government organizations to launch public affairs initiatives, thus requiring the corporate communication function to have an understanding of this function. The two pillars to organizing an effective lobbying effort are influential management and strategic planning. First and foremost, though, is an adequate infrastructure. Any company should know that the key to success is its organization (effective and efficient use of resources) and talent, coupled with the abilities to maneuver the proverbial minefield, build relationships with the key influencers, and close deals. Second is the process of developing a lobbying strategy—where to gain support and minimize opposition. Corporate executives should consider the following elements when developing a lobbying plan: people, cost and benefits, timing, place, campaign contributions, communication with the media, avoiding unnecessary conflicts, and maintaining confidentiality.

The American automotive industry came bumper to bumper with lobbying's critical role in the modern business environment in 2008, when the economic collapse crushed the country's top three automakers, General Motors, Ford, and Chrysler. The CEOs of all three auto behemoths—Rick Wagoner, Alan Mulally, and Robert Nardelli, respectively—made their way from Detroit to Washington in November 2008 to try to convince lawmakers to approve a bailout plan that would inject billions of dollars in federal aid into the ailing industry. As the companies' cash reserves dwindled quickly, Democratic and Republican leaders butted heads over granting automakers emergency bailout, with the former largely arguing in favor and the latter starkly opposed. Those in opposition to granting the aid argued on a number of platforms. Some said that the companies' leadership teams made their own beds, having managed their organizations poorly for years; others said that placing additional tax burdens on Americans who were already reeling from the economic collapse just to save the corporations was unfair, if not unethical; and still others argued that the automakers were hypocritical on their environmental positioning.

Supporters, on the other hand—and the automakers' CEOs themselves—argued that allowing the U.S. auto industry to go under would have a catastrophic ripple effect on the country's economy, wiping out hundreds of thousands of jobs. In the widespread media coverage of this Capitol Hill showdown, General Motors (GM) bore the brunt of the weight, having already been lobbying (read begging) the federal government to upend its otherwise inevitable demise. Traditional lobbying efforts certainly played the biggest role in the former America industry crown jewel's negotiation strategy, but digital communications proved to carry their weight as well. The company launched and maintained "GM Facts and Fiction" (*www.gmfactsandfiction.com*), a Web site in which "GM tells it like it is" by providing an array of information about the auto industry crisis and its potential effects on every American (see Figure 8.2). The site urged visitors to mobilize by writing their congresspersons in support of the bailout, allowed people to "get the word out" by e-mailing friends, and linked to coverage of the ongoing discussion on GM blogs.

Then, on November 17, 2008, GM executives posted a doom-and-gloom video on the Web site, as well as YouTube, that used scare tactics to inform the public about how the U.S. economy would be devastated by the company's collapse. The video's message was compelling, and it had a clear aim of influencing lobbyists, lawmakers, and the general public to support the proposed buy-out plan. The video shocked viewers with this ominous prediction: "What happens if the domestic auto industry collapses? In economic terms, the rapid termination of Detroit

Figure 8.2: "GM Facts and Fiction" Web site

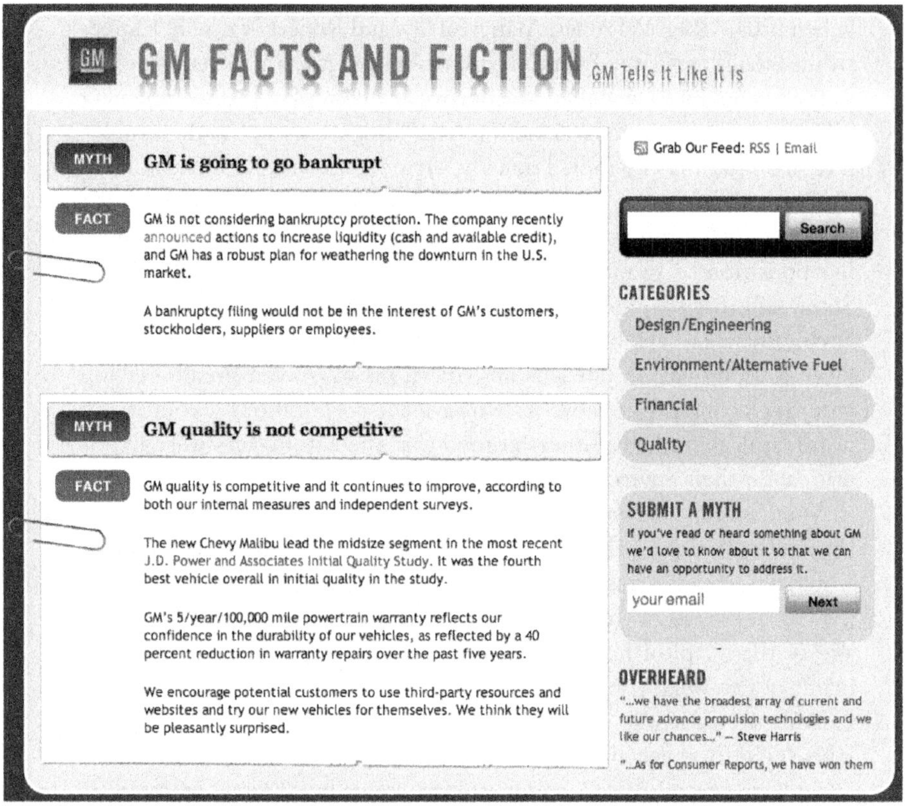

Three U.S. operations in 2009 would reduce U.S. personal income by over $150.7 billion in the first year. ..."

The use of online video got the attention of digital and traditional media alike, and conversations bubbled up on cyberplatforms such as Twitter and blogs. But GM execs may have misjudged the public's reaction to the video. Within a few days of being posted, it had garnered more than 200,000 views, but its rating was a sad two of six stars, and many viewers posted negative commentary. According to Owen Thomas, managing editor of tech gossip blog "Valleywag" (*www.valleywag.com*):

General Motors has posted its call for an auto-industry bailout directly to the Net, with predictably disastrous results. GM marketers have clearly fallen for the myth of Internet PR—that taking a company's message directly to the people through social media will give it a much friendlier reception than if it is filtered through the mainstream media. The reality? Slapping an infomercial on YouTube will generate far worse publicity than talking to friendly Detroit-based hacks on the automotive beat, who are every bit as dependent on the U.S. car industry for their paycheck as assembly-line workers are. ... The only upside for Detroit's message-makers: The instant YouTube reaction allows them to take their PR campaign back to the shop all the sooner.[29]

Regardless of the reaction—and the fact that analysts still gave the bailout proposal a less than favorable chance at succeeding—GM's video was just one more feather in the cap of digital communications, proving that Web 2.0 is no longer reserved for sexy brands, futuristic marketers, and tech-literate C-suites; it's a powerful tool that places influence in the hands of anyone who knows how to use it.

From Smoke-Filled Rooms to the World Wide Web: The Digital Age Descends on Washington

With the exponential growth of lobbying efforts from businesses, advocacy groups, and trade associations, pressure has never been greater on legislators in Washington and the statehouses. The explosive growth in lobbying has led to a boom in government relations positions and departments at the largest corporations—a development that has only been accelerated by the economic crisis, as evidenced by the automakers' life dependency on lobbyists' backing. The savviest companies have merged business strategies and techniques with lobbying efforts to create marketing campaigns around issues, both positive and negative.

The GM example highlighted in the preceding section is a good illustration of a company that probably leaned on lobbyists too little too late but that tried to regain ground by taking advantage of the ability of digital platforms to take messages to the masses. Microsoft, on the other hand, is a good example of a corporation that dominates lobbying the tech space and that does so in contrast to its competitors' comparatively measly efforts—a lesson competitors learned the hard way when they crossed paths with Microsoft in 2008.

With one of the largest lobbying platforms of all its Silicon Valley peers, the company spent nearly $9 million on lobbying in 2007 alone, according to statistics compiled by the Center for Responsive Politics.[30] Perhaps it learned its lesson after the disastrous public and economic fallout from the 1998 antitrust case brought against Microsoft by the Department of Justice and 20 states. This case developed out of an initial 1991 inquiry by the FTC that accused Microsoft of monopolistic behavior by bundling its Internet Explorer Web browser software with its Microsoft Windows operating system platform.[31] The case eventually settled on November 2, 2001, with Microsoft agreeing to share its application programming interfaces with third-party companies and to appoint a panel of three people who have full access to Microsoft's systems, records, and source code for five years to ensure compliance.[32]

But even with Microsoft's enhanced attention to lobbying, its contributions are minimal in comparison with many other corporate behemoths; in fact, the tech industry as a whole continues to lag in its lobbying efforts. Take Google. The world's leading search engine spent a mere $1.5 million in 2007; granted, that was 90 percent more than its $800,000 spent in 2006.[33]

Then there's Apple, a Wall Street darling, thanks to its ubiquitous iPod and iPhone platforms, which also trimmed its 2007 lobbying expenditure from $1.1 million to $720,000 while continuing to fend off challenges from the music industry and tech competitors, both of which have unleashed a barrage of monopolistic charges and complaints.[34] And Yahoo!, the top Google rival and target of a hostile takeover bid from Microsoft in early 2008, spent a mere $1.6 million in 2007, an almost 30 percent decline from 2006, while enlisting the same hired guns that have done work for Microsoft—that is, lobbyists Covington & Burling (for more on the Yahoo!-Microsoft deal that soured, see the next section).[35]

2 + 2 = 5? Understanding the Math Behind the Business Lobbying Equation

Even though Microsoft, Google, Yahoo!, and Apple are among the corporations driving the digital communications revolution, they are anathema to almost every other major industry doing business in the United States when it comes to government relations. These tech industry giants have a lot of ground to cover compared with other industries, such as health care, which is a major spender, having dropped $444.7 million on lobbying in 2007 alone.[36] According to *OpenSecrets.org*, organizations across all industries spent a total of $2.8 billion lobbying Congress in 2007, with 2008 figures expected to surpass the $3 billion mark.[37] That said, the total spend of all tech giants didn't crack the top 20 in Washington.

So, in the context of the current business environment, what's the lesson to be learned by the sharp contrasts in various industries' attention to lobbying? Given the past chapters' discussions about ways in which digital communications channels democratize access to information and, in turn, place corporate brands and reputations on the line, the implications once politics and government regulation enter the picture become all the more critical. After all, these stakeholder groups have a unique sphere of influence over companies' capabilities, processes, and abilities to control their profit margins.

This became all too clear for Google and Yahoo! in light of their still-unraveling advertising partnership flap. Announced in June 2008, the deal would allow Google to place paid sponsor ads alongside and embedded in select Yahoo! search results and vice versa.[38] When the companies initially came to the agreement, they predicted a new $800 million annual revenue opportunity to boost cash flow by nearly 45 percent to $450 million in the first 12 months of the deal.[39]

This opportunity for big profits notwithstanding, the deal also was considered to be a strategic move to derail Microsoft's attempted hostile takeover of Yahoo!; however, neither Yahoo! nor Google knew the hornets nest they were about to stir with such a public statement. Both companies thought that by offering Yahoo! and Google's ads at auction against one another, the deal would easily pass regulatory approval. But analysts and several major advertising agencies were skeptical that such a symbiotic relationship could really exist given Google's search technology dominance in the marketplace, not to mention its superior behavioral advertising embedded in its search platforms and products. "Yahoo is being a reseller of Google whenever it makes sense and that is likely to be a lot of the time given how much more effective Google Web search ads have proven to be," Global Crown Capital analyst Martin Pyykkonen said.[40]

Red flags were quickly raised by the burgeoning tech-savvy regulators at the Department of Justice (DOJ), too. The DOJ's scrutiny came on the heels of the advertising community's objection to the deal, which was based on fears that it ultimately would raise ad rates.[41] Within weeks, both Google and Yahoo! were announcing a delay to their deal to allow the DOJ to investigate possible antitrust violations. Both companies dismissed such a review with little fanfare, expressing little concern that the deal would be nixed. In a showing of brashness, both Yahoo! and Google stated that they would go ahead with the deal in early October whether or not the antitrust review was complete.[42]

Meanwhile, bloggers took note, constantly monitoring any public reference to the deal made by Google, Yahoo!, or Microsoft in the hope of reading tea leaves on the future of the big three search engines. The most vocal, of course, was Microsoft CEO Steve Ballmer, whose commentary popped up throughout the blogosphere.

As the volume of online conversations escalated, the DOJ showed no signs of taking a laid-back approach to the deal, having hired Sanford M. Litvack, a veteran antitrust lawyer, to help assess the evidence gathered by the department's own lawyers.[43] Yahoo! seemed more than willing to give into government regulators, whereas Google teetered on the brink of withdrawing from the deal. By the end of October 2008, Google was waving the proverbial white flag, saying that it would rather exit the deal than have government regulators dictate the agreement under antitrust terms.[44] Google officially called it quits a couple weeks later.

"After four months of review, including discussions of various possible changes to the agreement, it is clear that government regulators and some advertisers continue to have concerns about the agreement," said David Drummond, Google's chief legal officer, in a company blog post.

Why the sudden about-face? As it turns out, the cause was a combination of a botched lobbying effort, a group of farmers, and—what else?—the Internet. Google, it was discovered, had been humbled by the collective lobbying efforts of the National Association of Farmer Elected Committees and the National Latino Farmers and Ranchers Trade Association, which roused the DOJ from its slumber based on association members' concerns over how their Internet use would be affected.[45] It was a seemingly random claim with very little basis until another detail came to light: The farmers associations had hired The Raben Group—the same lobbying firm to which Microsoft had given $30,000 in the spring of 2008 when its efforts to purchase Yahoo! were rebuked by its shareholders and company executives.[46]

Microsoft's bold move to acquire Yahoo! for $47.5 billion in February 2008 had been a sign of the software giant's increased desire to compete head to head with Google and grab a bigger share of the online search market. Microsoft's mere 6.8 percent of total online ad revenue in 2007 was fourth behind Google (32.1 percent), Yahoo! (18.7 percent), and AOL (9.1 percent), respectively.[47] After over three months of back and forth negotiations between Microsoft CEO Steve Ballmer and Yahoo!'s Jerry Yang, an impasse resulted in a public embarrassment, leaving both companies battered and bruised in the eyes of investors.

But Microsoft was quick to bounce back. CEO Steve Ballmer, in an e-mail to employees that explained his decision to withdraw the offer, said that there was a strategy in place.[48] At the time, Microsoft's strategy appeared to be unclear. "It's not okay to say, 'We're going back to Plan A,'" said Charlie Di Bona, a securities analyst with Sanford C. Bernstein. "They need to say something that's credible and different. That's not Plan B, since they just gave up on Plan B. So what's Plan C?"[49]

Fast-forward to the very public announcement that Google would pull the plug on the Yahoo! ad auction deal, at which point blogs were blazing with speculation about when the next shoe was about to drop for Yahoo CEO Jerry Yang (it would apparently drop on November 18, when he announced his decision to resign from his post). As expected, Yang's enthusiasm over the now-defunct Google deal quickly shifted to a renewed courtship with "frienemy" Microsoft CEO Steve Ballmer, only to be publicly dumped on.

"We made an offer, we made another offer, . . . we moved on," Ballmer said. "We tried at one point to do a partnership around search . . . and that didn't work either, and we moved on and they moved on. We are not interested in going back and relooking at an acquisition. I don't know why they would be either, frankly."[50]

The economic landscape may have shifted from boom times to bust owing to the global economic crisis of 2008, but Microsoft remained tethered to its strategy, which appeared cryptic to investors at the time but became clearer when its aforementioned lobbying efforts aimed at breaking up the Yahoo!-Google ad deal came to light. After all, back when the Microsoft-Yahoo! deal collapsed, Ballmer made this statement: "Ultimately, our goal is to build the industry-leading business in search, online advertising, media and social networking. We are absolutely committed to being the leader in each of these areas."[51]

All this demonstrates how far Microsoft has come in maneuvering the political minefield compared with its search competitors. And while it's still too early to tell if Microsoft's lobbying lessons ultimately will pay off, the evidence is piling up in its favor. The economic crisis of 2008, combined with the demise of the Google-Yahoo! ad partnership, certainly tilted the balance in favor of Microsoft's ability to return to the table in a stronger position once again to make a play for Yahoo!—and soon to be knocking at Google's door to take back search ad revenue market share sooner rather than later.

Famous Last Words: "Change We can Believe in" Becomes the Mantra Heard 'Round the World

When the clock struck 12 noon on January 20, 2009, Barack Obama officially became the forty-fourth President of the United States of America. As quickly as power over the executive branch changed hands, so too did the digital face of one of government's most valuable digital properties: *www.whitehouse.gov*. At exactly 12:01 p.m. EST, the new version of the site went live, just as Obama was being sworn in by Supreme Court Chief Justice John Roberts, Jr. The revised platform, which boasted a large portrait of a smiling Obama alongside the words "Change Has Come to America," was just one more stop along Obama's ongoing journey toward the most digital presidency in the nation's history. Indeed, throughout Inauguration Day (as was the case in the days, weeks, and months leading up to and following Obama's election), the events taking place in Washington, DC, were both ceremoniously and unceremoniously followed on every digital platform imaginable, from streaming videos on news outlets' Web sites, to real-time updates on Twitter, to Flickr photo feeds.

Obama's "Change" platform, which was echoed loudly and constantly throughout the entire election process, continued into his first full day in office, during which time he instituted drastic changes that, he said, represented "a clean break from business as usual."[52]

Among the first policy changes Obama instituted were ones that demanded greater transparency and more disclosure from government and business alike. "Transparency and the rule of law will be the touchstones of this presidency," he said. "Starting today, every agency and department should know that this administration stands on the side not of those who seek to withhold information, but those who seek to make it known."[53] For someone who almost single-handedly redefined communications leading up to his inauguration by leveraging the power of connectivity made possible by Web platforms, this pledge gained even more credence.

Of course, only time will tell how much endurance Obama's initial call for transparency will have, but his earliest days in office spoke volumes. In the context of lobbying, outlined by the Microsoft-Yahoo!-Google example discussed earlier, the President ordered new rules of conduct that focused on accountability. His swift changes to the regulatory environment remained consistent with this notion as he demanded increased regulation to force businesses to operate more transparently.

This fresh stance ultimately would have a global appeal. In fact, according to PricewaterhouseCoopers' "Eleventh Annual Global CEO Survey," CEOs want governments to play a more prominent and proactive role on the international stage—both in promoting the convergence of global tax and regulatory frameworks and in leading efforts to address climate change.[54]

"It's understandable for businesses to evaluate regulations based on what's good for them. If it hurts their business, it's an example of 'over-regulation.' If it helps protect their market, it's a 'common sense' regulation," according to Tom Donohue, president and CEO of the U.S. Chamber of Commerce. "But what U.S. Chamber members want most are regulatory requirements that are consistent rather than contradictory, and rather than arbitrary—especially when it comes to doing business on both sides of the Atlantic."[55]

But business leaders aren't the only ones who are considering regulation as a means for increasing transparency and, in turn, public trust. In fact, it's the unanimous lack in trust worldwide—reiterated by the findings of the Tenth Annual Edelman Trust Barometer, which revealed that trust in business is at an all-time low[56]—that has prompted all stakeholders to call for government intervention in the form of increased regulation. When asked, "How strongly do you agree or disagree that your government should in the future impose stricter regulations and greater control over business across all industry sectors?" 65 percent of global Trust Barometer respondents claimed to agree.[57]

These realities of diminished public trust and increasing regulation have many effects on global business practices, but one is particularly relevant in the context of the influence of digital communications platforms over future strategies—collaborative business networks. Indeed, the PricewaterhouseCoopers CEO survey revealed that 57 percent of surveyed CEOs worldwide believe that collaborative networks will play a key part in future business models.[58] According to the survey:

The next decade could well prove to be an extraordinary era—one in which companies and governments work together to produce an environment capable of supporting wealth creation and social cohesion around the globe. The world is connected as it has never been before, and the power of collaboration is truly beginning to emerge. Technological advances have already enabled networked computing to become ubiquitous, and have created an infrastructure that can support collaboration across geographical distance and time zones. At the same time ... globalization is gradually eliminating many of the barriers to the movement of ideas, capital, labor, products and services. As a result, knowledge is migrating from being the preserve of the privileged few into a universal resource available to all—often at minimal cost.[59]

This statement is indicative of government relations' future, but there are steps being taken now that show a tangible move toward collaboration through technologies. At the 2009 World Economic Forum (WEF) held in Davos, Switzerland, three countries—Qatar, Singapore, and Switzerland—announced their sponsorship of an initiative that would define the new institutions of global cooperation among governments, businesses, and civil society organizations that are required to address the challenges presented in the twenty-first century, including those related to finance, health, the environment, and management of human resources.[60] Specifically, the initiative will use the global communications platform WELCOM, which is being developed by the WEF and is described as a set of "innovative tools for locating and accessing expertise, sharing knowledge, and meeting and working with peers. WELCOM empowers a multi-stakeholder approach to addressing the most pressing business and global governance challenges."[61]

According to Yaacob Ibrahim, minister of the environment and water resources of Singapore:

We have an increasingly interconnected world. We need to review our global institutions of global governance. The institutions established at Bretton Woods at the end of the Second World War need to be updated and improved to have appropriate global governance for the twenty-first century.[62]

This proposed project offers a glimpse into the future of global business' collaborative yet highly regulated relationship with governments, but it only scratches the surface of what is to come.

Conclusion

As this chapter demonstrates, the business of government, which includes lawmakers and corporations alike, has been slow to adopt Web 2.0 as a platform for communicating and messaging. Whether the reason is a lack of understanding or adherence to an old and outdated code of conduct, a rapidly changing business and political environment now mandates the adoption of digital communications strategies. The election of Barack Obama—a process that witnessed unprecedented use of online channels to reach and influence constituencies—proved that change has come to Washington, a place better known for gridlock and stagnation than fast-paced change and growth.

The transition to a new and change-friendly political regime happened alongside the most devastating economic collapse since the Great Depression. This crisis prompted a dramatic shift in the U.S. financial infrastructure, bringing in new regulatory models to bail out banking institutions that otherwise would have experienced imminent demise. But the path to governmental aid was not so smooth for the auto industry, which found itself lobbying the U.S. Congress—and the general public—for billions of dollars to reverse its quick spiral into bankruptcy. GM executives took this opportunity to digitize their communications on the topic, launching a Web site and creating an online video to swap support in its favor. This strategy was starkly contrasted by Google and Yahoo!'s lobbying prowess, as demonstrated by Microsoft's ability to outsmart the digital giants despite their industry domination. Precipitated by both a new administration and a necessary collaboration among business leaders, lobbyists, and lawmakers, the digital gap that divided these groups is finally beginning to close.

CHAPTER 9

HELP, MY AVATAR'S FALLEN AND HE CAN'T GET UP

CRISIS MANAGEMENT IN A VIRTUAL WORLD

President John F. Kennedy famously described crises by referring to the two brushstrokes used to write the word in the Chinese language, one standing for danger and the other for opportunity. There is an undercurrent of optimism in this characterization, but logic ultimately prevails. At least in business, crises often signal a tipping point—the moment at which change's momentum becomes unstoppable. Depending on the reaction to this change, its trajectory can kick upward and lead to bigger, better, and stronger organizations—the embodiment of learning from one's mistakes.

But the flip side of a crisis, in which the "victim" doesn't seize on potential opportunity and instead is overcome by danger, leaves many corporate institutions in ruins. And while corporate crises have existed as long as corporations themselves, their frequency and severity have increased exponentially in the context of the changing business environment for all the reasons discussed in previous chapters. Now more than ever, organizations' reputations—the backbone of a successful operation's brand and bottom line—are vulnerable to the innumerable unknowns that infiltrate every industry and that attack from every angle, thanks to digital communications channels. Corporate leaders, having seen their peers crumble against the pressures of unforeseen crises, are changing their business strategies and response mechanisms accordingly, but this isn't always enough to expect the unexpected. Preventive measures can do only so much; the rest is left to chance and to the skill with which corporate communication functions can take control of messaging once a crisis has been set into motion.

This chapter will explore the various catalysts for corporate crises in the modern digital environment by first considering the evolution of crisis communications to the present day. Through case studies of crises that were aided and abetted by digital channels, as well as their affected organizations' coping mechanisms, it will then outline a plan that companies can use to anticipate, manage, mitigate, and even prevent crises— or at least to turn whatever crisis does befall them into an opportunity for growth.

That Bitter Pill: Tylenol's Historic Crisis Response Reveals that the More Things Change, the Less They Stay the Same

More than two decades have passed since crisis swept across Johnson & Johnson's (J&J's) iconic Tylenol brand, but it still remains a textbook example—albeit a clichéd one—of how to communicate with stakeholders during a potential reputation meltdown. However, if you consider the event and Tylenol management's subsequent response in the context of modern business and communications, the outcome surely would go down in history, but it would be damned to the "what not to do" category of crisis response. In terms of response time, J&J's reaction would be deemed glacial today in a world of continuous news cycles generated by digital communications.

In late September and early October of 1982, seven people died after taking Tylenol capsules that had been laced with cyanide. At the time, J&J's household brand had close to 40 percent of the market for over-the-counter pain relievers. Within days of the first report of these poisonings, however, sales would drop by close to 90 percent.

According to Robert Andrews, then assistant director for public relations at J&J, news of the Tylenol-related deaths took the company's public relations (PR) department by surprise. "We got a call from a Chicago news reporter," he said. "He told us that the medical examiner there had just given a press conference, [that] ... people were dying from poisoned Tylenol. He wanted our comment. As it was the first knowledge we had here in this department, we told him we knew nothing about it. In that first call we learned more from the reporter than he did from us."[1]

Andrews' latter statement mirrors a modern reality: Media often know about unfolding crises before corporate executives do. However, the key difference is that despite the manner in which J&J's PR department learned of the poisonings, they still had time to execute a response that has been lauded by experts on crisis communications, marketing, and psychology as swift, caring, and triumphant. After all, despite losses exceeding $100 million immediately following the crisis, Tylenol came back stronger than ever within a matter of years. But how?

Instead of simply reacting to the critical situation, executives went on the offensive and pulled the product from the shelves of retailers, ultimately recalling more than 31 million bottles of the drug. They advised consumers not to use any Tylenol products via statements made to the press. Then CEO James Burke focused communications with all stakeholders, from consumers to employees to doctors, on the company's 306-word code of ethics, which had been J&J's guiding light since being penned in 1935. At the time of the crisis, Burke explained, "We had to put our money where our mouth was. We'd committed to putting the public first, and everybody in the company was looking to see if we'd live up to our pretensions."[2]

The first phase of the response—recalling Tylenol and telling consumers not to use any related products—was an unusual step for a massive corporation because it precipitated a $100 million loss. But it proved to be a strategic move in the long run; while initial media reports focused on the Tylenol-related deaths, this quickly shifted once it became clear that someone had tampered with the product and personally injected lethal doses of cyanide into capsules. J&J came to be viewed more as an innocent victim, the collateral damage of a deranged person's vindictive actions. The company's media relations juggernaut, which included corporate advertising, executive interviews, frequent press conferences, and a 1-800 hotline, helped to control the fallout. Once it was deemed safe for the product to return to shelves, the company's proactive response gave consumers confidence in the brand, in turn, making its reputation all the more resilient.

Reality Check: When It Comes to Crises Online, It Takes One to Know One

J&J's response to the Tylenol crisis may have held steady in 1982, but it benefited from a number of factors that don't exist today. First, that era's news cycle was regulated by time and geographic location—mere formalities that have become antiquated in the context of digital media's 24/7 cyber operations. Second, executives' control over messaging has nosedived with the emergence of digital communications channels. As every chapter of this book illustrates, crises take place early and often, and they affect every business function without bias. If anything, this reality has only increased the interdependency of these functions—an interdependency further facilitated by digital channels.

Finally, a lot has happened in the quarter century since the Tylenol crisis regarding public trust in corporations. Although far from perfect then, it has only deteriorated in the wake of corporate scandals such as Enron, WorldCom, and Tyco International, as well as the recent financial crisis. Now, companies are guilty until proven innocent; rarely if ever do skeptical stakeholders give corporations the benefit of the doubt. But that's not to say companies on the receiving end of a crisis are always at fault. Often factors outside its—or any human's—control create a situation of total upheaval. According to the Institute for Crisis Management, 19 percent of business crises do not originate with employees or management; the latter two account for 29 and 53 percent, respectively.[3] But the company as the perpetrator versus the company as the victim is the distinction on which public perception often hangs. This is why it's important for executives to understand the different types of crises before ever trying to manage one or another with an off-the-shelf strategy (for a breakdown of crisis classifications, see the following sidebar).

BUSINESS CRISIS CLASSIFICATION

The Institute for Crisis Management (ICM) defines a *business crisis* as any problem of disruption that triggers negative stakeholder reactions that could affect the organization's financial strength and ability to operate effectively. The institute identifies two overarching crises categories:

- *Sudden.* According to the ICM, between 1997 and 2007, only one-third of all business and organizational crises were sudden—that is, unexpected and unpredictable occurrences such as natural disasters or workplace violence.

- *Smoldering.* A crisis that starts out small and that should be recognized as a potential for trouble and fixed by someone within the organization before it becomes a public issue. The ICM estimates that in 2007, 65 percent of business crises were smoldering.

Within these broad categories, the ICM classifies crises into specific subgroups, including

- Catastrophes
- Casualty accidents
- Environmental
- Class-action lawsuits
- Consumer activism
- Defects and recalls
- Discrimination
- Executive dismissal
- Financial damages
- Hostile takeover
- Labor disputes
- Mismanagement
- Sexual harassment
- Whistle blowers
- White-collar crime
- Workplace violence

Source: Institute for Crisis Management, "Annual Crisis Report," *News Coverage of Business Crises During 2007* 17(1): page 2, March 2008.

Beyond understanding the different types of crises, executives must capitulate to social media's immeasurable influence over the speed with which crises manifest themselves and, in turn, infect corporate reputations. Just consider online search engine Google, and you'll begin to understand the havoc Web 2.0 can wreak on organizations. Today, a company's reputation is, for better or worse, whatever Google says it is. What's more, Google is the white elephant in any room, and this elephant never forgets. Any misstep that is recorded online becomes an entry in Google's vast library, in which information is catalogued in ways that trump the most meticulous Dewey Decimal System. But it

Figure 9.1: Crisis communications vehicles

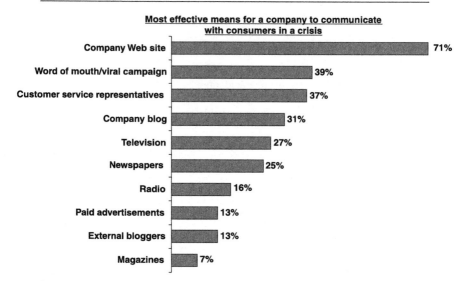

Source: "The 2008 *PR Week*/Burson-Marsteller CEO Survey," *PR Week*/Burson-Marsteller, November 14, 2008.

matters less and less whether online platforms are the ignition or extinguisher of a crisis; executives realize that the Web—especially company-owned channels such as the corporate Web site or corporate blog—is an effective means for communicating with stakeholders during a crisis (see Figure 9.1).

In the Tylenol tampering crisis, three of the top four communications vehicles cited in the Burson-Marsteller/*PR Week* CEO survey didn't exist: corporate Web site, word of mouth/viral (in the context of marketing), and company blog. The management team's aggressive media outreach, coupled with traditional advertising, communicated with stakeholders in a way that was widely viewed as honest, authentic, and transparent. Would the response have been the same today?

Mommies against Motrin: A Misunderstanding Leads to Twitter-Fueled Tantrums

J&J was dealt another image crisis in November 2008, 26 years after the infamous Tylenol debacle. Drastically less severe than the cyanide poisonings, the example still illustrates how quickly a story can be blown out of proportion in cyberspace; it also shows how the three digital means of communicating with consumers during crises—corporate Web site, viral marketing, and corporate blog—can come into play to both positive and negative effects. Piggybacking off the "International Babywearing Week" hosted by nonprofit organization Babywearing International, J&J's Motrin brand launched an online video ad on *www.motrin.com* that hinged on the concept of parents carrying babies around in slinglike carriers (the very definition of baby-wearing). The ad featured a voiceover from a baby-wearing mom, who said

> *Wearing your baby seems to be in fashion. I mean, in theory, it's a great idea. There's the front baby carrier, the sling, the shwing, the wrap, the pouch, and who knows what else they've come up with? Wear the baby on your side, your front, go hands-free. Supposedly it's a real bonding experience. They say that babies carried close to the bod tend to cry less than others, but what about me? Do moms that wear their babies cry more than those who don't? I sure do. These things put a ton of strain on your back, your neck, your shoulders—Did I mention your back? I mean, I'll put up with the pain, because it's a good kind of pain. It's for my kid, plus it totally makes me look like an official mom. And so, if I look tired and crazy, people will understand why.*

Clearly a subtle push for Motrin's pain-relieving properties—which bear the tagline "Motrin. We Feel Your Pain"—J&J executives wildly misjudged a key stakeholder group, who also happened to be the ad's target audience—mothers. The ad made its way to YouTube, and in a matter of hours, views of the ad on the video-sharing platform soared into the tens of thousands. In this case, however, more viewers didn't translate into a job well done. Microblogging site Twitter became the host of thousands of conversations between outraged mothers, who claimed the ad's message marginalized children as trendy accessories. Twitter users even set up a page dedicated to these diatribes, entitled "MotrinMoms." What's more, mommy bloggers, an extremely active demographic in the blogosphere, made the video their topic du jour, railing against the company and its subsidiary, McNeil Consumer Healthcare, the makers of Motrin.

The scale of damage in Motrin's marketing mishap and Tylenol's tampering crisis is incomparable—the latter had fatal consequences and also was a situation that the company couldn't have foreseen or controlled, whereas the former was purely a case of insensitive messaging that, had it been thought through, could have been avoided. But the moments after the crises were set into motion are most demonstrative of the differences brought on by digital communications platforms, especially in terms of the amount of time the company has to react.

In Tylenol's case, the first three of seven deaths occurred on September 29, 1982. On the morning of September 30, then Product Director of Tylenol Bill Carpenter received a phone call from a Chicago distributor asking if he was aware that three people had died, apparently from causes related to ingesting Tylenol (he was not). This kick-started a week-long period of intense activity in which the company issued a worldwide alert to the medical community, briefed the Food and Drug Administration, and publicized a $100,000 reward for information about the person(s) behind the tampering.[4] On October 5, the company issued a nationwide product recall. Just under two weeks after the first reported death, Tylenol's recovery campaign was set in motion, with all communications with stakeholders having been placed in the hands of the PR department.[5] By today's standards, two weeks of strategizing would be a lifetime, but the news cycle of the era made this time frame acceptable, if not commendable. Recalling the product—even a week later—was considered stoic given the inevitable profit loss the company would experience. On November 11, 1982, six weeks after the poisonings, J&J Chairman James Burke announced that the product would be reintroduced to the consumer market in tamper-proof packaging.

The Motrin crisis, on the other hand, required executives to react with a full communications strategy in a matter of minutes because that's how quickly news spreads with the modern media machine. The video was posted online on Saturday, November 15, 2008, and within hours, it was the most "tweeted" about topic on Twitter. By Sunday, a nine-minute video on YouTube showed screenshots of the angry Twitter posts alongside a montage of moms carrying their babies in slings. That same evening, "Tweeters" and bloggers reached an executive responsible for posting the ad by phone. As one blogger, Joyce Schwartz (*www.hollywood2020.blogs.com*), proclaimed, "Blogger Reaches Motrin Ad Agency Rep: Agency Appeared to [Know] NOTHING about TWITTER OUTRAGE."[6]

Much like the Tylenol crisis, corporate executives were informed of the spreading wildfire by the media; however, in 1982, the media was a traditional journalist, whereas in 2008, the media was a blogger. Regardless, an agency rep for the Motrin brand pulled down the video later that evening and replaced it with a note of apology from Kathy Widmer, vice president of marketing for McNeil Consumer Healthcare. She also sent an e-mail directly to those who most actively blogged against the ad over the previous weekend, which read

> *I am the Vice President of Marketing for McNeil Consumer Health-care. I have responsibility for the Motrin Brand, and am responding to concerns about recent advertising on our website. I am, myself, a mom of 3 daughters.*
>
> *We certainly did not mean to offend moms through our advertising. Instead, we had intended to demonstrate genuine sympathy and appreciation for all that parents do for their babies. We believe deeply that moms know best and we sincerely apologize for disappointing you. Please know that we take your feedback seriously and will take swift action with regard to this ad. We are in process of removing it from our website. It will take longer, unfortunately, for it to be removed from magazine print as it is currently on news stands and in distribution.[7]*

On November 17, 2008, Widmer posted another note to J&J's blog, JNJ BTW, admitting that the snafu had been a humbling experience (see Figure 9.2). One statement within her statement stood out as the ultimate lesson learned, regardless of the crisis at hand: "When you make a mistake—own up to it, and say you're sorry," she wrote. "Learn from that mistake." In both crises, executives from J&J took their own advice, and both brands' reputations rebounded accordingly. But recovery is often more hard fought and less easily won, as illustrated by the corporate victors and victims in the following sections.

Existential Crisis: Identifying Weak Spots to Withstand Wars Against Corporate Reputations

J&J's brand crises highlight a number of crisis communications components: Cyanide-laced Tylenol capsules ≠ Babywearing spoofs; response times to crises in predigital times ≠ those in the digital era; and traditional media ≠ social media (clearly, hell hath no fury like a mommy blogger scorned). Most important, though, the comparison set the stage for an analysis of the various vulnerabilities fueled by the modern business environment and how digital communications channels can exacerbate and mitigate crises in practically the same breath.

Figure 9.2: Treating the headache caused by Motrin's mommy misunderstanding

Divine Comedy Version 2.0: Dell Visits Dante's Seven Circles of Hell

As discussed in Chapter 4, Dell fell victim to its own ineptitude when a customer-service faux pas lit a fire beneath tech blogger Jeff Jarvis, whose missive against the company spawned the now-infamous period of "Dell hell." This is a textbook example of learning a lesson the hard way: Negative conversations percolated in the blogosphere, but Dell executives didn't have their ears to the proverbial computer screen, and by the time they noticed the army of anti-Dell activists, it was all but too late. At least one good thing came out of the reputation hit: It prompted Dell to finally enter the blogosphere on its own accord and launch what would be the first of many corporate blogs.

"The Dell story ... has become a classic case study. Rather than ignoring complaints, the company's executives embraced the new media," said Sir Martin Sorrell, group chief executive of WPP. "They set up Dell's own customer spaces, such as IdeaStorm, where people could record their experiences and post suggestions. Most importantly, Dell did not censor negative posts and reordered its customer services department to respond to the complaints. Within two years, Dell had halved negative online chatter about its products. It is hard to believe that an ad campaign with a cheery message would have achieved a similar result."[8]

But becoming literate in social media didn't make Dell immune to reputational crises. Case in point: In early 2008, the company shipped a number of laptop models with an error in the bottom row of letters (ZXCVBNM). Owing to a manufacturing glitch, each letter was shifted one key to the right—easy for the eye to oversee, but a clear malfunction once users' fingers met the keyboards. Dell issued two separate recalls, the second of which occurred when a keyboard supplier reshipped the already-recalled keyboards for a second time.

As one would expect, the error quickly made its way to the Web. Jake Gordon, recipient of one of the flawed Dell laptops, made an initial posting to photo-sharing site Flickr on May 1, 2008, showing pictures of the faulty keyboard (see Figure 9.3). Online news outlets immediately

Figure 9.3: Dell Vostro's faulty keyboard

picked up the story, and within 24 hours, Dell representatives were putting out fires throughout cyberspace, accepting blame for the flaw, and promising to replace all affected laptops. Seven days after Gordon's Flickr post, Dell commented on its corporate blog "Direct2Dell" and linked to a more in-depth statement on its "Small Business" blog, where Dell's Community Liaison Bill Bivin wrote, "Thanks to Flickr user Jake Gordon for alerting us to a problem with our Vostro 1310 and 1510 keyboard layout. He's the one that influenced Engadget and other blogs like Wired to write about the issue. There is no way to say it. ... we made a mistake and want to apologize to affected customers."[9]

Mistakes are an unavoidable by-product of doing business—especially doing business in a digitally connected world that continues to shrink. But Dell's multiple reputational crises, fueled largely by social media, brought the company to a relative reconciliation with its online stakeholders. Sure, it continues to stumble, but its inclination to respond quickly and transparently has been a key ingredient in its basic crisis communications strategy. A post penned by Chief Blogger Lionel Menchaca on the one-year anniversary of the launch of "Direct2Dell" launch summarizes a few lessons learned and best practices that all corporate executives would be wise to consider[10]:

- *Customers really are in control—and it's okay.*
- *Ignoring negative issues is not a viable strategy in the blogosphere.*
- *Maintaining a blog is a difficult balancing act.*
- *There are no shortcuts.*
- *If you open the lines of communication, customers will tell you what is wrong with your business.*
- *Innovation matters, but a little luck doesn't hurt.*
- *Probably the best time to launch a blog is when things aren't going so well.*

You Ain't Got No Alibi: Brands Busted for Ghost-Blogging Pay the Price

Menchaca's nod to transparency is a critical component of all online communications and especially those surrounding crises. But many corporate giants mistakenly thought they could outsmart the "digerati" by passing off company-sponsored blogs as those created by third-party ambassadors (in theory, making them more authentic and credible than praise on an official corporate blog). The self-inflicted wounds that come with this deception are representative of crises that easily could be avoided, yet company after company falls victim to temptation. Much like Sony's "All I Want for Christmas is a PSP" "flog" (fake blog) discussed in Chapter 4, Wal-Mart's effort at emulating a folksy customer-created platform backfired with considerable pomp and circumstance. "Wal-Marting Across America," launched on September 27, 2006, with its "authors" Laura and Jim setting out on a cross-country journey in their RV with plans to make pit stops in Wal-Mart parking lots. Laura and Jim chronicled their Kerouac-ian expedition by introducing readers to the kind-hearted and enthusiastic Wal-Mart employees they met along the way.

Soon, skeptics emerged online, questioning the true identity of the bloggers, as well as any possible connection to the company (a connection that was explicitly absent from the blog). The truth quickly showed itself: Jim and Laura were in fact real people, but their blog was supported by Working Families for Wal-Mart, an organization formed by the company's PR firm, Edelman, to counter the aggressive criticism from union-funded groups like Wal-Mart Watch and Wake Up Wal-Mart.[11] The realization that the blog was as unauthentic as they come ruffled the feathers of stakeholders, many of whom were already dubious of the company's frequently condemned business practices. Edelman CEO Richard Edelman addressed the faux pas on his blog, but only after more than a week elapsed from the time the story broke. He wrote

> *For the past several days, I have been listening to the blogging community discuss the cross-country tour that Edelman designed for Working Families for Wal-Mart.*
>
> *I want to acknowledge our error in failing to be transparent about the identity of the two bloggers from the outset. This is 100 percent our responsibility and our error, not the client's.*
>
> *Let me reiterate our support for the WOMMA [Word of Mouth Marketing Association] guidelines on transparency, which we helped to write. Our commitment is to openness and engagement because trust is not negotiable and we are working to be sure that commitment is delivered in all our programs.*[12]

5W Public Relations is another example of a PR agency that led its client directly into the lion's den by making online commentary under a pseudonym—only in this case its executives further soiled the firm's reputation by denying what hard evidence proved to be true.

Agriprocessors, a kosher slaughterhouse, hired 5W PR in the late spring of 2008 to manage a crisis brewing around allegations of labor violations and unkosher slaughter practices. In an effort to reverse the backlash against Agriprocessors, the firm actually inflamed the situation by impersonating well-respected Rabbi Morris Allen—an outspoken critic of Agriprocessors—on several influential blogs, using his name to puppet statements that supported the slaughterhouse. The strategy was a textbook example of ghostwriting gone wrong because the agency's executives vehemently denied any association with the impersonation once news emerged that Allen had nothing to do with the comments made in his name. These executives failed to realize that the Internet takes the fingerprint of every user in the form of an IP address—the piece of information that ultimately traced the blog comments back to the computer of a 5W employee. Busted.

5W did fulfill its responsibility to its client—in a way. It redirected negative attention away from Agriprocessors (who allegedly had no knowledge of the agency's subversive strategy) and pointed the finger directly at itself. Ron Torossian, CEO of 5W, said this in defense of his firm's wrongdoing:

> *A senior staff member failed to be transparent in dealing with client matters. He has taken full responsibility. Growing companies often have problems in their expansion, and we continue to strive for the highest performance. We have instituted internal measures to ensure this cannot happen again. We continue to strive for the highest ethical standards.*[13]

As it turns out, however, 5W's reputation would fare far better than Agriprocessors' in the long run because the story about the slaughterhouse's tainted image didn't end there; in fact, it began before the PR firm ever got involved. In May 2008, shortly after an immigration raid at the organization, "Postville Voices," "a blog by the people who live and work in Postville,"[14] was launched to defend the small Iowa town whose reputation was being tarnished by association—after all, it was home to Agriprocessors.

The blog sought to give voice to the plight of Postville residents, who felt they were being dragged down by the scandal. At the same time, it not-to-subtly defended the slaughterhouse's integrity and lambasted media for misrepresenting the facts surrounding allegations. The site also hosted videos of Agriprocessor employees speaking about their positive work experiences. The frequency of posts dwindled within a few months of the site's creation, but because interest in the scandal was renewed when violations of child labor laws were brought against the company in September 2008, an Associated Press reporter named Nigel Duara investigated the blog's legitimacy, only to find that it was at least partially run by Getzel Rubashkin, a member of the family who owns the kosher meatpacking plant.[15]

It proved to be yet another case of "astroturfing"—the act of designing deliberate, motive-driven communications to outwardly look like spontaneous, grassroots efforts. The irony of this ill-advised initiative was its synonymous occurrence alongside the 5W scam, yet Rubashkin didn't connect the dots and, even after being outted, aggressively defended his actions as . . . well, kosher. In the end, no amount of groveling or apologizing would have rescued Agriprocessors' reputation; on November 4, 2008, the company filed for bankruptcy, and 10 days later, the company's former CEO Sholom Rubashkin was arrested for bank fraud.

While the companies guilty of "astroturfing" have experienced varying degrees of reputation recovery, their mistakes by no means have been erased from the memories of stakeholders—or the Web. As stated previously, Google is the cyber elephant that never forgets—a fact that Edelman, Wal-Mart, Agriprocessors (whatever is left of it), and 5W PR (hopefully) will remember for a long time to come.

Gotcha! Internet Hoaxes Add a New Dimension to Online Crises

The companies discussed in the preceding section sabotaged their own reputations online, but some organizations fall victim to rogue Web users who use their digital prowess to attempt to sink brands for no apparent reason. Cases of identity theft, digital viruses, and Internet scams have plagued Web platforms practically since their conception, but that doesn't mean that all companies have learned to manage such risks over time. For example, the "I Love You" virus unleashed in 2000 cost businesses across a range of industries an estimated total of $10 billion in damages. Five years later, IBM released a report identifying the first viruses spreading beyond computers to attack and extract personal information from handheld devices such as mobile phones and personal digital assistants (PDAs)—the very tools on which profession-als, and certainly senior executives, rely to conduct daily business.[16]

Today, most online thieves are opting for more surreptitious tactics to steal confidential information. Viruses are now used more commonly to plant "Trojans" in personal or office computers—malicious software that steals sensitive information stored in a computer and relays it back to the criminal. "Phishing" is another popular tactic used by scammers who send spoof (but often legitimate-looking) e-mails to customers, posing as well-known companies and requesting personal information such as account passwords and Social Security numbers under the aus-pices of updating the company's online records. Banks are especially vulnerable to these types of scams. As a result of the ubiquity of derelict "digerati," a number of host-busting Web sites have emerged to keep stakeholders abreast of current scams (see the following sidebar).

HOAX-BUSTING WEB SITES

These third-party sites can be used to help identify, track, and debunk popular hoaxes:

- *Snopes.com*—investigative myth-busting Web site.
- *UrbanLegends.about.com*—an often-updated blog by David Emery that features an "Urban Legends" newsletter.
- *Hoax-Slayer.com*—debunks popular e-mail hoaxes with a monthly news-letter.
- *TruthorFiction.com*—a large directory of hoaxes and rumors by category.
- *HoaxBusters.org*—identifies popular Web hoaxes and scams.
- *VirusHoaxBusters.com*—offers guidelines and tips for identifying hoaxes, and lists current scams and viruses circulating on the Web.
- *Symantic.com*—tracks online attempts to defraud customers.
- *Vmyths.com*—identifies virus hoaxes and tells truths about computer security.

Sometimes, though, companies inadvertently open the door for scam-mers, as illustrated by Sony. In 2005, Sony's BMG Music Entertainment Division installed digital rights management (DRM) technology on its CDs without any notification to users. The technology automatically installed a "rootkit" program that embedded the DRM software into con-sumers' hard drives and subsequently exposed users' computers to security vulnerabilities, hackers, and the compromising of confidential data. News broke in the blogosphere first, where conversations percolated for days before company representatives ever acknowledged the problem. When Sony's use of hidden software became public, the company endured a maelstrom of criticism. It was forced to recall millions of CDs, executives were forced to make a humiliating public apology, the company faced a battery of lawsuits, and the brand suffered accordingly.

Other times, innocent jokes are misinterpreted and don't just affect one company; they go so far as to influence, say, the U.S. stock market. In what proved to be an April Fool's joke gone awry, Doug Kass, a short fund manager of Seabreeze Partners Short LLP and market pundit, issued a tongue-in-cheek statement on April 1, 2008, that he was raising his year-end price targets for the Standard & Poor's 500 to 1,666—a 26 percent gain.[17] The financial media picked up the story, only they didn't read between the lines and realize Kass' intended humor. Instead, top-tier news outlets, including *CNN Money*, the *Wall Street Journal*, *Bloomberg*, and *Barron's*, covered the joke as real news, in turn, causing equity futures to rally. Shortly after the market opened, the Dow was up more than 230 points, and the Nasdaq had gained almost 2 percent.[18]

Kass quickly realized his error in assuming that others would appreciate his humor, and he was forced to issue a mea culpa that same morning, which read: "I apologize to my partners, and to my friends, and especially to the SEC, for whom I have the greatest possible respect. I never intended markets to be manipulated in this manner. I was only trying to make some traders, who have been having a tough year, break a smile. ..."[19]

The smiles elicited by the joke were most likely of the wry variety, but Kass ultimately had the last laugh. His April Fool's spoof ended up being a springboard for a new CNBC show, called *The Mad Bull*, which Kass began hosting in June 2008. Regardless of the outcome, though, the scenario proved yet again that one voice on the Internet exercises impressive influence over corporate reputations and financial markets alike.

Virtual Vaccinations: Defense Mechanisms for Dodging, Managing, and/or Mitigating Crises in Cyberspace

A majority of corporate leaders still may take pause when presented with digital strategies as the primary means for reaching and influencing powerful stakeholders, but—as previous chapters (hopefully) have proven—these channels are becoming more and more central to successful communications strategies regardless of the business function or target audience. That said, the perceived loss of control, fueled by stakeholder empowerment, may be the biggest psychological impediment to widespread adoption of strategic digital plans, and the ubiquitous examples of Web-driven corporate crises only exacerbate this sentiment. This is precisely why organizations must keep their proverbial fingers to the pulse of the ever-changing business landscape and, in turn, build up their immunity to ominous online threats. Whether a crisis experience is past, present, or future for any given company, senior executives must take definitive steps to increase their tolerance of online tyranny.

A Crisis Came, Stakeholders Saw ... Now, Can Online Communications Conquer?

JetBlue Airways is a prime example of the modern reality of crisis management. Even if a crisis brewed completely offline, an offline-only or traditional crisis-management plan alone won't close the wound.

On February 14, 2007, a winter storm barreled through the Northeast region of the United States, hitting the New York metro area especially hard. As would be expected, local airports were crippled by the weather. Delays and cancellations prompted a backlog of planes on runways, and thousands of passengers buckled down for a long wait throughout the terminals. But the blizzard would prove to be the imperfect storm for JetBlue, which made a series of critical mistakes that would tarnish its sterling reputation for months to come.

At first, the airline's troubles weren't unlike those of its competitors: Delayed and canceled flights weren't unexpected given the weather conditions. But JetBlue execs took a gamble in hoping temperatures would rise enough to turn the sleet and snow into rain and therefore allow the planes to take off safely. With that prediction as their guiding light, the team at John F. Kennedy International Airport boarded six planes and permitted the aircrafts to push back from their respective gates. "We thought there would be these windows of opportunities to get planes off the ground, and we were relying on those weather forecasts," said Sebastian White, a corporate communications manager at JetBlue.[20]

When it became clear that the freezing rain wouldn't relent anytime soon, the executives planned to allow the six planes to alternate returning so that passengers could deplane because none of the planes were properly equipped with enough food and water to accommodate so many people for indefinite periods of time. To make matters worse, some of the bathrooms' toilets began to overflow, and passengers captured the "raw" footage on their cell phones and forwarded it on to family and friends. But then the equipment used to tow the aircraft back to the gates froze to the tarmac, and the situation deteriorated from there.

The jets were at a standstill for up to six hours before passengers finally deplaned, and one plane that landed at JFK didn't unload its passengers until nine hours after touching down. As for those inside the terminals waiting to board flights, their tempers flared as hours passed without any announcements about when they could expect to depart. Flight attendants, pilots, and JetBlue officials tried their best to alleviate tensions with frequent apologies, but the effort was futile, especially in light of what would happen in the following days.

Indeed, JetBlue customers turned to various sources to get information about their flight statuses in the days after what had already been dubbed the "Valentine's Day Massacre," but the platforms weren't able to handle the volume. The company's hotline greeted many callers with a recording that said, "We are experiences a high call volume. . . . we are unable to take your call."[21] What's more, JetBlue's Web site listed flights as on schedule for departure when, in reality, many had already been canceled. Numerous reports of lost luggage online inflamed an already raw situation.

So what was the company's response to the crisis that quickly threatened to deflate its reputation as a customer-service-oriented carrier? The management team took traditional crisis-management measures early on: They immediately issued press releases with apologies and promises of compensation to all affected passengers. On February 15, then CEO Bill Neeleman appeared on network and cable television morning shows explaining the debacle as the result of inadequate communication protocols to direct the company's 11,000 pilots and flight attendants, as well as a deficit of cross-trained employees who could work outside their area of expertise. According to Neeleman, "We had so many people in the company who wanted to help who weren't trained to help. We had an emergency control center full of people who didn't know what to do. I had flight attendants sitting in hotel rooms for three days who couldn't get a hold of us. I had pilots e-mailing me saying, 'I'm available; what do I do?'"[22]

The lack of cross-department communications and cross-discipline training constitutes separate issues, and they are issues that can be rectified by integrated digital strategies (for more on internal communications and training, see Chapter 5). For Neeleman and the rest of his crew, however, it was too late to initiate a robust digital strategy internally to overcome the challenges presented by the winter storm. So the damage control continued. Within days of the initial crisis, large "We're sorry" ads appeared in newspapers in JetBlue's main East Coast markets. The steps taken by the airline's communications team were by the book. Unfortunately, this book happened to be a battered hand-me-down from another era.

While executives buckled down and conducted damage control on the ground, the airline's reputation was in the midst of a turbulent storm in cyberspace. Photos, videos, and text messages from trapped passengers chronicled the chaos inside the grounded planes and crowded terminals and then were uploaded online and began circulating on blogs, discussion forums, and digital news outlets. Travelers populated sites like *www.jetbluehostage.com* with angry rants, and coverage of the crisis, its aftermath, and current JetBlue-related news continues to be posted to the blog. The creator of "JetBlue Hostage," Genevieve McCaw, described the community with her self-introduction:

> *My Name is Genevieve McCaw and I was a passenger on JetBlue #351 on Valentine's day along with my boyfriend Charlie. We were en route to LA for Valentine's day before we ended being held hostage for 11 hours on the frozen tarmac at JFK.*
>
> Jetbluehostage.com *is an archival site and online community. We post news articles, published blogs and official press releases and e-mails from JetBlue corporate. We also give the public an opportunity to voice their opinions and stories thru the comments sections and we publish e-mails that have been sent to us at jetbluehostage@gmail.com.*[23]

McCaw also created a MySpace page (*www.myspace.com/jetbluehostage*), but she wasn't the only consumer leveraging digital communications channels to express her discontent with the airline, nor was her blog the only platform disseminating reputation-damning messages. Clips of late-night comedy show hosts mocking JetBlue's predicament made their way to YouTube, and the media had no trouble locating sources willing to have their horror stories told. Meanwhile, Neeleman and his communications team were blogging; they even created a video of Neeleman apologizing and posted it to the corporate Web site and YouTube.

One week later, just as the airline's operations were returning to normal, the results were in, so to speak: The cancellations during the five-day period cost the airline an estimated $20 million in revenue and an additional $24 million in flight vouchers given to customers who were affected by the disruptions.[24] JetBlue subsequently lowered its operating margin forecast for the fiscal quarter and the year; investors immediately responded by selling off their shares of Jet Blue stock.[25] With this as his cross to bear, Neeleman faced an uphill battle to regain stakeholders' trust and to rebuild the company's dismembered reputation.

Lost and Found: SEO Buries—or Exhumes—Evidence of Crises Past

Three weeks after the JetBlue's "Valentine's Day Massacre," *Fast Company* interviewed CEO Bill Neeleman, whose frustration with how the situation unfolded was brutally obvious. "Look, I haven't slept in three weeks," he said. "I'm tired of talking. Emotionally, I am done. . . . I just want to go out and run the company."[26]

When pressed for insight into lessons learned and strategies for moving forward, Neeleman said:

> *For the 15th time, we've learned from this. That's why it's never going to happen again. . . . It's belts and suspenders. If your suspenders fall off, your belt keeps your pants up. You have to have contingency plans for everything. My job is to make sure no one ever forgets what happened.*[27]

That job would be an easy one because Neeleman wouldn't need to lift a finger to guarantee the immortality of the crisis; the Internet would do the dirty work for him. The vast digital collection of consumer accounts maintained a high profile online. The JetBlue communications team's focus on cranking out traditional press releases that were poorly optimized and therefore buried in search results made JetBlue's voice a mere whisper among the discord. This was a grave error in the company's response plan; search engine optimization (SEO) is an essential component of crisis communications because it helps to control what pages appear highest in search results (for more on SEO as a media relations tool, see Chapter 4). In the context of crises, executives can take steps to influence the information most easily found and accessed by stakeholders by (1) optimizing press releases or, better yet, social media releases and (2) using paid search.

Paid search differs from natural/organic search in that the latter's placement in results pages is determined solely by a search engine's algorithmic process, with no outside influence; paid search, on the other hand, is a form of marketing in which a company can purchase terms to have specific content appear on the first page of search results. These sites show up in the tinted block at the top of a Google results page, in the "Sponsored Links" site block that runs along the right side of the page, or in the "Ads by Google" sections of sites such as *NYTimes.com*.

Taco Bell put paid search to good use in late 2006 and early 2007 when an *E. coli* outbreak caused dozens of customers to become ill. Negative coverage exploded in digital and traditional news outlets alike. In addition to traditional crisis-management strategies such as executive interviews and press releases, the company's management also initiated a paid search-engine marketing (SEM) campaign, purchasing crucial search terms such as *taco bell + e. coli* so that the brand's bilingual microsites with its official corporate response would appear at the top of the results list on multiple search engines. These sites contained up-to-date information about the outbreak, affected locations, and the company's response, as well as a video message from CEO Greg Creed. This tactic garnered praise from bloggers and PR strategists, who commended the company for getting out in front of the crisis via proactive online communications.

JetBlue's failure to implement a paid SEM strategy only further crippled attempts to have its own messages overpower the caustic online commentary. However, what it failed to do on the Web, it compensated for on Capitol Hill—a point that can't be overlooked because it was largely responsible for JetBlue's reputation recovery. In February 2007, immediately following the airline's meltdown, members of Congress began to discuss legislation that would prevent air travelers from being trapped in grounded planes for excessive periods of time. This legislation, conceptualized as a passenger bill of rights, would standardize passenger compensation across all airlines that failed to meet levels of service deemed to be acceptable.

As this conversation gained momentum on Capitol Hill, Neeleman was already planning to implement a JetBlue Airways "Passenger Bill of Rights," which explicitly entitled passengers to vouchers for future travel if their flights were delayed for periods of time that the bill of rights identified as unreasonable. This left no ambiguity in terms of what customers could expect from the airline, and it also put JetBlue at risk for owing travelers millions of dollars as payback. On February 20, 2007, Neeleman officially announced the bill of rights, at which point the company's reputation began regaining altitude.

Come Hell or High Water: Digital Platforms Enhance Disaster Response

Although they seem to be the most prevalent when calling corporate crises to mind, not all disasters involve a business blunder. That said, uncontrollable and unpredictable crises such as natural catastrophes can be just as damaging to a brand if not managed properly. Consider an organization like The Home Depot. The world's largest home-improvement retailer is a natural go-to place for emergency preparation. After Hurricane Katrina devastated the Gulf Coast in 2005, the roll the company needed to play in disaster response became all too clear. This is why Home Depot's Atlanta-based corporate headquarters established a fully functional Hurricane Command Center to monitor and respond to supply-chain issues as they unfolded. But the center didn't have a means of communicating directly with customers during the critical hours of these natural disasters—that is, until now.

In 2008, Home Depot became the first commercial enterprise to use Twitter during a weather emergency to support customers and increase sales.[28] It was a drastic step for a company whose only prior social media effort was a YouTube channel with do-it-yourself videos and a few online polls and contests. But, according to Nick Ayres, Home Depot's interactive marketing manager, the company wanted to expand its use of digital platforms and "picked Twitter because it seemed like a low-cost, low-risk entry point."[29] Another Home Depot communications executive, Sarah Molinari, headed up the launch of the company's Twitter account (@*The-HomeDepot*) and began engaging with consumers. By the time Hurricane Gustav loomed off the Gulf Coast, she had a loyal following of "Twitterers," and the management team decided to test the platform as a crisis communications vehicle. Focusing on four message themes—timeliness, relevance, accuracy, and appropriateness—the communications team crafted its Twitter strategy. "To be honest, we weren't sure how the approach was going to go over or how effective it would be," Ayres said. "This was not going to be a hard-sell situation. We were not going to post: 'We still have generators, and you can buy them for $xx.'"[30]

Instead, Molinari hunkered down in the Hurricane Command Center and "tweeted" news in real time—the company's decision to keep 12 stores open all night in the hardest-hit areas. As the hours passed, her Twitter followers spiked to more than 1,000, and everyone from news media to the company's management logged online to stay up-to-date. Instead of acting as a passive bystander as the hurricane ripped across the region, Home Depot took a leadership role in its community and engaged stakeholders with authentic and helpful messages. Of course, the company's crisis response also gave it a competitive advantage over industry peers such as Lowe's, which had no social media presence during the catastrophe.

Although certainly at the forefront of twittering to manage and mitigate crises, Home Depot isn't the only example of a pioneer in this space. The American Red Cross (*www.twitter.com/redcross*) has used Twitter to dispatch information about shelter locations and survival tips during emergencies, including the 2008 Grand Canyon flood and Hurricane Gustav. The Red Cross' information was so timely that it was a primary resource for traditional media reporting on the disasters. The from-the-trenches nature of "Twitter-ed" reports has enabled some "digerati" to scoop major news outlets; elite blogger Robert Scobleizer (*www.scobleizer.com*) broke news of China's devastating 8.0 earthquake, which killed tens of thousands in August 2008, on Twitter an hour before it was confirmed by BBC[31] and approximately 45 minutes before it was announced by the U.S. Geological Survey.[32]

But is this completely open access to information that could be sensitive a double-edged sword? An intelligence report released by the U.S. Army identified a terrifying possibility—the use of Twitter as a communications tool for terrorists. The report specified three possible uses of Twitter by terrorists[33]:

1. Sending and receiving messages to and from other terrorist cell members
2. Detonating a roadside bomb
3. Following a soldier's tweets

The report also noted:

Twitter is already used by some members to post and/or support extremist ideologies and perspectives. For example, there are multiple pro and anti Hezbollah Tweets. In addition, extremist and terrorist use of Twitter could evolve over time to reflect tactics that are already evolving in use by "hacktivists" and activists for surveillance. This could theoretically be combined with targeting.[34]

This alternative perspective on the dangers of the democratic nature of digital communications has given pause to consideration of social media by national organizations, including the Department of Homeland Security (DHS) and the Homeland Security Institute (HSI). "HSI does not use social media programs, if what you have in mind is Twitter, Facebook and the like," HSI Fellow Charles Brownstein said in an interview with blogger Shel Israel. "We are not exploring how to weave social networking into HSI or DHS—but rather doing research into how national, state and local authorities can use social networking in *their* operations, and advising DHS on how it can promote such uses. There seems to me to be a number of ways."[35] He identified these ways as the following[36]:

- "First, emergency responders, especially the younger ones, use all of the same social media tools that you use. So, they are tuned into how Facebook was used at Virginia Tech by school authorities and students to gain a more accurate picture of events on the ground than the police, the mass media and the public had [during the April 16, 2007, shooting rampage that left 33 dead]. So their bosses want to know how to factor their own workers' uses into official operations. Police in the Phoenix area, the LA Fire Department and New York City are weaving Twitter into daily operations. So, from that point of view, we want to make sure that DHS does nothing to stop this from happening more—or, better yet, makes it legitimate for local authorities to spend block grant funds to find their own uses.
- Second, DHS can look at what information is readily made available by end users of social networking technology, and figure out how to incorporate that information into FEMA and other agency emergency response operations at command centers, such as common operating picture and logistics support systems. To some extent, this means

getting local authorities to figure out what works for them, doing some training, or at some point when its well-understood, offering assistance and promoting standards. Or, perhaps, it means designing and operating 'back end' information processing systems dedicated to effectively using the bits that individuals generate for their own purpose.

- Third, DHS can look at how the underlying common use infrastructure for social networking, such as application servers, terrestrial or mobile access links and data processing facilities, can be made or kept sufficient resilient, and reliable to be trustworthy in emergency situations."

The dichotomous nature of digital channels as both a blessing and a curse is a common theme in their emergence into the world of business communications, and this holds true for crisis management as well. But no amount of avoidance will keep online crises at bay, nor will vehement support for and implementation of digital platforms into communications strategies guarantee immunity. Ultimately, the key to survival is not unlike the best practices for digital communications during non-crises, including

- *Monitoring influential digital channels.* Knowing where your target stakeholders communicate with each other and search for information is the foundation of any communications strategy. On the bright side, for every online platform, there seems to be at least two monitoring services. These can be used at little or no cost to spot potential problems before they metastasize into full-blown crises (for a list of services for monitoring blogs and other Web channels, see Chapter 4).
- *Embracing transparency as communications' guiding light.* The access to information online is staggering by any standard, but succumbing to the temptation of sweeping dirty little secrets under the rug will come back to bite your organization's reputation in a big way. During a crisis, the best approach is to provide stakeholders with facts in the company's own domain, whether the Web site, corporate blog, or official Twitter account. What you choose to gloss over will become someone else's headliner, and the result could be crippling.
- *Taking advantage of SEO and SEM—even if you have to pay for it:* Paid search is worth considering in the wake of a crisis because the first place stakeholders usually turn for information is a search

engine. If the first page of search results contains only negative rants without any official statement from the company, the recovery period can be slow and riddled with setbacks. Besides optimizing all corporate content addressing the crisis for search, executives can buy search terms and pay for placement in visible areas of search results pages. It's not a homerun strategy, but it's far better than striking out.

- *Identifying affected audiences and customizing communications for each.* Crises affect different stakeholders in different ways, and lumping all groups together is a mistake. Companies should already be aware of their stakeholders' consumption habits; when crises strike, this information can be used to shape the ideal mix of distribution channels for reaching them in their natural environments.

- *Going out on a limb.* Traditional crisis-response plans don't translate into the digital era. That said, times of crisis aren't usually ones in which executives feel like taking big risks. But there is a fine balance between playing it safe and playing dumb; overlooking the benefits of digital crisis communications only stacks more cards against the afflicted organization.

Conclusion

Danger and opportunity may not seem like congruous concepts, but they have found common ground in the fourth dimension of cyberspace, in turn, giving increasingly crisis-prone organizations a roller-coaster ride through the beginnings of Modern Business, Version 2.0. The variables that traditionally acted as catalysts in crises have mutated and multiplied exponentially in the face of all the factors discussed throughout this book: an increasingly global marketplace, a turbulent economy, diverse stakeholder groups' growing influence, and most of all, the emergence of digital communications platforms, which make the business landscape morph almost daily.

What does this mean for corporate leaders? For starters, it requires a highly evolved mind-set in terms of embracing the uncertainties surrounding this changing environment. As the examples throughout this chapter demonstrated, crises that affect companies today are borne out of places that didn't exist ten, five—even three—years ago: A customer's complaint made on a blog crushes a behemoth brand's reputation, a misguided ad theme spirals out of control on Twitter, a practical joke initiated online drastically affects the U.S. stock market. Just as these crises spawned from digital platforms, so too were many of them solved when the Web was used by executives to regain control over messaging. Corporate blogs open the lines of communication between company leaders and their stakeholders, Twitter connects brands with consumers during emergencies, corporate Web sites become the go-to source for up-to-date information as an unexpected crisis gains momentum.

Essential to massaging danger into opportunity is the willingness of corporate leaders to hold—and not bite—the hand that feeds them. Stakeholders are already online, and they are starting—and extinguishing—fires for organizations across every industry. Executives fail to accept the power of digital communications at their own risk, and those who do accept it prosper. Fortune favors the bold.

DIGITAL DICTIONARY

Avatar A virtual representation of an individual who is engaged in an online game/virtual world. (See also *Second Life*.)

Blog (n.) Short for Web log; a Web page that is maintained by an individual or group for public consumption; defining characteristics include frequent updates, tone and content that reflect the author's views, and the ability for readers to post comments. (v.) To author a Web log.

Blogger A person who blogs.

Blogosphere The umbrella term used to as a reference for the ever-expanding universe of blogs that exists on the Internet.

Blogroll A list of links hosted on one blog that direct users to other blogs; usually comprised of blogs that the blog author references; helps to increase visibility of host blog in search engines; helps to expand a blog's community of readers.

Click-through A metric that defines the process of an individual clicking on a Web advertisement and then being redirected to a destination specified by the advertiser.

Crowdsourcing Outsourcing a task that traditionally would be performed by an employee to an undefined group or community.

Customer relationship management (CRM) The overall process of managing all interactions an organization has with its customers to influence their behaviors; includes customer service, marketing, and sales.

Del.icio.us A social bookmarking service that aggregates bookmarked Web pages based on users' actions, including tagging and sharing; gives users the ability to customize their own list of bookmarked pages, as well as to search for topics of interest by category and tags.

Digg A community-based Web site where users submit and/or rate online content based on what they like and don't like; submissions that earn a large number of "diggs" appear higher in Digg search results by category, sometimes even appearing on Digg.com's home page.

Extranet A network that exists online and acts like any other Web site but is accessible only to authorized users; often used to securely exchange information between organizations or groups without monopolizing bandwidth on an internal network. (See also *Intranet*.)

Facebook See *Social network*.

Feed A shortened version of a Web page that has been created for syndication and aggregation. (See also *RSS*.)

Feed aggregator An application that collects feeds from multiple sources based on a subscriber's preferences and then displays the results in a single consolidated view, either on a personal desktop or a Web browser. (See also RSS.)

Intranet A network that looks and acts like any other Web site but that belongs to an organization or group and is protected by a firewall; only grants access to individuals with authorization; usually exists on an organization's internal network.

Keyword A piece of text chosen by a Web site's administrator to help a search engine categorize and index the site, ultimately for the purpose of making it findable in search results; also referred to as *tag*.

LinkedIn A social networking site geared specifically toward professional users, who can create profiles, join groups, and maintain a list of their business contacts. (See also *Social network*.)

Mash-up A Web application that combines features and functions from multiple Web sites to create one integrated interactive platform.

Microblogging A form of blogging in which users write and publish brief posts (usually limited to 140 characters) via a variety of

channels, including text messaging, instant messaging. or the
Web. (See also *Twitter.*)

Microsite A platform within a Web site that has a separate URL
from its home page and is used to provide information
about/promote something specific within the company, such as a
product launch or a contest; often a temporary site that is
removed once its content is no longer relevant.

MySpace See *Social network.*

New media A generic term used to describe the emerging digital
platforms that enable the publication of content on the Web, as
well as communication among Internet users; used in relation to
"old" media forms, such as print newspapers and magazines.

Online newsroom A Web site that contains information about a
corporation or organization; online newsrooms are often
contained within corporate Web sites and act as a central location
for news, financial information, press releases, etc.

Page impression A metric that represents the exact number of
times a Web site is accessed by users; also refers to as *hits.*

Podcast An audio file that is posted to a Web site; listeners can
access the files by downloading them to a specific source or
streaming them online via an audio player.

RSS (Really Simple Syndication) The acronym used to describe
the syndication of Web content for aggregation and distribution
via customized feeds.

Search engine An online service such as Google that is designed to
search and index as many Web pages as possible within the World
Wide Web and then weighs them according to their purported
importance; looks for information based on keywords specified by
individual Web users; based on algorithms that are unique to each
individual search engine.

Search-engine marketing (SEM) Marketing efforts associated
with researching, submitting, and positioning an organization,
brand, product, service, Web site, etc. within search engines to
achieve maximum exposure in front of a highly targeted audience
of online users.

Search-engine optimization (SEO) The process of increasing the
number of visitors to a Web site by optimizing and weighting its
content so that it will be found and highly ranked by search
engines.

Second Life An Internet-based virtual world that allows registered users to create virtual representations of themselves, to interact and socialize with other users, and to engage in commerce by creating, buying, and/or trading virtual properties, products, and/or services. (See also *Avatar*.)

Social network An interactive Web platform such as Facebook, MySpace, and Linked that enables a user to create a customized profile that can be accessed and viewed by other network members who become "friends" or "contacts" of said user; establishes extended networks of individuals and communities.

Tag See *Keyword*.

Technorati A search engine that is programmed to specifically index, search, and track blogs and other forms of user-generated media.

Trackback A form of peer-to-peer communication designed to notify Web users about updates made to a specific Web property.

Traffic A metric that defines the total number of visitors to a Web site.

Tweet The slang term for a comment posted by a user on Twitter.

Tweeter A user of Twitter.

Twitter A microblogging service that allows users to send messages and read other users' messages, all of which are limited to 140 characters.

Unique visitor A metric that refers to an individual who visits a Web site more than once within a specified period of time; helps to measure traffic to a Web site more accurately by distinguishing between a user who visits a site once and a user who visits a page multiple times in rapid succession to artificially boost page views; measured according to unique IP addresses and therefore counted only once.

Viral marketing A technique that relies on word-of-mouth and peer-to-peer communications to spread marketing messages, usually via Web platforms including blogs, social networks, and e-mail.

Vlog Short for "video blog"; describes a blog that includes or consists of video clips that can be downloaded and/or streamed by visitors to the site.

Web 1.0 The term used to describe the first generation on the World Wide Web, which is largely defined by static Web sites that did not facilitate collaborative communications, the dissemination of user-generated content, or the creation of dynamic/interactive application.

Web 2.0 The term frequently used to describe the second generation on the World Wide Web, whose defining characteristics include interactive platforms and applications that allow Internet users to collaborate and share information online.

Web 3.0 The term used to define the third generation on the World Wide Web; it's definition remains highly speculative because its adoption is not yet universal, but many agree that it could be used to describe "intelligent" Web-based applications such as data mining and natural-language search that are driven largely by artificial intelligence technologies.

Wiki A collaborative Web site that consists of the perpetual collective work of many authors; can be created, edited, and/or modified.

YouTube A popular free video-sharing Web site that allows users to upload, view, and share video clips online.

Word-of-mouth (WOM) marketing A technique similar to viral marketing that relies on individuals and communities to build buzz about a brand, product, or service and to pass on information about it to their friends, therefore potentially reaching a larger audience than targeted marketing strategies would.

ENDNOTES

Chapter 1

1. Arthur W. Page Society, "The Authentic Enterprise CEO Report," December 2007.

2. 2008 Edelman Trust Barometer.

3. Marcia Vickers, Mike McNamee, Peter Coy, et al., "The Betrayed Investor," *BusinessWeek*, February 25, 2002, p. 105.

4. 2008 Edelman Trust Barometer.

5. *Ibid.*

6. K. G. Coffman and A. M. Odlyzko, "The Size and Growth Rate of the Internet," AT&T Labs, 1998. Retrieved at www.dtc.umn.edu/~odlyzko/doc/internet.size.pdf, July 8, 2008.

7. *www.nytco.com/company/milestones/timeline_1971.html*, retrieved July 8, 2008.

8. USC Annenberg Strategic Public Relations Center, "Media Myths and Realities: A Public of One," Media Usage Survey, 2007.

9. Project for Excellence in Journalism, "The State of the News Media," Washington, D.C., 2008.

10. *Ibid.*

11. Internet World Stats, Usage and Population Statistics, *www.internetworldstats.com*.

12. Arthur W. Page Society, "The Authentic Enterprise CEO Report," December 2007.

13. 2008 Edelman Trust Barometer.

14. IBM Corporation, "The Enterprise of the Future: Global CEO Study," Somers, New York, 2008, p. 48.

15. Marketing Leadership Council, a division of the Corporate Executive Board Company, "Business Model Transformation," Rosslyn, Virginia, 2007.

16. Ellen R. McGrattan and Edward C. Prescott, "Unmeasured Investment and the Puzzling U.S. Boom in the 1990s," National Bureau of Economic Research, Cambridge, Massachusetts, October 2007, p. 1.

17. *Ibid.*

18. IBM Global CEO Study, "The Enterprise of the Future," Somers, New York, 2008, p. 56.

19. *Ibid.*

20. *Ibid.*

21. "How Business Are Using Web 2.0: A McKinsey Global Survey," *McKinsey Quarterly*, March 2007.

22. Stephen Baker and Heather Green, "Beyond Blogs," *BusinessWeek*, June 2, 2008.

Chapter 2

1. Gibbon, Henry, "Global M&A breaks 2000 record: European M&A volume surpasses US$1.7trn following year of mega-mergers," Acquisitions Monthly, January 1, 2007.

2. Peter Eschbach and Jeremy Morgan, "Unlocking the Value of HP's Employee Portal," *PR News*, retrieved from www.prnewsonline.com/itsthepr/casestudy8, August 8, 2008.

3. Interview between Courtney Barnes and Diane Thieke and Alan Scott, April 2007.

4. *Ibid.*

5. Interview between Courtney Barnes and Mark Weiner, September 6, 2008.

6. *Ibid.*

7. Coverage by Courtney Barnes of the Arthur W. Page Society/Tuck School of Business Academic Symposium, Hanover, NH, May 21–23, 2007.

8. Interview between Jon Iwata and Courtney Barnes, via e-mail June 5, 2007.

9. Arthur W. Page Society, "The Authentic Enterprise CEO Report," December 2007.

10. "Fifth Annual Generally Accepted Practices Study," Strategic Public Relations Center, University of Southern California, May 18, 2008.

11. *Ibid.*

12. Weber Shandwick and Spencer Stuart, "The Rising CCO," www.spencer stuart.com/practices/corporate/, January 2008.

13. *Ibid.*

14. Interview between Paul Argenti and Sam Palmisano, December 2007.

15. Interview between Courtney Barnes and Jon Iwata, via e-mail June 5, 2007.

16. Corporate Leadership Council, a division of the Corporate Executive Board Corporation, *Succeeding in a Matrix Environment.* Washington, 2002.

17. IBM Corporation, "The Enterprise of the Future: IBM Global CEO Survey," Somers, New York, 2008, p. 41.

18. "Compete and Collaborate: What Is Success in a Connected World?" *PricewaterhouseCoopers 11th Annual Global CEO Survey*, 2008, p. 55.

19. Telephone interview between Courtney Barnes and Mike Davies, January 2007; featured in "Integrating Comms into All Activities in a Changing Business Environment, Part 2," *PR News*, February 19, 2007.

20. *Ibid.*

21. Tim Zimmermann, Maren Hauptmann, and Theresa Tenneberg, "Profitables Wachstum organisieren: Zentral steuern, dezentral führen," RolandBerger Strategy Consultants, 2008. (Translated from German.)

22. "GE Capital Reorg Focuses on Growth, Cost Savings," GE Reports blog, November 18, 2008, *www.gereports.com/ge-capital-reorg-focuses-on-growth-cost-savings/*; retrieved December 15, 2008.

23. Interview between Paul Argenti and Sam Palmisano, 2007.

24. *Ibid.*

25. *Ibid.*

26. Interview between Paul Argenti and Gerard Kleisterlee, 2007.

27. Communications Executive Council Benchmark Custom Report, "Themes in Communications Organizational Restructuring," October 2007. Cited from (author unknown), *Dictionary of Marketing Terms*," American Marketing Association, Chicago, Illinois, 2005.

Chapter 3

1. Jerome McCarthy and William Perreault, *Basic Marketing: A Global-Managerial Approach.* New York: McGraw-Hill, 1998.

2. Communications Executive Council, a division of the Corporate Executive Board Company, "Building Stakeholder Preference Through the Corporate Brand," Arlington, Virginia, 2008, pp. 16–21.

3. Carly Fiorina, *Tough Choices*. New York: Portfolio Hardcover, 2006, p. 179.

4. Communications Executive Council, a division of the Corporate Executive Board Company, "Building Stakeholder Preference Through the Corporate Brand," Arlington, Virginia, 2008, pp. 28–29.

5. Hardy Quentin, "Burning in HP's Brand," *Forbes*, July 25, 2003.

6. Marketing Leadership Council Executive Productivity Network, "Identifying Emerging Marketing Trends," interview with Michael Mendenhall, 2008.

7. *Ibid.*

8. Interview via e-mail between Courtney Barnes and Mark Weiner, September 6, 2008.

9. *Ibid.*

10. Veronis Suhler Stevenson (VSS) Forecast, released August 5, 2008; available at *www.vss.com/news/index.asp?d_News_ID=177*; downloaded August 10, 2008.

11. "IMC Defined," *Journal of Integrated Marketing Communications*, available at *http://jimc.medill.northwestern.edu/JIMCWebsite/site.htm*; downloaded August 11, 2008.

12. *Ibid.*

13. Market Research Executive Board, a division of the Corporate Executive Board Company, "Integrated Marketing Campaign Strategies Issues Brief," Arlington, Virginia, 2005.

14. Anonymous, "The Five Keys to Successful Integrated Marketing," *Primedia Insight*, January 31, 2005.

15. Interview via e-mail between Courtney Barnes and George Wright, October 2, 2008.

16. *Ibid.*

17. 2008 Edelman Trust Barometer.

18. Interview via e-mail between Courtney Barnes and Jason Alcorn, August 29, 2008.

19. Interview via e-mail between Courtney Barnes and George Wright, October 2, 2008.

20. Marketing Leadership Council Executive Productivity Network, "Identifying Emerging Marketing Trends," interview via e-mail with Michael Mendenhall, 2008.

21. Interview via e-mail between Courtney Barnes and Mark Weiner, September 6, 2008.

22. Interview via e-mail between Courtney Barnes and Mike Daniels, September 18, 2008.

23. Interview via e-mail between Courtney Barnes and Gregg Hale, September 23, 2008.

24. *Ibid.*

25. Interview via e-mail between Courtney Barnes and Heidi Sullivan, September 3, 2008.

26. Corporate Executive Board Marketing Leadership Council, "Executive Productivity Network: Stewarding the Brand's Voice," interview with Deborah Fell, 2008.

27. Interview via e-mail between Courtney Barnes and George Wright, October 2, 2008.

28. Interview via e-mail between Courtney Barnes and Shabbir Imber Safdar, August 29, 2008.

29. Interview via e-mail between Courtney Barnes and Zach Enterlin, October 9, 2008.

30. Interview via e-mail between Courtney Barnes and Jason Alcorn, August 29, 2008.

31. Michael Arrington, "Comcast, Twitter and the Chicken (Trust Me, I Have a Point)," April 6, 2008; available at *www.techcrunch.com/2008/04/06/comcast-twitter-and-the-chicken-trust-me-i-have-a-point/*; downloaded August 18, 2008.

32. *Ibid.*

33. *Ibid.*

34. Interview via e-mail between Courtney Barnes and Zach Enterlin, October 9, 2008.

35. Interview via e-mail between Courtney Barnes and Shabbir Imber Safdar, August 29, 2008.

36. *Ibid.*

37. Interview via e-mail between Courtney Barnes and Mark Weiner, September 6, 2008.

38. Interview via e-mail between Courtney Barnes and Mike Daniels, September 18, 2008.

Chapter 4

1. Sir Martin Sorrell, "Public Relations: The Story Behind a Remarkable Renaissance," Institute for Public Relations Annual Distinguished Lecture, New York, November 5, 2008.

2. Communications Executive Council, a division of the Corporate Executive Board Company, 2007 Communications Executive Council Member Poll, comScore Networks, Arbitron, Inc./Edison Media Research, Arlington, Virginia, 2007.

3. 2008 Edelman Trust Barometer.

4. Stephen Baker and Heather Green, "Beyond Blogs," *BusinessWeek*, June 2, 2008, p. 50.

5. *Ibid.*

6. Jose Antonio Vargas, "Blog Talk," August 27, 2008; available at *www. washingtonpost.com/wp-dyn/content/article/2008/08/26/AR2008082603072. html?nav=hcmodule*; downloaded September 2, 2008.

7. "Bloggers Play Key Role at Denver Convention," August 27, 2008; available at *www.cnn.com/2008/TECT.08/27/blogger.central.ap/index.html*; downloaded August 27, 2008.

8. Brian Wingfield and Joshua Zumbrun, "Convention Cutting," *Forbes.com*, August 12, 2008. Available at *www.forbes.com/2008/08/12/newspapers-media-conventions-biz-media-bw_jz_0812newsbiz.html*; retrieved August 27, 2008.

9. Interview via e-mail between Jon Iwata and Courtney Barnes, June 5, 2007.

10. Interview between Courtney Barnes and George Wright, New York, New York, October 2, 2008.

11. "Closing China's Starbucks," interview with Howard Schultz for CNN's Boardroom Master Class, November 12, 2007; available at *http://edition. cnn.com/2007/BUSINESS/10/01/boardroom.masterclass/index.html*; downloaded November 5, 2008.

12. Matt Marshall, "HP Announces an (Almost) Unbelievable Blogger Campaign," VentureBeat Digital Media, September 24, 2008; available at *http://venturebeat.com/2008/09/24/hp-announces-an-almost-unbelievable-blogger-campaign/*; downloaded October 1, 2008.

13. *Ibid.*

14. Interview via e-mail between Courtney Barnes and Katie Paine, October 26, 2008.

15. Sir Martin Sorrell, "Public Relations: The Story Behind a Remarkable Renaissance," Institute for Public Relations Annual Distinguished Lecture, New York, November 5, 2008.

16. *Ibid.*

17. Interview via e-mail between Courtney Barnes and Katie Paine, October 26, 2008.

18. *Ibid.*

19. "An Interview with Southwest Airlines: Social Media Use," p. 5; Communications Executive Council, a division of the Corporate Executive Board Company, Arlington, Virginia, November 2007.

20. *www.socialtext.net/bizblogs/index.cgi?fortune_500_business_blogging_wiki*; downloaded October 6, 2008.

21. *www.beingpeterkim.com/2008/09/ive-been-thinki.html*; downloaded October 6, 2008.

22. Bob Lutz, Keynote Speech delivered to the Public Relations Society of America International Conference, Detroit, MI, October 27, 2008.

23. Frank Washkuch, "State of Transition: Media Survey 2008," *PR Week*, March 30, 2008.

24. "An Interview with Southwest Airlines: Social Media Use," p. 5; Communications Executive Council, a division of the Corporate Executive Board Company, Arlington, Virginia, November 2007.

25. *Ibid.*

26. Laura Ramos, with Bradford J. Holmes, Charlene Li, Jeremiah K. Owyang, and Christina Less, "How to Derive Value from B2B Blogging," Forrester Research, Cambridge, Massachusetts, June 10, 2008.

27. *Ibid.*

28. Suzanne Marta, "It's Official: American Has a Blog," *Dallas Morning News*, April 14, 2008; available at *http://aviationblog.dallasnews.com/archives/2008/04/its-official-american-has-a-bl.html*; downloaded October 6, 2008.

29. Aarti Shah, "Game Changers," *PR Week*, August 11, 2008.

30. Patrick Seybold, "Welcome, You've Been Waiting," June 11, 2007; available at *http://blog.us.playstation.com/2007/06/11/welcome-you%e2%80%99ve-been-waiting/*; downloaded October 30, 2008.

31. Aarti Shah, "Game Changers," *PR Week*, August 11, 2008.

32. Patrick Ruffini, "Iowa Twitter Success," January 4, 2008; available at *www.patrickruffini.com/2008/01/04/iowa-twitter-success/*; downloaded October 13, 2008.

33. Interview via e-mail between Courtney Barnes and Heidi Sullivan, September 3, 2008.

34. Todd Andrlik, "Social Media Relations: Are You Ready for the Social Media Release and Social Media Newsroom?" presented at the Ragan Communications Social Media Summit, Chicago, Illinois, September 2007.

35. Bob Lutz, Keynote Speech at the 2008 Public Relations Society of America International Conference, Detroit, MI, October 27, 2008.

36. Todd Andrlik, "Social Media Relations: Are You Ready for the Social Media Release and Social Media Newsroom?" presented at the Ragan Communications Social Media Summit, Chicago, Illinois, September 2007.

37. Greg Jarboe, "Improving Your Search Engine Marketing and PR," *PR News* Next Practices Digital Summit, New York, New York, October 3, 2008.

38. Brian Solis, "SEC to Recognize Corporate Blogs as Public Disclosure: Can We Now Kill the Press Release?" *TechCrunch*, July 31, 2008; available at *www.techcrunch.com/2008/07/31/sec-to-recognize-corporate-blogs-as-public-disclosure-can-we-now-kill-the-press-release/*; downloaded October 20, 2008.

39. Lori Luechtefeld, "Steve Rubel on How Blogs Are Changing the Face of PR," *iMedia Connection*, October 7, 2008; available at *www.imediaconnection.com/content/20755.asp*; downloaded October 20, 2008.

40. Todd Andrlik, "Social Media Relations = The Release + Newsroom," September 30, 2007; available at *http://toddand.com/2007/09/30/social-media-relations-the-release-news-room/*; downloaded October 30, 2008.

41. Andrew Barnett, "PR, Meet Search: Rethinking Digital Communications," presented at *PR News* Next Practices Digital Summit, New York, October 3, 2008.

42. "How Search Engines Work," February 17, 2006; available at *www.webopedia.com/DidYouKnow/Internet/2003/HowWebSearchEnginesWork.asp*; downloaded October 21, 2008.

43. Institute for Public Relations, "You Are Now Free to Link PR and Sales," November 10, 2005.

44. Sir Martin Sorrell, "Public Relations: The Story Behind a Remarkable Renaissance," Institute for Public Relations Annual Distinguished Lecture, New York, November 5, 2008.

45. Andrew Barnett, "PR, Meet Search: Rethinking Digital Communications," presented at the *PR News* Digital PR Next Practices Summit, New York, October 3, 2008.

Chapter 5

1. "Eleventh Annual Global CEO Survey," PricewaterhouseCoopers, Belfast, Northern Ireland, 2008, p. 39.

2. Matt Gonring, "Assessing the Value of Communication: A Special report from the IABC Research Foundation and Watson Wyatt Worldwide," *Communication World*, January 2004.

3. Richard M. Able, "The Importance of Leadership and Culture to M&A Success," Human Capital Institute and Towers Perrin, January 16, 2007.

4. "Eleventh Annual Global CEO Survey," PricewaterhouseCoopers, Belfast, Northern Ireland, 2008, p. 39.

5. "Building Stakeholder Preference Through the Corporate Brand," research from the Communications Executive Council, a division of the Corporate Executive Board Company, Arlington, Virginia, 2007.

6. *Ibid.*

7. *Ibid.*

8. *Ibid.*

9. Interview between Paul Argenti and Sam Palmisano, 2007.

10. Lynn Dorsett, Michael A. Fontaine, and Tony O'Driscoll, "Redefining Manager Interaction at IBM," IBM Institute for Business Value, 2002.

11. Interview between Paul Argenti and Sam Palmisano, 2007.

12. Lynn Dorsett, Michael A. Fontaine, and Tony O'Driscoll, "Redefining Manager Interaction at IBM," IBM Institute for Business Value, 2002.

13. Gary Bendt, "Breaking It Down for Internal Communicators," January 30, 2008; available at *www.garykoelling.com/?q=node/370*; downloaded October 31, 2008.

14. *Ibid.*

15. *Ibid.*

16. *Ibid.*

17. "The Authentic Enterprise," Arthur W. Page Society, 2007.

18. "Eleventh Annual Global CEO Survey," PricewaterhouseCoopers, Belfast, Northern Ireland, 2008, p. 42.

19. "Generation Y: The Millennials: Ready or Not, Here They Come," NAS Insights, NAS Recruitment Communications, Cleveland, Ohio, 2006.

20. Bureau of Census, Educational Attainment in the United States, "The Millennials: Americans Born 1977 to 1994," Bureau of the Census, Washington, 2002.

21. "When Watching a Movie Could Get You Hired: A 2.0 Approach to Modern-Day Talent Management," *PR News*, June 9, 2008.

22. Aili McConnon, "The Name of the Game Is Work," *BusinessWeek*, August 13, 2007; available at *www.businessweek.com/innovate/content/ aug2007/id20070813_467743.htm*; downloaded October 29, 2008.

23. *Ibid.*

24. "Online Networking Sites Capture Interest of Hiring Managers," Robert Half Finance and Accounting, Menlo Park, California, 2008.

25. "Eleventh Annual Global CEO Survey," PricewaterhouseCoopers, Belfast, Northern Ireland, 2008. Pg. 48.

26. *Ibid.*

27. Aili McConnon, "The Name of the Game Is Work," *BusinessWeek*, August 13, 2007; available at *www.businessweek.com/innovate/content/ aug2007/id20070813_467743.htm*; downloaded October 29, 2008.

28. *Awareness, Inc., Powers Online Web 2.0 Community for JetBlue*, YouTube video posted, April 28, 2008; available at *www.youtube.com/watch?v=*

faU08bLNvuM&eurl=http://newlearningplaybook.com/blog/2008/05/13/jet-blue-university-uses-own-faculty-to-test-social-media-tools/; downloaded November 5, 2008.

29. Mark Jen, "First Day on the Job, First Post on the Blog," January 17, 2005; available at *http://99zeros.blogspot.com/2005_01_01_archive.html*; downloaded October 30, 2008.

30. Mark Jen, "First Day on the Job, First Post on the Blog," February 11, 2005; available at *http://99zeros.blogspot.com/2005_01_01_archive.html*; downloaded October 30, 2008.

31. IBM Social Computing Guidelines; available at *www.ibm.com/blogs/zz/en/guidelines.html*; downloaded October 31, 2008.

32. "An Interview with Southwest Airlines: Social Media Use," Communications Executive Council, a division of the Corporate Executive Board Company, Arlington, Virginia, November 2007.

33. Del Jones, "Sun CEO Sees Competitive Advantage in Blogging," *USA Today*, June 26, 2006; available at *www.usatoday.com/tech/news/2006-06-25-exec-sun_x.htm*; downloaded October 31, 2008.

34. "Putting the Success in Succession Planning: Fostering Thought Leadership," *PR News*, April 21, 2008.

35. Interview between Paul Argenti and Sam Palmisano, 2007.

Chapter 6

1. National Investor Relations Institute, NIRI Corporate Web site, *www.niri.org*.

2. Sir Martin Sorrell, "Public Relations: The Story Behind a Remarkable Renaissance," Institute for Public Relations Annual Distinguished Lecture, New York, November 5, 2008.

3. *Ibid.*

4. National Institute of Investor Relations, "Origins of NIRI," 2008; available at *www.niri.org/about/origins_ch1.cfm*; downloaded October 19, 2008.

5. *Ibid.*

6. National Institute of Investor Relations, "Survey of Activist Investors," Vienna, Virginia, September 2007.

7. Emanuel Zur, *The Power of Reputation: Hedge Fund Activists*. New York: Stern School of Business, New York University, 2007, p. 40 (IPREO Buy-Side Survey, Investor Relations Roundtable research).

8. Corporate Executive Board, "Proactive Approaches to Managing Shareholder Activism," Investor Relations Roundtable, a division of the Corporate Executive Board Company, 2007, p. 19.

9. CFO Executive Board, a division of the Corporate Executive Board Company, "Best Practices in Shareholder Activism Management Response," Arlington, Virginia, March 2005.

10. Steven Levingston, "Icahn, Time Warner End Fight," *Washington Post*, February 18, 2006, p. D1.

11. "Carl Icahn Launches 'The Icahn Report,'" June 23, 2008; available at *www.mediabuyerplanner.com/2008/06/23/carl-icahn-launches-the-icahn-report/*; downloaded October 22, 2008.

12. "Anatomy of a Meltdown: The Credit Crisis," available at *www.washingtonpost.com/wp-srv/business/creditcrisis/*; downloaded October 9, 2008.

13. Investor Relations Roundtable, a division of the Corporate Executive Board Company, "IR's Role in Risk Communication in Times of Market Turmoil," Arlington, Virginia, October 2008.

14. Investor Relations Roundtable, a division of the Corporate Executive Board Company, "Activating the Financial Brand," Arlington, Virginia, 2008.

15. Holmes Report, "Investment Professionals Believe Communications Adds or Subtracts Value," London, United Kingdom, July 2007.

16. *Ibid.*

17. Investor Relations Roundtable, a division of the Corporate Executive Board Company, "Investor Relations Organizational Structures," Arlington, Virginia, March 2007.

18. Investor Relations Roundtable, a division of the Corporate Executive Board, "Budget, Spending, and Staffing FAQs," Arlington, Virginia, July 2007.

19. *Ibid.*

20. Jeff Smith, "How Do They Do It? Best IR Programs," presentation at 2008 NIRI Annual Conference, San Diego, California, June 10, 2008.

21. *Ibid.*

22. Louis Thompson, "Challenges and Solutions for Effective Investor Relations," presentation to the World Money Show, Orlando, Florida, February 2006.

23. Maureen Wolff-Reid and Brooke Fumbanks, "Measures That Matter," presented at the National Investor Relations Institute Annual Conference, San Diego, California, June 2008.

24. Daly, Rich, "Broadridge Financial Solutions, Inc., F4Q08 Earnings Call Transcript," August 14, 2008.

25. National Investor Relations Institute, "NIRI Annual Report Survey," August 2006.

26. Dominic Jones, "Reflections on 2008 Annual Report Season," IR Web Report, June 3, 2008; available at *www.irwebreport.com/daily/2008/06/03/reflections-on-2008-annual-report-season/*; downloaded October 22, 2008.

27. Dominic Jones, "SEC Does First Conference Call with Bloggers," IR Web Report, April 18, 2008; available at *www.irwebreport.com/daily/2008/04/18/sec-does-first-conference-call-with-bloggers/*; downloaded October 23, 2008.

28. "The Interactive Video Annual Report," presented at the National Investor Relations Institute e-Learning Forum, January 8, 2008.

29. Investor Relations Roundtable, a division of the Corporate Executive Board Company, "IR 2006 Agenda Poll's Budget and Spend," Arlington, Virginia, 2006.

30. *IR Magazine*'s "2006 Investor Perception Study."

31. Investor Relations Roundtable, a division of the Corporate Executive Board, "Attributes of World Class Investor Relations Web Sites," Arlington, Virginia, 2007.

32. "Improving Your IR Web Site," presentation delivered at the National Investor Relations Institute's e-Learning Forum, October 28, 2008.

33. Michael Arrington, "Naveen Jain's Latest Scam: Intelius," May 29, 2008; available at *www.techcrunch.com/2008/05/29/naveen-jains-intelius-prepares-to-go-public-how-much-of-their-revenue-is-a-scam/*; downloaded October 22, 2008.

34. "Yahoos Won't Work for Microsoft," February 14, 2008; available at *www.techyouruniverse.com/technology/yahoos-wont-work-for-microsoft*; downloaded October 22, 2008.

35. Lynn Tyson, "Welcome to 21st Century IR," Dell Shares IR Blog, November 1, 2007; available at *http://dellshares.dell.com/archive/2007/11.aspx*; downloaded October 17, 2008.

36. Rob Williams, "Dell Shares—An IR Blog, Social Media and Why It Matters," presentation at National Investor Relations Institute Annual Conference, San Diego, California, June 10, 2008.

37. *Ibid.*

38. *Ibid.*

39. *Ibid.*

40. Social Media Influence, "Does the Corporate IR Team Need a Blog?" Custom Communications, May 13, 2008; available at *http://customcom.typepad.com/social_media_influence/2008/05/does-the-corpor.html#more*; downloaded October 17, 2008.

41. Telephone interview between Courtney Barnes and Jon Sullivan, August 22, 2008.

42. *Ibid.*

43. *Ibid.*

44. *Ibid.*

45. CFO Executive Board, a division of the Corporate Executive Board Company, "Best Practices in Shareholder Activism Management Response," Arlington, Virginia, March 2005.

Chapter 7

1. Sam Palmisano, "A Smarter Planet: The Next Leadership Agenda," presented at the Council on Foreign Relations Annual Meeting, New York, November 6, 2008.

2. David Vogel, "CSR Doesn't Pay," Forbes.com, October 16, 2008; available at *www.forbes.com/2008/10/16/csr-doesnt-pay-lead-corprespons08-cx_dv_1016vogel.htmlwhere*; downloaded October 30, 2008.

3. Howard Schultz, *Pour Your Heart into It.* New York: Hyperion, 1997, p. 131.

4. "The GS Sustained Focus List," Goldman Sachs, New York, June 22, 2007.

5. "Perception of Corporate Responsibility Linked to Reputation," news release from the Reputation Institute and the Boston College Center for Corporate Citizenship, Boston, October 17, 2008.

6. Tara Weiss, Matthew Kirdahy, and Klaus Kneale, "CEOs on CSR," Forbes.com, October 16, 2008; available at *www.forbes.com/2008/10/16/ceos-csr-critics-lead-corprespons08-cx_tw_mk_kk_1016ceos.html*; downloaded October 30, 2008.

7. *www.sourcewatch.org.*

8. "GE Launches Ecomagination to Develop Environmental Technologies; Company-Wide Focus on Addressing Pressing Challenges," media release, Fairfield, Connecticut, May 9, 2005.

9. Wendy Melillo and Steve Miller, "Companies Find It's Not Easy Marketing Green," *Brandweek, http://www.brandweek.com/bw/esearch/article_display.jsp?vnu_content_id=1002877873*; July 24, 2006.

10. Jeremiah Owyang, "Case Study: Dissecting the Dell Regeneration Graffiti Facebook Campaign," Web Strategist blog, March 24, 2008; available at. *www.web-strategist.com/blog/2008/03/24/case-study-dissecting-the-dell-regeneration-graffiti-facebook-campaign/*; downloaded November 19, 2008.

11. "Earth Movers: Timberland Takes Green Marketing Online," *New Hampshire Business Review, http://www.thefreelibrary.com/Earth+movers:+Timberland+takes+green+marketing+online.-a0181115208*, June 20, 2008.

12. *www.earthkeeper.com*; downloaded October 21, 2008.

13. Timberland news release distributed via Business Wire, November 5, 2008; available at *http://studio-5.financialcontent.com/chron?GUID=7070762&Page=MediaViewer&ChannelID=3191*; downloaded November 12, 2008.

14. Interview via e-mail between Courtney Barnes and Katie O'Brien, August 6, 2008; campaign press release.

15. Interview via e-mail between Courtney Barnes and Reggie Bradford, August 6, 2008 (for "The Flavor of Philanthropy: A Spunky Brand Goes Social in the Name of Peace, Love and Ice Cream," *PR News*, August 11, 2008).

16. "Rethinking Corporate Social Responsibility," Fleishman-Hillard/– National Consumers League Study, 2006.

17. Shikha Dalal, "Viral Video Volunteerism: A New Peak in Corporate Creativity," on Philanthropy.com, October 15, 2008; available at *www.onphilanthropy.com/site/News2?page=NewsArticle&id=7623*, downloaded November 15, 2008.

18. "Corporate Responsibility and Sustainability Communications: Who's Listening, Who's Leading? What Matters Most?" research report released by Edelman in conjunction with Boston College Center for Corporate Citizenship, Net Impact and the World Business Council for Sustainable Development, Boston, 2008.

19. *Ibid.*

20. "The GS Sustain Focus List," Goldman Sachs, New York, June 22, 2007.

21. Telephone interview between Courtney Barnes and Erin Dobson, March 17, 2008, for "CSR Awards Issue," *PR News*, March 24, 2008.

22. *www.ford.com/aboutford/microsites/sustainability-report-2006-07/impacts Materiality.htm*; downloaded November 16, 2008.

23. "The GS Sustain Focus List," Goldman Sachs, New York, June 22, 2007.

Chapter 8

1. Andrew Nachison, "Two Thirds of Americans View Traditional Journalism as 'Out of Touch,'" WE Media online, February 28, 2008; available at *http://ifocos.org/2008/02/27/two-thirds-of-americans-view-traditional-journalism-as-%E2%80%98out-of-touch%E2%80%99/*; retrieved November 9, 2008.

2. *www.ciozone.com/index.php/Case-Studies/The-Barackobama.com-Difference.html*.

3. *Ibid.*

4. Holly Davis, "Resource Interactive: Millennials Put Age before Race in Presidential Choice," October 21, 2008; available at *www.marketwatch.com/ news/story/millennials-put-age-before-race/story.aspx?guid=%7B3BC76E38- 1161-4174-9103-5E1FEEA9C67B%7D&dist=hppr.*, retrieved October 26, 2008.

5. *Ibid.*

6. *Ibid.*

7. Micah Sifry, "The Obama Machine," NPR Sunday Soapbox blog, October 26, 2008; available at *www.npr.org/blogs/sundaysoapbox/2008/10/the_potential_ of_the_obama_mac.html*; retrieved October 30, 2008.

8. *Ibid.*

9. *Ibid.*

10. Catherine Holahan, "John McCain Is Way Behind Online," *Business Week*, June 27, 2008; available at *www.businessweek.com/technology/content/ jun2008/tc20080626_575590.htm.*

11. *Ibid.*

12. Micah Sifry, "The Obama Machine," NPR Sunday Soapbox blog, October 26, 2008; available at *www.npr.org/blogs/sundaysoapbox/2008/10/ the_potential_of_the_obama_mac.html.*

13. Heather Havenstein, "McCain Revamps McCainSpace Social Net," *Computerworld*, August 30, 2008; available at *www.computerworld.com/ action/article.do?command=viewArticleBasic&articleId=9113838.*

14. *www.hitwise.com/political-data-center/key-candidates.php.*

15. *www.techpresident.com/youtube.*

16. Heather Havenstein, "Obama Still Dominates in Web 2.0 World, Internet Searches," *New York Times*, October 22, 2008; available at *www.nytimes.com/external/idg/2008/10/22/22idg-Obama-still-dom.html.*

17. *www.techpresident.com/scrape_plot/technorati.*

18. Jake Tapper, "Music Video Has a Crush on Obama," *ABC News Online*, June 13, 2007; available at *http://abcnews.go.com/Politics/Story?id=3275802& page=1*; retrieved November 9, 2008.

19. "Music Video Creators Have a 'crush on Obama,'" interview with Kauffman and Relles on MSNBC.com, June 14, 2007; available at *http:// video.msn.com/?mkt=en-us&brand=msnbc&tab=m5&rf=http://www.msnbc. msn.com/id/16438329/&fg=&from=00&vid=e199a3f2-d7b6-4ead-b4d7- d8f9561de1f0&playlist=videoByTag:mk:us:vs:1:tag:hotvideo_m_edpicks:ns: MSNVideo_Top_Cat:ps:10:sd:-1:ind:1:ff:8A*; retrieved November 9, 2008.

20. Erin Carlson, "Will the Obama Girl Win a YouTube Award?" Associated Press, March 20, 2008; available at *http://news.yahoo.com/s/ap/20080320/ ap_en_ot/youtube_awards*; retrieved November 9, 2008.

21. John Gibson, "Crush' Video Good for Obama," Fox News Channel, June 14, 2007; available at http://www.foxnews.com/story/0,2933,282694,00. html; retrieved November 9, 2008.

22. "Obama Responds to Crush," *DesMoines Register*, June 18, 2007.

23. "Fireside Chat Microphone, 1930s," National Museum of American History, Smithsonian Institution; available at *http://americanhistory.si. edu/exhibitions/small_exhibition.cfm?key=1267&exkey=143&pagekey=246*; retrieved July 7, 2008.

24. David Kirkpatrick, "In Transition, Ties to Lobbying," *New York Times Online*, November 14, 2008; available at *www.nytimes.com/2008/11/15/ us/politics/15transition.html?_r=2&hp&oref=slogin&oref=slogin*; retrieved November 16, 2008.

25. Paul A. Argenti, *Corporate Communication*, 5th ed. New York: McGraw-Hill, 2003.

26. Holly Brasher and David Lowery, *The Corporate Context of Lobbying*. Berkeley, CA: Berkeley Electronic Press, 2006.

27. Paul A. Argenti, *Corporate Communication*, 5th ed. New York: McGraw-Hill, 2003.

28. *www.answers.com/topic/pac*; retrieved November 1, 2008.

29. Owen Thomas, "GM's Scare Tactics Fail to Win Over YouTube Users," Valleywag.com, November 17, 2008; available at *http://valleywag.com/ 5091311/gms-scare-tactics-fail-to-win-over-youtube-users*; retrieved November 19, 2008.

30. Ken Schachter, "Microsoft Leads in Lobbying Largess," Red Herring Web site, April 28, 2008; available at *www.redherring.com/Home/24187*; retrieved November 1, 2008.

31. Rajiv Chandrasekaran, "Microsoft Attacks Credibility of Intel Exec," WashingtonPost.com, November 13, 1998; available at *www.washingtonpost. com/wp-srv/business/longterm/microsoft/stories/1998/microsoft111398.htm*; retrieved November 1, 2008.

32. Microsoft Consent Decree; available *www.usdoj.gov/atr/cases/f201200/ 201205a.htm*; retrieved November 1, 2008.

33. Ken Schachter, "Microsoft Leads in Lobbying Largess," Red Herring Website, April 28, 2008; available at *www.redherring.com/Home/24187*; retrieved November 1, 2008.

34. *Ibid.*

35. *Ibid.*

36. *Ibid.*

37. *www.opensecrets.org/lobby/index.php*; retrieved November 1, 2008.

38. Michele Gershberg and Anupreeta Das, "Yahoo Reaches Google Ad Deal, Microsoft Talks Fail," Reuters Web site, June 12, 2008; available at

www.reuters.com/article/topNews/idUSN1247863820080612?feedType=RSS &feedName=topNews; retrieved November 1, 2008.

39. *Ibid.*

40. *Ibid.*

41. Brian Kraemer, "Google Considers Walking Away from Yahoo Ad Deal," The Channel Wire blog, October 31, 2008; available at *www.crn. com/software/211800539*; retrieved November 1, 2008.

42. Miguel Helft, "Google and Yahoo Delay Ad Deal for Antitrust Review," *New York Times Online*, October 3, 2008; available at *www.nytimes. com/2008/10/04/technology/internet/04google.html*; retrieved November 1, 2008.

43. *Ibid.*

44. Brian Kraemer, "Google Considers Walking Away from Yahoo Ad Deal," The Channel Wire blog, October 31, 2008; available at *www.crn.com/software/211800539*; retrieved November 1, 2008.

45. Stephanie Clifford, "Google Learns Lessons in the Ways of Washington," *New York Times Online*, October 15, 2008; available at *www.nytimes. com/2008/10/20/business/media/20lobby.html?_r=1&partner=rssnyt&emc= rss&oref=slogin*; retrieved November 2, 2008.

46. *Ibid.*

47. Robert A. Guth and Kevin J. Delaney, "Microsoft, Yahoo Discussed Deal," *Wall Street Journal Online*, May 5, 2008; available at *http:// online.wsj.com/article/SB117827827757492168.html*; retrieved November 2, 2008.

48. Benjamin Romano, "With Yahoo Deal's Collapse, Stymied Microsoft Must Find New Online Strategy," *Seattle Times Online*, May 5, 2008; available at *http://seattletimes.nwsource.com/html/microsoft/2004392575_ microsoft05.html*; retrieved November 2, 2008.

49. *Ibid.*

50. "Ballmer to Yahoo: Not Interested," The Channel Wire blog, November 7, 2008; available at *www.crn.com/software/212001243*; retrieved November 9, 2008.

51. *Ibid.*

52. Sheryl Gay Stolberg, "On First Day, Obama Quickly Sets a New Tone," *New York Times*, January 21, 2009; available at *www.nytimes.com/ 2009/01/22/us/politics/22obama.html?_r=1&scp=3&sq=%22business%20as% 20usual%22&st=cse*; retrieved January 28, 2009.

53. *Ibid.*

54. "Regulate and Collaborate: What Is Success in a Connected World?" PricewaterhouseCoopers Eleventh Annual Global CEO Survey, Belfast, Northern Ireland, 2008.

55. *Ibid.*

56. 2009 Edelman Trust Barometer, January 2009.

57. *Ibid.*

58. "Regulate and Collaborate: What Is Success in a Connected World?" PricewaterhouseCoopers Eleventh Annual Global CEO Survey, Belfast, Northern Ireland, 2008.

59. *Ibid.*

60. Don Tapscott, "Bretton Woods 2.0?" *BusinessWeek*, January 30, 2009; available at *www.businessweek.com/careers/managementiq/archives/2009/01/bretton_woods_2.html*; downloaded January 31, 2009.

61. *Ibid.*

62. *Ibid.*

Chapter 9

1. "Crisis Communication Strategies: The Johnson & Johnson Tylenol Crisis," Department of Defense Joint Course in Communication, Class 02-C, Team 1; available at *www.ou.edu/deptcomm/dodjcc/groups/02C2/Johnson%20&%20Johnson.htm*; retrieved November 21, 2008.

2. Brian O'Reilly, "Managing: J&J Is on a Roll," *Fortune*, December 26, 1994, p. 109.

3. Institute for Crisis Management, "Annual Crisis Report," *News Coverage of Business Crises During 2007* 17(1): page 2, March 2008.

4. Rohit Deshpandé, "McNeil Consumer Products Company: Tylenol," case study based on an earlier case developed by John Deighton, Assistant Professor of Business Administration, Amos Tuck School of Business Administration, Dartmouth College, Hanover, NH, 1992.

5. *Ibid.*

6. *http://hollywood2020.blogs.com/hollywood2020/2008/11/hollywood2020ne.html*; retrieved November 24, 2008.

7. Lisa Belkin, "Moms and Motrin," November 17, 2008; available at *http://parenting.blogs.nytimes.com/2008/11/17/moms-and-motrin/*; retrieved November 25, 2008.

8. Sir Martin Sorrell, "Public Relations: The Story Behind a Remarkable Renaissance," Institute for Public Relations Annual Distinguished Lecture, New York, November 5, 2008.

9. Bill Bivin, "Europe Vostro Keyboard Issue: What We're Doing," Dell's Small Business Blog, May 8, 2008; available at *http://en.community.dell.com/blogs/smallbusiness/archive/2008/05/08/europe-vostro-keyboard-issue-what-we-re-doing.aspx*; retrieved November 24, 2008.

10. Lionel Menchaca, "Direct2Dell One Year Later," Direct2Dell, July 14, 2007; available at *http://en.community.dell.com/blogs/direct2dell/archive/2007/07/14/20884.aspx*; retrieved November 24, 2008.

11. Pallavi Gogoi, "Wal-Mart's Jim and Laura: The Real Story," *Business-Week.com*, October 9, 2006; available at *www.businessweek.com/bwdaily/dnflash/content/oct2006/db20061009_579137.htm*; retrieved November 24, 2008.

12. Richard Edelman, "A Commitment," 6 a.m. blog, October 16, 2006; available at *www.edelman.com/speak_up/blog/archives/2006/10/a_commitment.html*; retrieved November 24, 2008.

13. Lynda Waddington, "Misconduct by Agriprocessors' PR Firm Has Rabi Considering Legal Options," *Iowa Independent*, July 18, 2008; available at *http://iowaindependent.com/2595/misconduct-by-agriprocessors-pr-firm-has-rabbi-considering-legal-options*; retrieved November 24, 2008.

14. *www.postvillevoices.com*; retrieved November 24, 2008.

15. Lynda Waddington, "Rubashkin Starts and Defends 'Grassroots' Blog," *Iowa Independent*, October 7, 2008; available at *http://iowaindependent.com/6690/rubashkin-starts-and-defends-grassroots-blog*; retrieved November 24, 2008.

16. Rhymer Rigby, "Software Menaces Are Moving with the Times," *Financial Times*, July 22, 2005.

17. "Internet Hoax Gooses Stock Market," The Big Picture, April 1, 2008; available at *http://bigpicture.typepad.com/comments/2008/04/internet-hoax-g.html*; retrieved November 25, 2008.

18. *Ibid.*

19. *Ibid.*

20. Gregory G. Efthimiou, "JetBlue Airways: Regaining Altitude," *Arthur W. Page Society's Annual Case Study Competition Journal*, p. 27, 2008.

21. Gregory G. Efthimiou, "JetBlue Airways: Regaining Altitude," *Arthur W. Page Society's Annual Case Study Competition Journal*, p. 28, 2008.

22. J. Bailey, "JetBlue Cancels More Flights, Leading to Passenger Discord," *New York Times*, *http://query.nytimes.com/gst/fullpage.html?res=9F06E1DE153EF93BA25751C0A9619C8B63&sec=&spon=*, February 18, 2007.

23. *http://jetbluehostage.blogspot.com/*; retrieved November 26, 2008.

24. J. Bailey, "JetBlue Cancels More Flights, Leading to Passenger Discord," *New York Times*, *http://query.nytimes.com/gst/fullpage.html?res=9F06E1DE153EF93BA25751C0A9619C8B63&sec=&spon=*, February 18, 2007.

25. P. Korkki, "Investors Mostly Glum in a Short Trading Week," *New York Times*, February 27, 2007, p. C10.

26. Chuck Salter, "Lessons from the Tarmac," *Fast Company* 115:31, 2007.

27. *Ibid.*

28. Shel Israel, "SM Global Report: Home Depot's Nick Ayres: The Return on Hurricane Tweeting," Global Neighbourhoods blog, October 27, 2008; available at *http://redcouch.typepad.com/weblog/2008/10/home-depot.html*; retrieved November 30, 2008.

29. *Ibid.*

30. *Ibid.*

31. Shel Israel, "Twitterville Table of Contents—Part 2," Global Neighbour-hoods blog, November 23, 2008; available at *http://redcouch.typepad.com/weblog/2008/11/twitterville-1.html*; retrieved November 30, 2008.

32. Shel Israel, "SM Global Report: Homeland Security's Charles Brown-stein: Using Social Media in Disasters," Global Neighbourhoods: SM Global Report, September 23, 2008; available at *http://redcouch.typepad.com/weblog/sm_global_report/index.html*; retrieved November 30, 2008.

33. Ian Paul, "Reality Check: Terrorists Using Twitter?" *PC World, http://www.pcworld.com/article/152927/reality_check_terrorists_using_twitter.html*; October 30, 2008.

34. Heather Havenstein, "U.S. Army Lays Out Scenarios with Terrorists Using Twitter," *New York Times Online*, October 27, 2007; available at *www.nytimes.com/external/idg/2008/10/27/27idg-US-Army-lays.html*; retrieved November 30, 2008.

35. Shel Israel, "SM Global Report: Homeland Security's Charles Brownstein: Using Social Media in Disasters," Global Neighbourhoods: SM Global Report, September 23, 2008; available at *http://redcouch.typepad.com/weblog/sm_global_report/index.html*; retrieved November 30, 2008.

36. *Ibid.*

INDEX

ABOUT THE AUTHORS

Professor Paul Argenti has taught management and corporate communication starting in 1977 at the Harvard Business School, at the Columbia Business School from 1979 to 1981, and since 1981 as a faculty member at Dartmouth's Tuck School of Business. He has also taught as a visiting professor at the International University of Japan, the Helsinki School of Economics, Erasmus University in the Netherlands, London Business School, and Singapore Management University. He currently serves as Faculty Director for the Tuck First Year Projects, Tuck's Leadership and Strategic Impact Program, and Tuck's executive programs for Novartis.

His most recent books include: *Strategic Corporate Communication*, published in 2007 in India by Tata/McGraw-Hill, *The Power of Corporate Communication* (coauthored with UCLA's Janis Forman) published by McGraw-Hill, and *The Fast Forward MBA Pocket Reference* (second edition), released through Wiley. He also published a fifth edition of his textbook for McGraw-Hill/Irwin in 2008 entitled *Corporate Communication*. Professor Argenti has written and edited numerous articles for academic publications and practitioner journals such as *Harvard Business Review*, *California Management Review*, and *Sloan Management Review*.

Professor Argenti is a Fulbright Scholar and a winner of the Pathfinder Award in 2007 from the Institute for Public Relations for the excellence of his research over a long career. He serves on the Board of Trustees for the Arthur W. Page Society. Finally, he has consulted and run training programs for hundreds of companies including General Electric, ING, Sony, Novartis, and Goldman Sachs.

Courtney M. Barnes is cofounder and principal member of Think Communications, a strategic communications advisory that helps organizational leaders establish and enhance their executive voice and influence through the strategic use of social media.

Barnes is also the editor of *PR News*, where she manages editorial content and writes on corporate communications and public relations, with particular expertise digital communications, integration and leadership/management issues. In addition to her writing and editing responsibilities, Barnes is an active guest lecturer for executive education programs and industry events.

Barnes has contributed to thought leadership pieces that have appeared in academic and business journals, including the *Harvard Business Review* and the *Journal of Business Strategy*. Prior to joining *PR News* as editor, Barnes was an associate with Communications Consulting Worldwide, a multidisciplinary consulting unit of Fleishman-Hillard. She has also worked for *Condé Nast Traveler* and *Washingtonian* magazines.

Barnes graduated from Northwestern University's Medill School of Journalism with a B.S. in journalism and a B.A. in Middle Eastern Studies.

CPSIA information can be obtained at www.ICGtesting.com
Printed in the USA
BVOW11*1734170116

433181BV00001B/1/P